PENGUIN BOOKS S0-AZK-594

MARY WOLLSTONECRAFT

Eleanor Flexner was born in New York and educated at the Lincoln School of Teachers College,
Swarthmore College, and Oxford. She is the
author of *Century of Struggle: The Woman's
Rights Movement in the United States*, published
in 1959 and often called the basic historical text
of the modern feminist movement. Since 1957,
Miss Flexner has lived in Northampton, Massachusetts. She describes herself as "a moderate"
who vehemently favors equal rights, equal
opportunity, and equal pay for women.

ELEANOR FLEXNER

Mary Wollstonecraft

A BIOGRAPHY

PENGUIN BOOKS INC *Baltimore, Maryland*

Penguin Books Inc
7110 Ambassador Road
Baltimore, Maryland 21207, U.S.A.

First published by Coward, McCann & Geoghegan, Inc., New York, 1972
Published by Penguin Books 1973

Printed in the United States of America

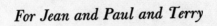

For Jean and Paul and Terry

Acknowledgments

My THANKS are due to the following who have been of assistance to me in writing this book:

To Mr. Carl H. Pforzheimer, Jr., for permission to use the Abinger Mss. microfilm in the possession of the Pforzheimer Library.

To Lord Abinger for permission to quote excerpts from the Wollstonecraft family letters belonging to him.

To the staff of the Pforzheimer Library for their encouragement and assistance, most particularly Mr. Kenneth N. Cameron, editor of Volumes I–IV of *Shelley and His Circle*, and Mrs. Doucet Devin Fischer for her help in deciphering numerous Wollstonecraft letters.

To the Goldsmiths' Company of the City of London, for copies of the Primrose Street leases to Edward Wollstonecraft.

To Mr. Jeffrey Ede, keeper of Public Records, H.M. Record Office, London; Mrs. Violet Durgin, reference librarian of the Forbes Library, Northampton, Massachusetts; the staff of the William Allen Neilson Library of Smith College, Northampton; Mr. H. E. Whiteley, borough librarian and curator of the Beverley Public Library; Mr. S. Stephenson, member of the Beverley Photographic Society; Liverpool City Libraries, for permission to reprint the letters of Mary Wollstonecraft to William Roscoe, in Appendix E.

To Harper & Row, for permission to quote from Edna St. Vincent Millay's "To a Poet Who Died Young" (*Collected Poems*, pp. 91–92) the lines on p. 257.

To New Directions Publishers, for permission to quote from Dylan Thomas' "Over Sir John's Hill" (*Collected Poems*, p. 187) the lines on p. 28.

Further acknowledgments will be found in the reference notes.

I am grateful to the trustees of the John Simon Guggenheim Foundation for a year's fellowship which made possible research abroad.

Contents

Illustrations follow page 160

Preface

The woman who first effectively challenged the age-old image of her sex as lesser and subservient human beings lived a short and stormy life in late-eighteenth-century England. Mary Wollstonecraft was only thirty-eight years old when she died in 1797. She wrote one book in which she articulated her protest and her ideas of what education and equality of opportunity might accomplish, not just for women but for society as a whole: *A Vindication of the Rights of Woman*, published in 1792.

It is not given to many books to exert as powerful an influence as the *Vindication* has done, although its effect was delayed and for decades it was largely unread. Until the middle of the nineteenth century the condition of women remained very much what it had been when Mary Wollstonecraft was goaded into her echoing protest: Very few were educated, almost no occupations were open to those who needed to earn a livelihood, and women could neither vote nor hold office. Married women did not even exist as a legal entity; they could not enter a legal complaint, appear in court, or retain counsel.

What is so astonishing about the *Vindication* is not that Mary wrote it, but that she was alone in raising the issues that she did, in a period of social change first signaled by the rebellion of the American colonies against British rule and then by the tremendous upheaval of the French Revolution. Hers was the only audible voice raised to assert that women, as well as men, had an inalienable right to freedom, that they too were human beings. In an age becoming aware of the exploitation of the slave, whose leading minds revolted at the African trade in human bodies, almost no one else echoed her belief in the importance, or even existence, of women as thinking persons.

Mary's viewpoint was shaped to an unusual degree, not by study or intercourse with her contemporaries, but by the circumstances of her own life and that of other women whom she knew: by their struggles against poverty and debt; by the frustration of minds she herself knew to be capable of achievement but denied their potential development by a society which decreed that women—any woman, all women—lacked the capacity to reason or even think. At the other end of the social scale she witnessed the corruption brought about by wealth and idleness on women of a different class.

Her arguments in *A Vindication of the Rights of Woman,* therefore, are for the most part neither philosophical nor theoretical. Without the circumstances of her own life, Mary Wollstonecraft could not have written the book she did. If she had been granted the educational opportunities, the leisure and security for study she longed for, she might have been just another bluestocking, as the small number of educated women who became scholars or writers were called by their contemporaries. But she would not have written the incandescent *Vindication* rooted in her own life. The woman who emerged from that life, Mary Wollstonecraft as she really was—by turns reasonable and angry beyond all reason; devout and hopeful, then despairing; contemptuous of women, but even more contemptuous of men corrupted by their power over women, wasteful of their opportunities, and irresponsible in the discharge of their obligations—such a woman could not write with gentility or restraint. Instead she wrote a classic.

Because she drew her ideas mostly from her own experience

and that of other women she knew, rich and poor, this study of Mary Wollstonecraft has laid more emphasis on her life than on the intellectual trends of the period in which she lived. That highly complex era—it has been variously called the Enlightenment, the Age of Reason, the Age of Revolution—has been discussed by philosophers, political and social scientists, literary critics, theologians, and historians. While drawing on their work and that of earlier biographers of Mary Wollstonecraft, I have chosen instead to ask how it came about that this particular woman, virtually alone among her contemporaries, demanded that the "rights of man" be extended to women and that women be allowed to enter their full human heritage.

Mary wrote nothing else comparable in significance to *A Vindication of the Rights of Woman*. She was just turning back to the problems of women in the last year of her life. We can only wonder whether she might have written more books or pamphlets which equaled its eloquence and thereby helped the movement for equal rights to an earlier start. She died in childbirth a few months after her thirty-eighth birthday. She speaks to us today across a gap of almost two centuries with a voice of courage and hope.

ELEANOR FLEXNER

Northampton, Massachusetts
November, 1971

I here throw down my gauntlet, and deny the existence of sexual virtues, not excepting modesty. For man and woman, truth, if I understand the meaning of the word, must be the same . . . women, I allow, may have different duties to fulfil; but they are *human* duties, and the principles that should regulate them, I sturdily maintain, must be the same. To become respectable, the exercise of their understanding is necessary; there is no other foundation for independence of character. . . .

—MARY WOLLSTONECRAFT, *A Vindication of the Rights of Woman*

We are Turks with the affections of our women, and have made them subscribe to our doctrine too. We let their bodies go abroad liberally enough, with smiles and ringlets and pink bonnets to disguise them instead of veils and yakmaks. But their souls must be seen by only one man, and they obey not unwillingly, and consent to remain at home as our slaves—ministering to us and doing drudgery for us.

—WILLIAM THACKERAY, *Vanity Fair*

MARY WOLLSTONECRAFT

CHAPTER I

As the Twig Is Bent (1759-78)

THE BIRTH OF A GIRL CHILD in London to the wife of a young silk weaver in the year 1759 was of no moment to anyone but her family, who probably wished that she had been a second son—boys could earn their keep when they grew up; most girls were of little use except eventually to bear children, preferably sons, in their turn. But a first daughter would be a help around the house, and so Mary Wollstonecraft had at least that much in her favor to begin with.

For the daughter of a tradesman, the prospects were clearly limited. If lucky, she would marry another tradesman, have his children, and—usually sooner than later—go to her grave. If unlucky, she could end up as an indentured servant, in a poorhouse, or, after having been a prostitute, in prison. She would do far better to marry, whatever the circumstances.

Actually, Mary's prospects were better than those of most girls in her class. This was due, not primarily to her parents, but to her grandfather Edward Wollstonecraft, "weaver and citizen of London," who possessed unusual ideas and ability and whose ambi-

tion extended far beyond his trade. He wished to become a
"gentleman," and he understood that the way to a better situation
for himself and his family (to three generations of which he gave
his name) lay through property—not so much its ownership as its
use.

Between 1753 and 1755 Edward Wollstonecraft leased land
belonging to the "Worshipful Company of Goldsmiths" on Primrose Street in the Spitalfields area which was the center of the
London silk-weaving industry. There he built three blocks of
houses accommodating some thirty tenants, whose rents would
be the mainstay of the family's income for sixty-odd years.[1]

His oldest son, Edward John Wollstonecraft, was apprenticed to
his father during the usual seven-year period, ending in 1757.[2] At
that time he married an Irish woman, Elizabeth Dickson, who came
from "a good family" in Ballyshannon, County Donegal, in the
northwest corner of Ireland.[3] Their first child was a boy, named
Edward Bland Wollstonecraft. Then came Mary, born April 27,
1759; another daughter, named Elizabeth, followed soon after.

The family had by then moved into the suburbs of London,
somewhere in Essex, where still another daughter, Everina, was
born.[4] In 1765, when Mary was six years old, there is finally a
clear record of their whereabouts, in Barking, a village and river
port eight miles east of London. The parish poor-rate books (which
help us from here on to trace the itinerant Wollstonecraft family
the length and breadth of Britain) record Edward Wollstonecraft
as "late weaver," paying a fairly high poor rate, or tax for the support of the parish poor, of 25 pounds 9 pence, indicating that he
had bought or leased a substantial house on a good-sized piece of
land.[5] Here a fifth child was born, a son named James.

By now Edward John Wollstonecraft had left his trade and
become a farmer, either because silk weaving had fallen on hard
times (as happened periodically), or because he did not care for
it, or because he shared his father's ambition to better his station,
an ambition which was driving any number of men who had
made money in the city to seek a more attractive life and greater
prestige through entry into the landlord class. One way was to
rent and farm property, increasing one's income until one could
eventually buy an estate, no matter how small.[6]

The possibilities were indeed appealing. Yet at best farming demanded skill and patience. This was particularly true at the time, because enormous changes were taking place in English agriculture. Smaller holdings and open common lands were being steadily enclosed into large holdings; more modern methods of cultivation and fertilizing were making agriculture increasingly productive—and competitive. Farming, for an inexperienced or less than industrious practitioner, could be an exacting, even risky occupation.

Unfortunately for Edward John Wollstonecraft—and his family —he had been able to gratify his restless urge for a new way of life because his father's death in February, 1765, left him with substantial means. The terms of the old man's will cast a long shadow over three generations of Wollstonecrafts.[7] He divided his property into thirds, of which his oldest son (Edward John) received one portion, a daughter the second third, and a grandson—Mary's brother—the remaining share. The will seems to us at this remove a strange mixture of canniness and sheer folly: Mistrustful of his son-in-law, old Edward safeguarded the portion of his daughter and the interest of her children by setting up a trust. He established no such safeguard for the portion of his grandson Edward Bland, in spite of the fact that the latter's father would have the legal management of young Edward's portion during his minority.

What Edward John got was the leaseholds of the rented property, which gave him the apartment house rents, and a collectible debt amounting to 3,000 pounds. His son—then less than ten years old—got the leasehold to another piece of property and a share (value unspecified, but it could have been considerable) in an East India merchant ship.

If Mary's father had been a reasonably good provider, if he had stuck to his trade, or if he had shown some aptitude and determination in the new occupation he had chosen, then his family would have been well provided for, and we might never have heard anything at all of Mary Wollstonecraft. Matters turned out very differently, though, because Edward John Wollstonecraft was the last person to have turned farmer. It was not in the man's nature to settle down or to persevere in the face of difficulties.

Anything was preferable, even the most ill-considered moves and changes.

From Barking, a pleasant place where the Wollstonecrafts were on social terms with the leading family (the wealthy and influential Gascoynes), they moved again in 1768, this time to the north of England, near Beverley, a market town near Hull in east Yorkshire. Again we do not know why, nor do we know why the move was such a distance and to an area where farming would necessarily be different because of alterations in the soil and climate. Local tradition has assigned the Wollstonecraft farm to the village of Walkington a few miles southeast of Beverley. But within three years they had moved into Beverley itself, where they lived in the smaller of the town's two marketplaces (called the Wednesday Market) and where the sixth and last child, a son named Charles, was born.[8]

In Beverley, at the age of eleven, we first get to know Mary Wollstonecraft as a person, through the vivid letters she wrote her "best" friend, a girl named Jane Arden.[9] Mary loved Beverley, not just for Jane's sake; she remembered it well and with good reason. The widely traveled Arthur Young described it as "very pretty, well and regularly built, very clean and well-paved; the streets broad and handsome."[10] Even today the town retains its individual character. Its greatest glory is the church of St. John of Beverley, a magnificent Gothic structure second only to cathedrals like York and Ely, which must have left a lasting impression on the child Mary. But even more meaningful to her was the vast rolling pasture, or common, that stretched out on three sides of the town, still today guaranteed in perpetuity for the benefit and pleasure of the inhabitants. One section, called Westwood from an earlier day before its trees were cut down, was the favorite playground of the Wollstonecraft children, and there Mary learned—and never forgot—the value of active outdoor games in building a healthy body. There too she stored up the knowledge and love of growing things—birds and insects and flowers which she would use in her books for children—and there she found respite from too-early responsibilities and from the nagging petty restrictions imposed on her by her parents.

There were other reasons why romping on Westwood was a lifesaver for the young girl. Edward John's shortcomings were becoming an open secret and scandal. Years later Mary wrote to her dearest Beverley friend:

It is almost needless to tell you that my father's violent temper and extravagant turn of mind, was the principal cause of my unhappiness and that of the rest of the family. The good folk of Beverley (like those of most country towns) were ever ready to find out their neighbors' faults, and to animadvert on them; many people did not scruple to prognosticate the ruin of the whole family, and the way he went on justified them for doing so.

Mary herself was becoming aware of increasing friction between her parents and of her father's mounting irascibility, even brutality. Although her brother, senior by several years, was apparently her mother's favorite and although the mother seems to have been unsympathetic, even harsh, toward Mary, it was nevertheless the girl who assumed the role of the mother's protector when she was threatened by her husband's temper:

She would often throw herself between the despot and his victim, with the purpose to receive upon her own person the blows that might be directed against her mother. She has even laid [sic] whole nights upon the landing-place near their chamber-door, when, mistakenly, or with reason, she apprehended that her father might break out into paroxysms of violence.[11]

These episodes probably began during Mary's early teens and were a major cause of many problems later in her life. She was fortunate that she could escape to the freedom and boisterous games on Westwood. Warm and loving by nature, she lavished affection on her younger brothers and sisters, and her friends, particularly Jane Arden, whose home afforded her another sanctuary from the rising tensions at home. There she was welcome, among a family with different values from her own, and even shared in some of Jane's lessons from her father. John Arden was a teacher (the Beverley poll books list him as a "philosopher") and the first intellectual influence in Mary Wollstonecraft's life. Jane was diametrically Mary's opposite: cheerful, even-tempered and popular.[12] (The fact that Mary was none of these first emerges in her letters to Jane.) The girls shared the usual girlish flutterings and first awareness of boys, *a* boy. ("I could have been far happier with two persons I could name," Mary wrote her friend "—don't be jealous—the other is not a lady. . . .")

Her letters show that already at sixteen her vocabulary, spelling, and ability to express herself, as well as her literary tastes and general curiosity, were above the norm for anyone from her environment, especially a girl. More painfully, they also display the qualities which were to complicate her personal relationships all her life; she was already possessive, and highly sensitive. The slightest affront, often fancied rather than real, caused intense feelings of rejection and anger. If Jane slighted her (as Mary thought), she flew into a fit of jealousy and wrote bitter letters raking up past grievances:

> I once thought myself worthy of your friendship. I thank you for bringing me to a right sense of myself. When I have been at your house with Miss J—— the greatest respect has been paid to her: everything handed to her first; in short as if she were a superior being. Your Mama too behaved with more politeness to her.

Jane tried to smooth matters over, but Mary found it hard to make peace. She wrote of herself, with acute self-knowledge for an adolescent: "I am a little singular in my thought of love and friendship. I must have first place or none. . . . I cannot bear a slight from those I love."

Sometime late in the year 1774 the Wollstonecraft family left Beverley and returned south; whatever the reason, we do not know it. Probably farming was proving too much for Edward John; perhaps he was running away from debts. He settled next in Hoxton, a small but somewhat dreary village a few miles north of London. Mary's first and best-known biographer, her husband, William Godwin, wrote that he next became involved in "a commercial speculation of some sort" which turned out badly; after a year and a half he gave it up.

This would have meant using money—of his own or borrowed —for investment. We can speculate that if his share of the inheritance was beginning to run out, Mr. Wollstonecraft may have used money derived from the bequest to his son, "the Cruttenden East Indiaman, John Bowland now or late commander."[13] Young Edward Bland Wollstonecraft would be approaching his majority. He was no longer living at home but was articled to a London solicitor, housed and fed by him like any apprentice for a five- or six-year term, the sole means of preparing for that profession. His father might have been tempted to take the risk of using so lucrative a source of ready cash while he still had the opportunity to do so.

The most plausible argument for such an explanation is that such a venture's failure and loss of the money would go a long way toward explaining the appalling neglect of his father by the son in later years, when Mr. Wollstonecraft was repeatedly destitute and his son did not send him the money from the Primrose Street rentals which were legitimately his.

Meanwhile, Edward John was becoming increasingly unstable and ill tempered, and the sixteen-year-old Mary was literally being driven out of her home in search of a place where she could read and study by day and sleep without interruption at night. She found refuge with her next-door neighbors, a gentle and affectionate elderly couple named Clare. Mr. Clare was a retired, semi-invalid clergyman who seldom went outdoors and was afflicted with some physical deformity (he may have been a hunchback). There was nothing in the relationship between husband and wife to arouse tension or dread; moreover, the couple loved books, lending them to Mary and often reading aloud.

As they came to love Mary, the Clares realized that she needed something they could not give her, a congenial friend her own age. One day when she was paying a visit to friends who lived in Newington Butts, a village south of London, Mrs. Clare took Mary along. There her meeting with the oldest daughter of the Blood family, Frances, or Fanny as she was called, made an impression on Mary which was still vivid when she described it to William Godwin some twenty years later:

The first object that caught her sight, was a young woman of slender and elegant form, and eighteen years of age, busily employed in feeding and managing some children, born of the same parents, but considerably inferior to her in age. The impression which Mary received from a scene, which so happily accorded with her two most cherished conceptions, the picturesque and the affectionate, was indelible; and before the interview was concluded, she had taken, in her heart, the vows of an eternal friendship.[14]

Mary soon came to regard Fanny as superior in all accomplishments. Fanny played and sang, both talents assiduously cultivated by eighteenth-century ladies. She was an excellent needlewoman and could draw "with exquisite fidelity and neatness"— gifts which she put to good use in the support of her family. By contrast with her beautiful script, Mary's hurried scrawl was nearly illegible.

But the greatest gift Fanny brought to her new friend was the experience of loving without fear or self-consciousness. Unlike the turbulent friendship with Jane Arden, there were no quarrels, jealousies, or even differences of opinion during those first years. Nothing marred the relationship which became, in Godwin's words, "so fervent as for years to have constituted the ruling passion of her mind." Mary herself wrote her earlier friend Jane that she had found:

> . . . a friend, whom I love better than all the world beside, a friend to whom I am bound by every tie of gratitude and inclination: to live with this friend is the height of my ambition, and indeed it is the most rational wish I could make, as her conversation is not more agreeable than improving. I could dwell forever on her praises, and you wo (d) not wonder at it, if you knew the many favors she has conferred on me, and the many valuable qualifications she possesses; she has a masculine understanding, and sound judgment, yet she has every feminine virtue. . . .

To live with Fanny now became Mary's dream. Although she had shown some normal teen-age interest in boys, we hear no more of them. From now until Fanny married and left Mary, she thought only in terms of a life shared with one whom she loved, as she once wrote, "better than life itself." We could write off such phrases as youthful exaggeration, if it were not for the fact that Mary lived up to them. Repeatedly during Fanny's lifetime she proved her loyalty to Fanny above all others. As long as Fanny lived, her interests and those of her family took precedence, something of which Mary's brothers and sisters were uncomfortably aware.

Many teen-agers go through a phase of "crushes" which they outgrow. It is a more difficult, drawn-out process for those who, like Mary Wollstonecraft, never found a normal outlet for their childish affections or experienced the stability and security of their parents' love for their children and for each other. What is surprising is that she *did* outgrow it—after Fanny Blood died.

To the appeal of Fanny's beauty and talent and her response to Mary's love, there was added another factor: Her predicament at home strongly resembled Mary's. While there was no indication that he abused his family, Mr. Blood did nothing to support them. That burden fell on his wife and oldest daughter. Fanny drew and painted. Mrs. Blood sewed "sometimes from four in the morning until she could not see at night." By the time she was seventeen Mary Wollstonecraft knew at first hand the desperate plight of women compelled to earn their own livelihood and that of others dependent on them.

The pleasures of Mary's association with the Clares and of her friendship with Fanny were shattered sometime in 1776, when Edward John Wollstonecraft, unsuccessful in his "commercial speculation," left Hoxton to make another try at farming. This time he chose Wales, perhaps to get as far away as possible from any previous attempt and leave his reputation behind him. He took his family to Carmarthenshire, in the southeast corner of Wales, and settled in the village of Laugharne, a beautiful spot at the mouth of the Towy River, famous today as an artists' resort and as the home for many years of the poet Dylan Thomas. It was surrounded by hills and water, with views of distant headlands and beyond them the Irish Sea. Down the Towy River floated fishermen's coracles—light, round boats with the occupant wielding only a paddle. A ruined castle behind the village dated from the twelfth century. Strange birds swooped over the estuary:

Over Sir John's hill
The hawk on fire hangs still
In a hoisted cloud at drop of dusk . . .
. . . slowly the fishing holy stalking heron
In the river Towy below bows his tilted headstone.[15]

The beauties of the place sank deep into Mary's consciousness; years later she wrote of the castle and also that familiar figure, the Welsh harpist, for whom people sat up all night when he stayed at an inn. But in general Laugharne was a lonely spot for the Wollstonecrafts, despite their friendship with a family named Allen, whose two daughters later married into the wealthy Wedgwood family and would cross the paths of the Wollstonecraft girls again. Edward John once more displayed his chronic restlessness and preference for the city: "business or pleasure took him often to London." The business might have entailed looking after the Primrose Street houses, but such a preoccupation hardly made for an assiduous farmer. Eventually something like a family revolt, combined with his own predilections, brought him back to the London area. This time they settled in a place largely of Mary's choosing: the village of Walworth, near the Bloods' home in Newington Butts.

Mary's ascendancy was not due only to her age and the fact that she was now, at eighteen, the oldest child at home. At some point Mr. Wollstonecraft had become so badly entangled financially that he used part of money settled on his daughters to extricate himself. Mary's statement, in a letter to Jane Arden, is forthright; he took it, and she agreed to relinquish her share. Apparently that of the others was not so lightly relinquished; there is mention, years later, of Everina's "annuity." Where the money came from remains a mystery; there was no provision for the girls in old Wollstonecraft's will, and no other source has come to light.[16] In any event Mary now possessed some influence over her father—enough to dictate where he should settle and lay down certain conditions for her not leaving home, something she was now considering. She was promised a room of her own and other "requisites of study."

These conditions apparently were not observed, but it was another year before Mary was able to break away. She was still sufficiently concerned about her mother to yield to her "intreaties and tears" when a position as companion presented itself, even after all the arrangements had been made. There were other ties as well—to the younger children and to Fanny.

Edward Bland was already living away from home, and he married in 1778.[17] The following year he began to practice as a solicitor.[18] His marriage made no real difference—it was already abundantly clear that he was not interested in the welfare of his family and would do as little for his parents or brothers and sisters as he could get away with.

Sometime late in 1778, Mary finally left home, to be companion to a Mrs. Dawson in the famous watering place of Bath. It was a decision she came to only after prolonged and anguished struggle, and we can conclude that she did so only because it had become literally impossible for her to live any longer at home.

CHAPTER II

Forge of Adversity (1778–82)

THE ENORMOUS WEALTH pouring into England from the Empire rapidly growing overseas, in India, in North America, wealth spent by the landed nobility and the mercantile class on sumptuous new mansions in London and in the countryside, was nowhere more blatantly in evidence than in the resort of Bath. Here the sick came to "take the waters," and the rich as well, to take their ease and display their opulence.

The old city lay not far from Bristol Channel in a natural amphitheater of hills which provided the perfect setting for its tiers of terraces and squares, the outstanding example of neoclassical or Palladian architecture in England.

> The houses are so elegant, the streets so beautiful, the prospects so enchanting, I could fill whole pages upon pages upon the beauty of the place and the country [wrote Fanny Burney]. . . . Tuesday morning we spent in walking all over the town, viewing the beautiful Circus, the company-crowded Pumproom, and the exquisite Crescent, which, to all the excellences of architecture that adorns the Circus, adds all the delights of nature that beautify the Parades.[1]

Thanks to royal patronage and to its longtime master of cere-
monies Beau Nash, who insisted on a high level of decorum and
gentility, Bath had become unique among British watering resorts
as the center of society, drawing the nobility, the new rich and
the middle class bent on aping both. The pace of life was feverish
and giddy, the atmosphere portentously trivial, since Bath catered
to the hypochondriacal, as well as to the ostentatious. Jane
Austen's novels were still to come, but it had already been richly
described by Smollett and Sheridan. Fanny Burney grew sated
with the uninterrupted round of visits:

> I begin to grow most heartily sick and tired of this constant
> round of visiting, and these eternal new acquaintances . . . I
> really have at present no pleasure in any party, from the trouble
> and tiresomeness of being engaged to so many.[2]

Certainly it was an extraordinary milieu for a young woman
of Mary Wollstonecraft's limited social experience. When she
alighted, cramped and weary, from the twenty-hour coach trip
from London, she was taken to Milsom Street where Mrs. Dawson
lived, and Milsom Street, "whether in or out of the Season . . . (is)
the very magnet of Bath, and if there is any company or movement in the city, Milsom Street is the pulse of it." It had been
from a shop in Milsom Street that Anne Elliott "as she sat near
the window, descried, most decidedly and distinctly, Captain
Wentworth walking down the street."[3]

Mrs. Dawson was the widow of a well-to-do London merchant
whose son owned a house in Bath where his mother lived. Mary
took the post with the knowledge that Mrs. Dawson was hard to
please and that a succession of women had tried to fill it and
failed. Perhaps she had an advantage over them; Mrs. Dawson
could hardly have been more intransigent than her own father.
She knew, moreover, that she had little choice. A woman in
eighteenth-century England had so few options as to be almost
unimaginable to us today. For the overwhelming majority there
was only one—marriage. For a single woman with no independent source of income, only three respectable ways of making a
living were open: to teach in a school; to serve as governess in a
well-to-do family; or to be a companion to an older woman. The

first two, even with the inadequate educational standards for girls that then existed, required the three R's, dancing, music, and French and thus demanded of Mary (as of most contemporary women) more than she could perform. To be a companion to a woman like Mrs. Dawson was her only hope, and with her limited worldly experience and connections she had been fortunate to obtain such a position.

Given the circumstances of the time, it was not a bad situation. Mrs. Dawson spent her summers in Southampton or Windsor, where Mary accompanied her; in Southampton she enjoyed the sea bathing, and people were so hospitable that she was sorry to leave the place. When Mrs. Dawson went away on a visit from Windsor leaving her alone in the house, Mary was free to spend her time as she chose. If Mrs. Dawson was difficult and demanding, she was also a woman who had traveled and whose conversation gave Mary the opportunity to widen her own horizons.

Mary was also able to renew her friendship with Jane Arden, whose father was living in Bath, giving lectures and teaching, as he had in Beverley, young ladies and gentlemen "at home or at his house, Geography, the Elements of Astronomy, and Use of the Globe and Maps." Mary saw his advertisement in the newspaper and paid a call. She learned that Jane was a governess nearby in rural Somerset, and the young women resumed correspondence. On at least one occasion when Jane visited her family in Bath, Mary saw her again.

There were other amenities. Mary was given time off from her work to visit her family and Fanny. In Windsor she liked driving through the countryside, especially in the Royal Forest, and she went frequently to the beautiful chapel in the castle. She does not seem to have taken advantage of Bath's unusual theatrical offerings, which gave visitors a choice of the Elizabethan and Restoration dramatists. The only references to entertainment in her letters are to the balls and assemblies which formed the staple of Bath's fashionable social life.

In this predominant aspect of life in Bath Mary took as little part as possible. But she could not avoid being exposed to it; it flowed on all around her, in the streets and shops, on the promenades, and probably even in Mrs. Dawson's drawing room. It was

Mary's first exposure, and it sank deeply into her consciousness—particularly what she saw of fashionable, idle, and irresponsible women. The images she stored up here were to furnish Mary Wollstonecraft with some of the outrage which would later stir generations of feminists to action.

Mary was increasingly unhappy in Bath. Not only was its atmosphere uncongenial, but her position grated on her temperament. An independent turn of mind, an assertive character which was to become increasingly more obvious, and a restless intelligence did not fit her for a position whose prime requisite was conformity to someone else's taste and whims. But other forces were also at work. Her letters dwell on her poor health and spirits. We get a picture of a young woman already prematurely grave and almost self-consciously moralistic and philosophical.

Over and beyond any immediate causes for depression such as Fanny's absence, her family's problems, and the life of Bath, there is already evident a deep-seated malaise, a chronic depression which made Mary Wollstonecraft unhappy in almost every situation in which she found herself during the greater portion of her life. Granted that she had abundant cause for frustration and worry and often faced difficult and unpleasant situations, the fact remains that she lacked the kind of resilience and optimism that enabled more fortunate dispositions to make the best of matters.

Modern psychiatry has identified some of the symptoms of which Mary constantly complained—lassitude, depression, acute headaches, and digestive difficulties—as symptoms of deeply repressed anger. She had ample reasons for it—at a society which thwarted women; at a father who had thrown away a comfortable endowment and mistreated both wife and children; and at a mother with inadequate understanding. The fact that literature shows us many such women, not to mention such dramatic examples as George Eliot and Florence Nightingale, only proves that the social pressures and personal frustrations from which Mary suffered to an unusual degree have been inflicted on others and still are.

Mary Wollstonecraft's mainstay against difficulties, whether practical or psychological, was her religious faith. Until the last five years of her life she was a deeply religious woman. By the time she married the freethinker William Godwin her beliefs had undergone a radical change (to the relief of most of her biographers, including her husband, who had little sympathy with her religious commitment). But from adolescence until she was thirty-two years old, her faith enabled her against great odds to accept and bear a heavy load of responsibility and unhappiness. Far from rendering her gloomy and despondent or morbid, religion was the principal aid that enabled her to surmount these tendencies in her character:

From Bath she wrote to Jane Arden:

> I hinted to you in my last letter that I had not been very happy—indeed, I have been far otherwise: Pain and disappointment have constantly attended me since I left Beverley. I do not however repine at the dispensations of Providence, for my philosophy as well as my religion will ever teach me to look on misfortunes as blessings, which like a bitter potion is disagreeable to the palate tho' 'tis grateful to the Stomach—I hope mine have not been thrown away on me, but that I am both the wiser and better for them.[4]

This is not a point of view which commends itself to modern skepticism or indeed to many of her own contemporaries, including her family. There were not many with whom she could share her religious convictions: Jane, Fanny's brother George, and clerical friends. She also lavished religious admonitions on her youngest sister, Everina, until the latter rebelled.

One of the reasons Mary worried so much about her family while she was with Mrs. Dawson was the lack of satisfactory communication. When letters did come, Mary showed herself painfully sensitive, another trait that clouded her relationships with people all her life. She wrote to her sister Elizabeth (whom the family always called Eliza):

> I this morning received your letter which was truly welcome to me, as I found by it you still remember me; but I must say, I should like to be remembered in a kinder manner. There is an air of irony through your whole epistle which hurts me exceedingly; I would willingly put the most favorable construc-

tion on it—yet, it still displeases me. I hate formality and compliments, one affectionate word would give me more pleasure than all the pretty things that come from the head; but have nothing to say to the heart. Two or three expressions in your last particularly displeased me, you mention my *condescension* and early enquiries—I know not what to make of those words. . . . As to Everina's illness my Father only mentioned it in a careless manner to me, and I did not imagine it had been so bad, even now I am ignorant of the nature of her complaint tho' I am very anxious about it.

You don't do me justice in supposing I seldom think of you— the happiness of my family is nearer my heart than you imagine —perhaps, too near for my own health or peace.

For my anxiety preys on me, and is of no use to you. You don't say a word of my mother. I take it for granted she is well —tho' of late she has not even desired to be remembered to me. Some time or the other, in this world or a better, she may be convinced of my regard—and then may think I deserve not to be thought so harshly of. . . .[5]

This letter is revealing in many ways. There was no communication between mother and daughter although Mary hungered for it. She could not reveal her feelings to her mother because they were so ambivalent, compounded of pity, contempt for what she regarded as her mother's submissiveness to her husband, and resentment of Mrs. Wollstonecraft's treatment of herself. (There is mention in one of her novels of the mother's reception of a childish confidence from her daughter: She laughed at her.[6])

"I take it for granted she is well . . . of late she has not even desired to be remembered to me." Did Mary already sense that her mother was far from well and dread the summons that eventually reached her? Sometime during or after the year 1780, she was called home to nurse Mrs. Wollstonecraft in her last illness. Mary alluded to the disease as "a dropsy, attended by many other disagreeable complaints"; today we would call it edema, the abnormal retention of fluid in the body which can be due to cancer or a heart or kidney condition. If it was a long-drawn-out cancer, the illness would have been excruciatingly painful, since laudanum, a derivative of opium and the only opiate known at the time, would diminish in efficacy with constant use.

Mrs. Wollstonecraft would allow no one but Mary to care for her and was an exacting patient. Mary grew exhausted and resentful, and there does not seem to have been any kind of reconciliation between them before the mother died. Her last words, "A little patience and all will be over," have been quoted by Mary as a fitting valedictory to one who has fared almost as badly at the hands of Mary's biographers and of Mary herself (in her novels) as her husband.[7] One verdict is of "a timid woman, [who] soon lost all dignity of character in the face of [her husband's behavior]." Godwin called her "the first and most submissive of his subjects."[8]

There is no evidence to support such a conclusion. If her treatment of Mary was unduly harsh, this would indicate rigidity rather than weakness. Perhaps Mrs. Wollstonecraft was trying to offset the absence of steady paternal authority by firm handling of a girl who was a tomboy. (Perhaps she also sensed the intensity of Mary's anger at her father and tried to harness it.) Her lack of warmth can be understood in light of her own disappointment— with her husband, with her whole life—and the effort it cost to hold her own against her husband's violence and lack of judgment.

Yet hold her own against Edward John Wollstonecraft she did. She must have. There is no other explanation for the fact that for twenty-five years the family kept together—in the face of the ruin of their fortunes, frequent changes of domicile, and Edward John's vagaries. When Elizabeth Dickson Wollstonecraft died in 1782, three of her six children had been launched into the world. All of them turned out surprisingly well, when one considers the example their father set them, the difficulty of making a way without means or influential connections, and the hazards facing women who had to earn their way.

It is true that the four younger children would have had a difficult time without Mary's assistance—but someone formed Mary's character, and all of them had the makings of resourcefulness and independence. There is no basis in fact for the strictures of those who have written Mary's kindred off as millstones hung around her neck.[9]

It could so easily have been otherwise; many a younger son

ended on the gallows or in debtors' prison, many a girl as an indentured servant or prostitute. Although several of the younger Wollstonecrafts made rough weather of it, none of them lost his footing permanently; in a society which cared nothing for those who encountered misfortune, this was an unusual showing. Mary has received the credit, but surely some of it is due her mother. She was not a spineless nonentity, but a woman of quite different mettle. In the face of a growing family and steadily worsening prospects, she kept going. She endured the travel, the constant settling in strange homes and strange communities, the uprooting of whatever slender ties she may have made outside her home, the uncertainty of the future. Her greatest gift to her daughter— one that Mary herself never realized—was her example: In the face of sharp changes of fortune, of violence and lovelessness, she never gave up. Mary derived from her a similar toughness of fiber, the ability to persist under great stress. When she shouldered the care of her younger brothers and sisters, adventured alone and first as a single woman in the literary world of London, went to revolutionary Paris, fought for a man's love when it was dead for the sake of their infant daughter, Mary Wollstonecraft was more like her mother than she ever knew.

In 1780, two years before his wife's death and while Mary was still at Mrs. Dawson's, Mr. Wollstonecraft had again moved his family from Walworth, where Mary had left them, to Enfield, another village north of London.[10] Since his stay in Wales, he had abandoned all pretense at farming, "it appearing to be now less a source of profit than of loss."[11] After his wife's death he moved back to Laugharne, taking with him only his twelve-year-old youngest son, Charles. He also remarried, an act which further alienated his oldest daughter. Mary's last novel, *Maria, or The Wrongs of Woman*, describes her stepmother as a kind of "upper servant," perhaps a housekeeper;[12] according to the book, her father saw fit to do his courting, and the woman to accept his advances, during his wife's illness, but as so often happens with Mary's books, it is almost impossible to disentangle fact from fiction. We know only that such a marriage did take place and that Mary's strong feelings about her stepmother were rooted in her own exhaustion and her ambivalent feelings about both her parents. In fairness it should be pointed out that in later years the second Mrs. Wollstonecraft earned the grudging respect of at least one of her stepchildren (Eliza) by her efforts to control her husband's increasingly violent and spendthrift ways. Moreover, she succeeded in keeping him settled at Laugharne for the remaining twenty-one years of his life, which, given his restless temperament, was no mean achievement.[13]

Meanwhile, the family had dissolved. James had gone to sea at the age of fourteen in 1780 as "captain's servant," a career he was to pursue with some interruptions until his death.[14] The two younger girls lived with Edward for a brief period, an unpleasant experience for both of them; Edward was as unloved by the rest of his family as his father. The only person who left Enfield for a happier existence was Mary, who could at last with a clear conscience do what she had wanted to do for so long—go live with Fanny. The Blood family had meanwhile moved farther out of London, to the village of Walham Green, west of the city and not far from the Putney Bridge over the Thames River. Mary was made doubly welcome, for Fanny's sake and because she could add her efforts to help support the family.

For six months Mary took part in a graphic demonstration of the burden carried by women who lacked any marketable skills. The poverty at the Bloods' was more acute than any Mary had known previously. Despite their debts, the Wollstonecrafts had been able to send some of their children away to school and keep a servant. At the Bloods', the grinding struggle for enough to eat was unceasing. Mrs. Blood, Fanny, and Mary worked from sunup until daylight gave out (they could not afford expensive lamplight). Sometimes the family's income was less than a guinea a week. On occasion the work and the strain it involved made Mary actually ill, and her eyes suffered severely.[15]

There were, of course, compensations. She was genuinely fond of Mrs. Blood, whom she called "our mother." She formed a long-term friendship with Fanny's brother George. And she was living under the same roof with Fanny, a prospect she had long looked forward to. But proximity also brought confirmation of what she had long suspected, that Fanny's health was deteriorating. This was cause for deep concern; in those days serious illness was tantamount to sentence of death, especially with the added burdens of poverty and hard work.

Moreover, Mary came to realize painfully that while Fanny's companionship was all she asked for, her presence was not enough for Fanny. In fact, she was in love—with an Irishman named Hugh Skeys, who was in the wine business and spent a good deal of time in Portugal. Skeys was interested in Fanny but could not come to a decision, and the affair dragged along for several years. Mary later blamed Skeys' hesitation for the fact that Fanny's illness eventually killed her. The long-drawn-out uncertainty cannot have done her any good.

By the end of 1782 there was a plan under consideration for Fanny to go to Portugal, either for the sake of her health or to marry Skeys there, and for Mary to accompany her. However, the wedding did not take place until February, 1785; long before this date, Mary had left the Bloods.

On October 10, 1782, Eliza Wollstonecraft—who had been living with her brother Edward—was married to Meridith Bishop, "of the Parish of St. Mary Bermondsey in the County of Surry a Batchelor of the age of twenty-one." All that is known of Bishop is that he was a friend of Hugh Skeys. The circumstances suggest that the marriage was not a matter of choice for one or perhaps even both parties. It took place by special license, since Eliza was still a legal minor, and required the consent of the bride's father, by then in Wales, and the posting by her brother Edward of a bond of 200 pounds (which was matched by Bishop), payable to the court in case the marriage did not take place.[16] Only a few weeks later, a daughter was born and named Mary.

Whether she or Bishop were forced into the marriage, Eliza was ill equipped for such a situation or for motherhood under the best of circumstances. Like all the Wollstonecraft children, she carried the scars of unhappy childhood, and she now suffered what today would be called an acute postpartum breakdown.

Mary was summoned from Walham Green to nurse her sister and found her in a condition bordering on insanity. She wrote to Everina, who was still living with Edward and his wife:[17]

I cannot yet give you any certain account of Bess, or form a rational conjecture with respect to the termination of her disorder. She has not had a violent fit of frenzy since I saw you, but her mind is in a most unsettled state . . . a number of wild whims float on her imagination, and fall from her unconnectedly. . . . She seems to think she has been very ill used, and in short, till I see some more favorable symptoms, I shall only suppose that her malady has assumed a new and more distressing appearance.

To complicate the situation, Bishop's own temperament was mercurial (a friend described him as being "either a lion or a spaniel"), and he also became ill. Very soon Mary began to form the opinion that Eliza could not remain with her husband; she came to think not of a temporary removal of her sister until the latter had recovered her health, but of a lasting separation. Mary did not at once make up her mind, and she wrote that "my heart almost broke while Bishop reasons the case"; but she eventually proposed it as the only possibility for both him and Eliza to consider, and once she had made up her mind it proved unshakable.

The period during which matters moved to a crisis was a harrowing one. Mary sent Everina frequent bulletins.

I have nothing to tell you, my dear girl, that will give you pleasure. Yesterday was a dismal day, long and dreary. Bishop was very ill, etc., etc. He is much better today, but misery haunts this house in one shape or another . . . to attempt to lead or govern a weak mind is impossible; it will ever press forward to what it wishes, regardless of impediments, and, with a selfish eagerness, believe what it desires practicable, though the contrary is clear as noonday. My spirits are harried with listening to pros and cons; and my head is so confused, that I sometimes say no when I mean yes. . . . May my habitation never be fixed among the tribe that can't look beyond the present gratification, that draw fixed conclusions from general rules, that attend to the literal meaning only, and, because a thing ought to be, expect that it will come to pass. . . .

Clearly Bishop wanted to keep his wife and maintain his family intact. Mary's reference to "the present gratification" has been

interpreted as his insistence on his marital rights and has therefore led to his portrayal as an inconsiderate and sensual man. But
taken in context with the rest of the sentence, it seems to show
only that he believed his marriage could be saved. The "general
rules," "literal meaning," and "belief that because a thing ought to
be, expect that it will come to pass" refer to the marriage vows
which the couple had solemnly undertaken, to remain united "for
richer or poorer, in sickness or in sorrow, till death do us part," in
the beautiful words of the Anglican marriage service. To Mary's
mind they were irrelevant in this situation since she was convinced that Bishop had only one motive: "To gratify the ruling
passion, he would command all the rest." Even the arguments he
advanced concerning the welfare of the child did not shake her.

If Eliza were to leave her husband, where would she go? She
was in no condition to work out a solution. It was Mary who took
and maintained the initiative throughout the whole unhappy
affair. She wrote Everina asking her to find out if Edward would
again give Eliza a home, but he refused. Mary then decided on a
hazardous course: She would take Eliza away from Bishop, and
they would make a home together.

Not only was such a step against all considerations of propriety,
but Meridith Bishop would have public opinion solidly behind
him if he took steps to secure the return of his wife, and he would
be within his rights. Despite these facts, her own acute fears, and
Eliza's half-crazed condition, Mary went ahead with her plan. She
had only the slim assistance that Fanny and Everina were able
to give her. Fanny took some of Mary and Eliza's belongings to a
shop in the Strand (a street running west from the city limits to
Charing Cross). One morning early in January while Bishop was
out, the two women took a coach, switching to another on the
way in order to avoid being followed, to the house of a Mrs. Dodd
"opposite the Mermaid, Church Street, Hackney." Eliza became
so hysterical during the escape that she actually bit her wedding
ring to pieces.

For several days the two women cowered in their room at Mrs.
Dodd's, expecting the worst. Mary sent Everina almost daily
letters.

My heart beats with the arrival of every coach, and a knocking at the door almost throws me into a *fit*. . . . I hope B. will not discover us, for I would sooner face a Lion—yet the door never opens but I expect to see him panting for breath. Ask Ned how we are to behave if he should find us out, for Bess is determined not to return. Can he force her? But I'll not suppose it, yet I can think of nothing else. She is sleepy, and going to bed; my agitated mind will not permit me. Don't tell Charles or any creature! Oh! let me entreat you to be careful, for Bess does not dread him now as much as I do. . . . She looks now very wild. Heaven protect us! I almost wish for a husband, for I want someone to support me.

Although the sisters had only three guineas between them, they were not friendless. The Bloods, despite their poverty, offered them a home. Mrs. Clare, who had befriended Mary in Hoxton, also offered them money. Bishop did nothing beyond calling at Edward's home and demanding that his wife return to him for the sake of their child. Nor does Edward seem to have made any strenuous effort to locate the runaways. He did refuse any aid to her and Mary.

Mary's action has been hailed by latter-day feminists as the best thing she could do for a sister driven insane by the man she married. Unfortunately there is nothing to show that Mary *first* tried to remove Eliza on a *temporary* basis, on the chance that she might recover her balance and then be able to save her marriage, or that Bishop refused to permit such a step. Although we know very little about Bishop, there is evidence that he was either sufficiently generous or anxious to enlist the goodwill of his sister-in-law, to lend her 20 pounds to help the Bloods out of serious difficulty, at a time when Mary was already contemplating taking Eliza away from him!

But Mary was incapable of making any objective judgment of Meridith Bishop. Instead, what she saw in Bishop was her own father—violent, unstable, abusing a sister who was for Mary the helpless image of her mother. Perhaps the Bishops' marriage could not have been saved—but we can hardly take Mary's word for it, since she had transferred to Bishop all the anger, revulsion —and fear—she had felt toward her father and to Eliza the frustrated and protective pity she had felt for a woman at the mercy of a man she herself hated. No wonder she had written Everina, "Bess does not dread him now as much as I do." She had done what she had so often done as a girl—stepped between husband and wife to protect the latter. But this time, because Mary was an adult, she had done what she could never have done for her mother; she had taken Eliza away from her husband.

In the process of transference she had also lost the ability to consider anybody's welfare except Eliza's, including that of the newly born child. Unlike its mother, Mary thought very little about the third life involved in the tragedy:

> Bess's mind was so harassed with the fear of being discovered, and the thought of leaving the child, that she could not have stood it very long . . . she cannot help sighing about poor little Mary, whom she loved tenderly; and on this score I both love and pity her. The poor brat! it had got a little hold on my affections; some time or other I hope we shall get it.

In judging the Eliza Bishop of later years—her endlessly querulous letters, her irritability, her outbursts of hysterical anger —something must be written off to the traumatic experience of her marriage and the loss of her child. That separation left a life-long scar. Years later she would write, after parting from another child to whom she had been governess: "This is the *last* child I will ever love! while I have the power of loving!"[18]

The experience also sowed in Eliza the seeds of later deep-seated resentment against Mary, who had assumed the obligation to care and provide for her, separated her from her child, and yet would later make it clear to her sisters that Fanny Blood came first in her affections and her responsibilities. Mary was always to be more critical of Eliza than of Everina, and no real sympathy ever developed between them.

CHAPTER III

The School on the Green (1783–86)

IN TAKING ELIZA BISHOP AWAY from her husband, Mary Wollstone-craft at twenty-three displayed for the first time qualities that would set her apart from other women and force her out of the mold of conventional eighteenth-century womanhood. She had shown decision and courage (no courage is greater than that which overrides acute fear) and had laid the basis for growing confidence in her own judgment.

In some respects she was brilliantly justified. Meridith Bishop and little Mary were not heard of again. But the problem of how Mary and Eliza were to maintain themselves remained. Fanny and Mrs. Clare suggested that they open a small shop selling perfumes and haberdashery, which might be stocked for a matter of fifty pounds, and that Edward might provide it. (Because she thought Edward did not approve of her, Fanny declared she would never live with the sisters, "lest he should be averse from assisting them, from a notion that I should live with them."[1]) Edward declined to assist his sisters—he probably felt he had done as much or more than they deserved in putting up the bond

for Eliza's marriage, and he had his own law practice and reputation and a growing family to think of, and what was the use of
his helping Mary if she persisted in helping others when she
could not even take care of herself?

When Mary suggested that the three of them rent a small
house and support themselves by sewing, drawing, and painting,
Fanny had to point out to Everina the realities of the situation:

> . . . Half a guinea a week . . . would just pay for furnished lodg-
> ings for three persons to pig together. As for needle-work, it is
> utterly impossible they could earn more than half a guinea a
> week between them, supposing they had constant employment,
> which is of all things the most uncertain. Mary's sight and
> health are so bad, I am sure she could never endure such
> drudgery. . . . As for what assistance they could give me at the
> paints, we might be ruined before they could arrive at any pro-
> ficiency at the art.

Fanny's letter shows vividly the narrow range of options facing
women of this class and the conditions under which women without training or education—and this would include the overwhelming majority—scrabbled for a living. In the end it was decided that Mary, Eliza, and Fanny would open a school; it would
cost much less than a shop to open and operate, and the income,
especially if there were boarders as well as day students, would
be steadier. A lady "who gave Fanny five guineas for two drawings and (who) will assist us," advised them to settle in Islington,
a village north of London adjacent to Hackney, where the fugi-
tives had lodged. This was probably Mrs. Burgh, the widow of a
scholarly clergyman and schoolmaster, who was to be a strong
source of support to Mary in the future. When enough pupils
failed to materialize in Islington, the women again took her advice and moved to nearby Newington Green, where Mrs. Burgh
herself lived. There she was able to exert enough influence to
bring them some twenty pupils in the course of two or three
weeks.

Mary and Fanny were fortunate in other ways when they
settled at Newington Green. It was still an unspoiled village, a
horseback ride past gardens and across the fields, away from

London. Around "the Green" had gathered a kindly and congenial circle of people who made up a highly individual community, and among them Mary found herself for the first time in
a stimulating environment. Both mind and heart were nourished
by intercourse with a group who were unique not only in Mary's
experience but in England.[2]

Intellectual life centered on the small Dissenting chapel at one
end of the Green, then Presbyterian (it survives today as a
Unitarian congregation). But it was not the stern brand of Dissent
inherited from the Puritans; it generated an atmosphere far more
akin in its gentle and warm human concerns to that which ema-
nated from the Quakers or from the later Evangelical school
which centered on the Clapham Sect at the turn of the century.
Much of this tone was due to Richard Price, the chapel's principal
preacher from 1758 to 1783, a man of broad interests and tower-
ing scholarly eminence. He was widely known as a preacher and
theologian, philosopher, actuary, mathematician in public finance
and political science. His friends reflected his wide interests: the
philosopher David Hume, the scientist Joseph Priestley, the
banker Thomas Rogers, the liberal theologian Andrew Kippis,
and the American agent for the colonies, Benjamin Franklin. In
addition, Price was a most lovable human being, with a simplicity
and humor that endeared him to children and overflowing with
kindness for those in trouble.

How much immediate personal contact Mary Wollstonecraft
had with him is not clear. She testified that he had been "uncom-
monly friendly" to her, and she always thought that some of the
help Mrs. Burgh later extended to her really came from Price. He
continued to live at the Green for a number of years after giving
up his ministry, but Mary can have heard him preach only at
evening service for a few months after she arrived, and he had
abandoned morning service even earlier.[3]

Until now her horizon had necessarily been a narrow one,
bound up as her life had been with the problems of her own family and the Bloods and of earning a living. None of her reading
would have prepared her for the breadth of Price's knowledge,
but his simplicity and humility would have reached her, and his
charm, which was not a thing of manners but sprang from his

benign love of men and of God. "He would talk and read the Bible to us," wrote Samuel Rogers, then a youngster, "so wonderfully till he would send us to bed in a frame of mind as heavenly as his own." Loving-kindness was a quality that would affect Mary even more deeply than most people. In Price for the first time in her experience she found it matched to a first-rate intelligence, and it must have played its part not only in stirring her own mind to activity but in the changes her religious beliefs would gradually undergo.

While the diarist Samuel Rogers remembered Mary sitting in the chapel in an adjacent pew, she was never a contributing member and, because of the heavy burden of her school, probably attended only irregularly.[4] The preacher she may have heard was Joseph Towers, who succeeded Price and, like him, was a man of liberal, not to say radical, sympathies. Another influence on Mary that should not be overlooked was that of James Burgh. He had been dead ten years when she arrived at the Green, but having recognized Mary's unusual gifts, his widow would hardly have failed to give her the writings of her late husband to read; there are passages in his treatise on *The Dignity of Human Nature* which find an echo in Mary's later work on the rights of women. Mary's personal relationship with Mrs. Burgh was sufficiently close to make her feel a particular concern about repaying sums the widow lent her.

Other familiar figures in the circle to which Mary had access were Thomas Rogers (Samuel Rogers' father), a banker whose benevolent sympathies extended far beyond his financial interests and who was a keen student of theology, literature, and philosophy; Joseph Priestley; and the Anglican clergyman John Hewlett, who had an influence on Mary's life out of all proportion to his own modest achievements as a classicist.

However attractive the social atmosphere at the Green might have been, Mary's overriding concern was the school. She had launched it with Eliza and Fanny, but the main burden fell on her, not only because the others were in poor health, but because it was in her independent, even aggressive nature to shoulder such a load. Not only did she run the school, with all the varied concerns it involved—care of the boarding pupils, hiring servants, dealing with parents—but she also taught. If she was ambitious and tried to impart some of the knowledge she had absorbed from John Arden (such as "the globes") and from Mr. Clare, such extras would involve study and preparation and constitute an additional demand on her energies.

Mary also *learned* from her school. Children of all ages were nothing new to her. But in the school her experience broadened; she reflected on what she observed in her pupils and in the behavior of the parents who brought their children to her and, in some instances, lived with her.

At some point the little group was joined by young Everina Wollstonecraft; she may have come to replace Fanny Blood. For Hugh Skeys at long last made up his mind, and early in January, 1785, Fanny left for Lisbon, where she was married on February 24. Added to Mary's sense of loss at her going was the old feeling of dread—for Fanny was already sufficiently ill for Mary to see little hope for her recovery, even in the milder climate of Portugal.

The summons Mary expected came in less than a year, but meanwhile, there were letters from Fanny, making mild fun of her husband and of her married state:

> [March 20, 1785. He is] a good sort of creature and has enough common sense to let his cat of a wife follow her own inclinations in almost everything—and is even delighted when he sees me in spirits long enough to coquette with the men, who to do them justice, are not backward in this respect. . . . I am sorry to add that he is too much inclined to pay attention to his wife than any other woman—but 'tis a fault a little time no doubt will cure. . . .

She wrote in this manner (there is no missing the double edge of the last sentence) to Mary's sisters; none of her letters to Mary have survived.

Despite its promising start, the school was already encountering difficulties. During the summer of 1785 Mary lost the services of a Miss Mason who had been of great practical help to her in caring for the house. In September she lost a good lodger, a Mrs. Campbell, and was unable to replace the contribution her board had made to the household income. She wrote to George Blood in Ireland that she was "plagued with bad servants added to the other cares that attend the management of a family . . . our affairs here do not wear the most smiling aspect."[5]

In addition to the problem of getting Mr. Blood a job—a recurring vexation—George himself had been a source of anxiety. He had been articled to an attorney near Newington Green, a man named Palmer, in the hope that he could be launched in a profitable profession as young Edward Wollstonecraft had been. However, Palmer was arrested on a charge of forgery. Mary took George into her home. When bailiffs arrived to question him, she provided money for him to get away, and eventually he made his way to Ireland. There she wrote to him that the charge being investigated by the bailiffs was not his complicity with Palmer's alleged forgery but the fathering of a child of one of Palmer's servants. Mary refused to believe it ("I suppose the child is Palmer's, or many fathers may dispute the honor"), but the story got out. There was gossip and criticism, since all the neighbors did not share the liberalism and tolerance of the Burgh-Price-Rogers circle, and the matter did the school no good.

Her worries over the school and the Bloods and Fanny's health began to erode the optimism with which Mary had begun. Only to George did she reveal her black depression:

[July 3, 1785] I have lost all relish for life and my almost broken heart is only cheered by the prospect of death. I may be years a-dying, tho, and so I ought to be patient. For at this time to wish myself away would be selfish.

She also unburdened herself to George over her difficulties with her sisters.

[July 21, 1785] My spirits are fled and I am incapable of joy . . . we have so many tattling females—I have no creature to be unreserved to. Eliza and Averina [sic] are so different that I would as soon fly as open my heart to them—How my social comforts have dropped away—Fanny first and then you went over the hills and far away—I am resigned to my fate, but that gloomy kind of resignation that is akin to despair—my heart—my affection cannot fix here and without someone to love this world is a desart [sic] to me. . . .

It has been suggested that Mary's depression at this time arose from disappointment over a love affair with, or an attachment to, an Anglican clergyman named Joshua Waterhouse. The whole business is mysterious because none of her acquaintances ever mentioned Waterhouse, and he seems to have been an example of the less admirable cleric of his day, a man of dissipated tastes who eventually became a miser and recluse and was murdered by a house thief in Huntingdonshire in 1827![6]

The first and only time his name was publicly linked to Mary's was after his violent death. Strewn over the kitchen floor, after the thief had ransacked the house, were found numerous love letters which the Reverend Mr. Waterhouse had received from various ladies; the only name mentioned in a newspaper account is that of Mary Wollstonecraft; whether she wrote Waterhouse one letter or dozens and what their contents really amounted to, we do not know. We might dismiss the episode as too dubious to consider on the basis of such evidence, if Mary herself, in several letters to George Blood, had not referred to a mutual acquaintance by the fanciful name of "Neptune"![7]

Possibly there was an attachment of some sort, which may or may not have coincided with her dark mood just now. It can be argued on more substantial evidence that her depression at this time was due in good part to the bleak circumstances of her life. When she wrote George that she was harassed by suspense, "a dread of I cannot tell what," she was also describing the classic syndrome of deeply repressed anger, the same anger which was rooted in her traumatic childhood experiences and had more recently been reinforced by her encounter with Meridith Bishop (perhaps also Hugh Skeys). Today we know that, far from diminishing with the passage of time, such anger accumulates throughout a lifetime, until the breaking or explosion point is reached. Both Mary Wollstonecraft's physical ailments and her depressions were, to a very large extent, psychosomatic in origin and nature.

What kept her going, despite weariness and anguish, was her sense of responsibility, particularly for her two sisters, and her faith. This latter has been decried as sentimentality or "the desperate resignation of the baffled idealist."[8] But to Mary Wollstonecraft the belief that her troubles were a preparation for future happiness, a necessary stage of spiritual trial and strengthening for a hereafter prepared for those who strove to be worthy of it, was as strong a reality as the vicissitudes which beset her. Shared faith was one of the strongest elements in her affection for George Blood, whom she loved almost more than her own family, not only because he was Fanny's brother but because she could share her struggles with him:

> [July 21, 1785] I have a motherly tenderness for you, and my heart dances when I make any new discovery of goodness in you—It gives me the sincerest satisfaction to find that you look for comfort only where it is to be met with—and that Being in whom we trust will not desert you! . . . I feel . . . most particularly attached to those who are [word illegible] of the promises and who travel on the thorny path with the same *Christian hopes* that render my severe trials a cause of thankfulness—when I *can* think.

There was the catch, of course; she could not always be this logical. Feelings overcame her—irritation at her sisters, rebellion at the hopelessness of the future, loneliness. She would not have been human if she had not vacillated between belief and apparent unbelief—even the saints went through such struggles. But she always came back to the central, living core of trust; "that Being who is gone before to prepare a mansion for us, must cleanse our hearts and make us fit for it."[9]

In September, 1785, came the summons for which Mary had been waiting ever since Fanny Blood had left England to marry Hugh Skeys. Fanny was pregnant and ill; she wanted Mary to come out to Lisbon and be with her during her confinement.

The fact that Mary responded to her call was only one more instance of her deep feeling for Fanny. (It was very much akin to some of her father's actions when by an impulsive action, whatever the motive, he jeopardized his family's welfare.) Now, by responding to Fanny, she was endangering the future of both the sisters for whom she had assumed responsibility. In leaving the school in the hands of Eliza, then twenty-two, and the even younger Everina, she was imposing a burden they were incapable of carrying—and Mary must have known her sisters well enough to understand this. Moreover, she was also confirming their belief that Fanny (who had gone away, to a husband of her own choosing!) still mattered more to Mary than they did, with no husband to look out for them. Certainly the journey would not help close the gap between Mary and her oldest brother, who already considered her irresponsible. Finally, her departure would shake the confidence of parents whose children were in the school.

Perhaps Mary was impelled by more than her feelings for Fanny when she decided to go. Whether or not she realized it, she was running away from a situation that was too much for her, just as her father had done. She did the same thing repeatedly in the course of her life—for instance, when she went to revolutionary Paris in 1792. When Mary came up against the intolerable, she tried to escape from it. It is only fair to point out that her mother, for whom Mary had so little regard, did not run away. She had endowed her eldest daughter with her capacity for perseverance—but only up to a point. There were times when the father's escapist strain became dominant and when Mary tried to shift her responsibilities—or run. The journey to Portugal was one of those occasions.

Some of the results of her decision were apparent even before she left for what seemed likely to be an absence of several months. A Mrs. Cockburn announced she would advise three possible boarders against coming to the Wollstonecraft establishment. However, Mary found support, as well as opposition; Mrs. Burgh lent her money for the costly journey (Mary always believed the money really came from Dr. Price). It could of course be repaid only from the proceeds of the school and therefore by the joint efforts of the three sisters, a circumstance which would hardly be lost on Eliza and Everina.

By November Mary was on her way. There were times when it appeared that it would be a one-way voyage. The thirteen-day passage across the Bay of Biscay was stormy:

> The sea was so rough, and we had such hard gales of wind, the captain was afraid we would be dismasted . . . the water came in at the cabin windows, and the ship rolled about in such a manner, it was dangerous to stir. The women were sea-sick the whole time. . . .[10]

Not, however, Mary, for whom the climax of the grim journey was the illness of a fellow passenger whom no one else was well enough or willing to nurse and whose symptoms were a painful preview of what awaited her. She reached Lisbon to find Fanny already in labor; four hours after her arrival the child was born, healthy but "puny." Despite a brief interval of improvement, Fanny Skeys died on November 29, 1785.

Mary's stay in Portugal was brief. She saw Fanny buried, then took the first ship back to England, all within a month of her arrival.

Fanny's death had a far-reaching effect on her friend. As long as she lived, she filled Mary's need for "a particular affection" which was the heritage of her rejected childhood. Whether Mary would ever have outgrown her compulsion to sacrifice everything and everyone else on Fanny's behalf if she had lived, we do not know. If Skeys had made Fanny unhappy, Mary might have come to her rescue as she had to Eliza's. The pattern of intense devotion and possessiveness was to repeat itself again in Mary's life. Fanny's death released Mary from the need for further acts of devotion to her friend and freed her to grow into greater maturity, but it did not alter the basic pattern of her nature.

CHAPTER IV

Thoughts on the Education of Daughters (1786)

MARY'S VOYAGE BACK TO ENGLAND was even worse than the trip out; during four stormy weeks, it often seemed as if the ship would founder. When it encountered a French vessel in the Bay of Biscay in even worse straits, the English captain refused to take its crew and passengers on board, a risky operation at best, and gave as his pretext that he did not have enough food aboard for all. Characteristically, it was Mary alone who challenged him; she threatened, if he failed to attempt a rescue, to reveal his dereliction when they reached shore. He backed down, and the transfer was safely carried out.

On her way to Newington Green, Mary passed through London. The experiences of the past few weeks—Fanny's death, the two hazardous boat journeys—had sharpened her perceptions, and she saw darker aspects of London life that had previously gone unnoticed. Not long afterward she wrote of her autobiographical heroine in the novel *Mary*:

As she passed through the streets [of London] in an hackney-coach, disgust and horror alternately filled her mind. She met

some women drunk; and the manners of those who attacked the
sailors, made her shrink into herself and exclaim, are these my
fellow-creatures! . . . She saw vulgarity, dirt and vice—her soul
sickened; this was the first time such complicated misery had
obtruded itself on her sight—Forgetting her own grief, she gave
the world a much indebted tear; mourned for a world in ruins.[1]

The London that she saw early in 1786 was the focus of misery
for a country suffering from a half century of almost continuous
warfare, aimed at achieving a balance of power in Europe and
building a colonial empire. In the end the war for the independence of the American colonies injected an idealistic note
into the endless seesaw struggle. When the Peace of Paris was
signed in 1783, its most important outcome was the establishment
of an independent nation founded on democratic principles in the
Western Hemisphere.

But to the average Englishman, whether country gentleman,
yeoman or merchant or the flotsam and jetsam already crowded
into stinking slums, it made very little difference except the cessa-
tion of casualty lists. The victories of Clive in India and the
British fleet half a world away had no direct impact on every-
day living. That they would contribute to revolutionizing a way of
life by pumping vast wealth into the island kingdom was not
immediately visible. Wealth itself was nothing new in England,
which had been ruled during much of the eighteenth century by
an oligarchy of some seventy Whig landed families, whose lavish
way of life made a model for the new rich to imitate or outdo.

What was new was the inexorable rise in prices and the flow of
impoverished families from villages whose common lands were
being enclosed to the cities in search of bread. That flow was
becoming intensified by a sharp population rise, owing to the discovery that cleanliness was a deterrent to infant mortality at
birth, a discovery which would steadily increase the pressure of
poverty.

The younger Pitt, only twenty-six years old, was Prime Minister. He had a strong interest in badly needed parliamentary reform. Although the House of Commons numbered such brilliant
liberals as Burke, Fox, Sheridan, and Wilberforce among its members, most seats were at the disposal of the great landlords and

were dispensed as patronage. In 1768 in the entire country there had been only 160,000 voters, who held the franchise on the basis of an outmoded set of property rights; in twenty years, matters had not improved. There was no channel for public dissatisfaction to express itself except through violence or rioting such as the anti-Catholic outbursts of 1780. The same limited group of landlords dispensed the majority of clerical appointments or livings without regard for the merits or qualifications of the appointee or the number of livings he already held.

The industrial development which would shortly compound England's wealth, on the one hand, and the miseries of her poor, on the other, had just begun in some sections of the country. The groundwork had been laid for revolutionizing the textile industries—wool, cotton, and silk alike—by the invention of machines for spinning thread and for mechanized weaving that would do the work that had previously required many hands.

Mary Wollstonecraft, now twenty-seven years old, was aware of little or none of these developments when she passed through London early in 1786, and the enormity of its "complicated misery" struck at her heart. But she gave it only passing thought, for her fears were centered on what awaited her at Newington Green. She found the reality even worse than she expected.

A Mrs. Disney who had been boarding while her three children attended the school had fallen out with Eliza and Everina and was on the point of leaving; when she did so, it was without paying Mary all the money she owed her. Other pupils had already been withdrawn. With the diminished number of students, Mary could no longer afford the rent of a large house. There was also her debt to Mrs. Burgh, and others now began to accumulate. She still had the older Bloods on her hands, although George, now settled in a position in Dublin, was just beginning to help them. Tradesmen harassed her, and the outlook, she wrote George, was gloomy. Nevertheless, she rejected his suggestion that she come to Ireland, since that would amount to repudiating her debts:

> I am indeed very much distressed at present, and my future prospects are still more gloomy—yet nothing should induce me to fly from England. My creditors have a right to do what they

please with me, should I not be able to satisfy their demands.
. . . Should our present plan fail [the school], I cannot even
guess what the girls will do. My brother, I am sure, will not
receive them, and they are not calculated to struggle with the
world. Eliza, in particular, is very helpless. Their situation has
made me very uneasy—and as to your father and mother, they
have been a continual weight on my spirits. You have removed
part of the load, for I now hope you would be able to keep them
from perishing, should my affairs grow desperate. . . .[2]

Mary's father was in Wales, presumably living on the rents
from the Primrose Street houses, but who was collecting them
and looking after the property, we do not know.

In the general gloom, one event pointed the way to Mary
Wollstonecraft's future: She wrote and published her first book, in
1786. The proceeds—10 guineas—paid the fare of the two older
Bloods to Dublin, where George assumed responsibility for them.
It was the Reverend John Hewlett who not only suggested to
her that she try to write a book, but introduced her to the man
who published it, Joseph Johnson.[3]

The theme of *Thoughts on the Education of Daughters* grew
naturally out of her experiences with her school during the past
three years. It is a collection of short essays on the care of children, their upbringing and education, with particular emphasis
on the training of girls. Here can be traced in seed form some of
the ideas which would later be more fully developed in *A Vindication of the Rights of Woman*. It lacks the ornate phrases and
flowery verbiage that still characterized both prose and poetry in
the late eighteenth century and that makes so much of Mary's
later writing unpalatable to modern readers. Instead, the style is
simple and direct, the sentences are short and lucid, and the sequence of ideas is clear and natural. For its time, it is an astonishing first book, and it is not surprising that Joseph Johnson, familiar with the trash being written on how to equip young ladies with
the needed social graces, marked down Mary Wollstonecraft as
an unusual woman.

Mary was, of course, writing for a public limited by the ability
to read and to buy books, found largely in the growing middle
class, the country gentry, and the aristocracy. It made sense,

therefore, when she urged that children be educated by their parents rather than servants, not only because they must be taught and reasoned with—which most servants were not equipped to do—from their earliest years, but because love was so essential to their upbringing. The home should be harmonious and happy, and the child governed by love rather than constraint or punishment.

> It is only in the years of childhood that the happiness of a human being depends on others—and to embitter those years by needless restraints is cruel. To conciliate the affections, affection should be shown, and a little proof of it ought always to be given . . . punishment should be reserved for serious offenses: violation of the truth, cruelty to animals, inferiors, or those kinds of follies which lead to vice.[4]

It would be interesting to know whether Mary was already familiar with Jean Jacques Rousseau's *Emile* (published in 1762) and had read John Locke's classic on education, *An Essay Concerning Human Understanding* (1690). Rousseau's work was a reaction against the rigidity and formalism of education on the Continent, particularly in France, where it was controlled by the Catholic Church; Mary was to take bitter exception to some of Rousseau's theories on the education of girls in her *Vindication of the Rights of Woman*. Although John Locke did not write specifically about the education of girls, many of Mary's ideas, which she put into practice in her school, paralleled his. He too was concerned with the child's bodily health, with sufficient sleep, a sensible diet, and plenty of exercise. "Gamesome humor" and the "noise and bustle of their play" were part of a child's educational process. Teaching should be by example, never "by rote" or with reliance on authority. Even more congenial to Mary's ideas would be his opposition to any attempt to "curb or humble" a child's mind and his insistence on fostering its interest and curiosity.

But Locke put the formation of a good character and what he called "wisdom" ahead of learning, by which he meant study and intellectual discipline. He was concerned with the education of a young gentleman of means and position at the close of the seventeenth century. When Mary Wollstonecraft put her emphasis instead on awakening and training the intellect, in particular the intellect of a *woman*, she was arguing without precedent, at a time when the mere existence of a woman's mind not only was in question, but was of no interest to anyone, women included.

In *Thoughts on the Education of Daughters*, her ideas were still in a very embryonic state. She argued that from the earliest age, every attempt should be made to develop children's intelligence: "Whenever a child asks a question, it should always have a reasonable answer given to it." Curiosity should be stimulated: "Many things with respect to the animal and vegetable world may be examined in an amusing way; and this is an innocent source of pleasure within everybody's reach."

No progressive teacher today could put the case for learning how to reason more compellingly: "Above all, teach them to combine their ideas. It is of more use than can be conceived, for a child to learn to compare things that are similar in some respects and different in others. I wish them to be taught to think."

"I wish them to be taught to think." In a book on the education of girls, this phrase alone showed how far ahead of her time the writer already stood.

Yet despite her emphasis on the development of the mind—in contrast with the vogue for external accomplishments such as dancing, drawing, manners, and the rest of the frippery which then passed for female education—Mary Wollstonecraft insisted strongly on the importance of woman's role in the home:

> No employment of the mind is a sufficient excuse for neglecting domestic duties, and I cannot conceive that they are incompatible. A woman may fit herself to be the companion and friend of a man of sense, and yet know how to take care of his family.

In another passage she wrote that the goal of education and training was "to prepare a woman to fulfill the duties of a wife and mother." Later feminists who professed the thought of Mary Wollstonecraft as their creed dropped this aspect of it entirely.

In a chapter of her book entitled "Unfortunate Situations," Mary Wollstonecraft described the plight of the young woman whose parents had spent or lost all their means and who, like herself, might be thrown on the world to earn her livelihood as teacher, governess, or companion. It is bad enough for such a young woman to be "companion," she wrote, "to a rich cousin. It is infinitely worse to live with strangers, who are so intolerably tyrannical. . . . It is impossible to enumerate the many hours of anguish such a person must spend. She is alone, shut out from equality, and confidence. . . ." Teaching was little better: "A teacher at a school is only a kind of upper servant, who has more work than menial ones. A governess to young ladies is equally disagreeable." Some sixty years later, when matters had changed all too little, Charlotte Brontë would write *Villette*, describing the plight of a teacher, and *Jane Eyre*, about a governess, bearing eloquent witness to the truth of Mary's words.

In later years, Mary Wollstonecraft demanded substantive changes in education and opportunities in new fields for women, even the vote. But now she was still hampered by her lack of experience and intellectual development. Her ideas were still fragmentary, limited, and largely subjective. The great leap ahead in her thinking was still several years away. Even the emotional problems of a young woman (referred to in that earlier and simpler time as "the passions"!) are here discussed in terms of individual experience, perhaps her own:

> I am very far from thinking love irresistible, and not to be conquered. "If weak women go astray," it is they and not the stars that are to be blamed. A resolute effort will almost always overcome difficulties. I knew a woman very early in life attached to an agreeable man, yet she saw his faults; his principles unfixed, and his prodigal turn would have obliged her to have restrained every benevolent emotion of her heart. She exerted her influence to improve him, but in vain did she try for years to do this. Convinced of the impossibility, she determined not to marry him, though she was forced to encounter poverty and its attendants.

Was the woman Mary and the man Joshua Waterhouse? She would prove on other occasions remarkably tenacious in her efforts to improve or remold people. Nothing but trouble ever came from her inability to distinguish between the younger brothers and sisters whom she tried to mother and develop into responsible adults and the men with whom she fell in love, who were not all she thought that they should be, yet stubbornly resisted her efforts to change them!

In her book, as in her own life, Mary's last resort was religious faith, and she offered it as such to the unhappy among her readers:

> Yet if a young woman falls into [so much misery] she ought not to be discontented. Good must ultimately arise from everything, to those who look beyond the infancy of their being; and here the comfort of a good conscience is our only stable support. The main business of our lives is to be virtuous; and He who is training us up for immortal bliss, knows best that trials will contribute to make us so. . . . The Almighty is then the kind parent, who chastens and educates, and indulges us not when it would tend to our hurt. . . .

Mary never lost her belief that "the main business of our lives is to be virtuous," but that purpose became vastly enlarged in scope as her comprehension deepened. She came to realize that such a purpose could be accomplished in more ways than just passive submission to the will of God and to demand drastic changes in society's attitude to and expectations for women.

Mary returned to Newington Green from Portugal in February, 1786; by spring matters at the school had reached a crisis. She moved into the home of a Mrs. Blackburn, with only one servant, and her sisters began looking for positions, one as a companion, the other as a teacher. Eliza in particular found the prospect terrifying and would have preferred to go on living with Mary, but Mary seems to have refused. Eliza, she wrote to George Blood, "could not give up the world or live in the style I intend to, if it was possible to earn a scanty living together."[5]

Poor Eliza! For many years she was to face greater, more constant unhappiness than her more gifted sister, shifting from one position to another as each in turn became intolerable. Everina fared better because she had a more resilient temperament and also a better relationship with her oldest sister. Between Eliza and Mary a barrier grew up. Mary complained often to George about Eliza's perpetual whine and how impossible it was to write freely to her for fear of depressing her mercurial spirits still further.

By the end of June Everina was back in Edward's household (where she could make herself useful helping to care for two small children). Eliza, recommended by the ever staunch Mrs. Burgh, was at Mrs. Sampell's school in Market Harborough, a midland town a dozen miles from Leicester. Mary herself was teaching eleven pupils of her "old flock" entirely by herself and studying French with "an excellent master."

Her letters to George Blood during that summer of 1786 are black with depression. But when George wrote once more urging her to come and live with his family, she again refused. This time she admitted that it was not just a question of facing her responsibilities to her creditors. She could not "live with your Father and condescend to practice those *arts* which are *necessary* to keep him in temper."[6]

Then suddenly in midsummer matters became more hopeful. Mary accepted an offer—one among several—of a position in Ireland which she heard of through another Anglican clergyman, the Reverend John Prior, a teacher and housemaster at Eton. The salary would be 40 pounds a year, of which Mary would be able to save a considerable amount toward paying off her debts. She was to be governess to the younger children of Lord Kingsborough, a great landowner in County Cork. She would meet the Kingsborough girls at the Priors' in Eton and travel to Ireland with them, and in this expectation she prepared to leave Newington Green in late September or early October.[7]

Her last weeks at the Green were embittered by Edward's refusal to help her pay her most pressing debts: "Edward behaved very rude to me, and has not assisted me in the smallest degree." Once again Mrs. Burgh came to the rescue and lent her enough so that she could leave England without fear of any legal action being taken against her.[8] Richard Price too showed her renewed kindness although his wife had just died and he himself was planning to move away from Newington Green.

Yet at this time when she was preparing to take the dreaded post of governess in a great house, Mary was already thinking further ahead.

The terms held out to her [by the Kingsboroughs] were such that she determined to accept, at the same time resolving to retain the situation only for a short time. She was desirous however first to accumulate a small sum of money, which should enable her to consider at leisure the different literary engagements that might offer, and provide in some degree for the eventual deficiency of her earliest attempts.[9]

Already Mary had glimpsed the possibility of turning her first contact with the publisher Joseph Johnson to further account, to escape from the rat race of work she despised. She had glimpsed something better at the Green and had demonstrated with her first book that it was not beyond her reach. Perhaps this vision explains Mary's loathing for her position at the Kingsboroughs and the unhappiness of the next year.

She had an unpleasant foretaste of the kind of life in store for her while she waited for the Kingsborough girls at Eton. At the Priors' house she had an inside view of the great "public school" and the social life that revolved around it. She disliked both intensely. It was Bath all over again and she hated its frivolity, its superficiality, and its endless puerile witticisms which ran chiefly to puns—"nothing but dress and ridicule going forward," she wrote to Everina.[10]

In the distasteful atmosphere of Eton, Mary succumbed to her emotions. She was twenty-seven years old, but the thought of going so far away from home (although any real "home" was nonexistent) frightened her. There was no longer a Fanny to be cherished, and Mary's deeply loving nature required some outlet. Although she could not tolerate her sisters when they all were under the same roof together, her feelings swung to the opposite pole at the thought of a long separation. She wrote Everina:

How grateful to me was your tender unaffected letter—I nearly wept over it—for I was in a melting mood. . . . A whole train of nerve disorders have taken possession of me . . . you will be surprised to hear that a disappointment with respect to your visit made me almost faint on Friday. . . . When shall we meet? Your image haunts me and I could take my poor timid girl to my bosom and shield her from the mean winds—and if it is possible from the contagion of folly—or the inroads of sorrow.

Everina was finding life in Edward's household difficult, and Mary exhorted her sister to try to find another situation: "How earnestly I wish you out of his house. If you possibly can, try to exert yourself or you will fall a prey to melancholy. You require kindness . . . but those you are with are the merest earthworms."

Instead of coming to Eton, the Kingsboroughs changed their plans. They went back to Ireland without Mary, leaving her to travel in the company of the butler and his wife, their house-keeper. The couple were "beyond measure civil and attentive," so Mary had no cause for complaint, and the boat crossing from Holyhead to Dublin was enlivened by the company of a young clergyman who proved "an agreeable companion . . . intelligent, with that kind of politeness which arises from sensibility."[11] This may have been Henry Gabell, a newly ordained graduate of Oxford going to take up a position in the north of Ireland. In Dublin she spent several days visiting the Bloods and renewing ties with an old friend she and Fanny had known, Betty Delane. For the Bloods, she need have no further financial concern: "Old Blood is now settled in a very elligible [*sic*] place, the income of which will enable him to live very comfortably. This is a weight off my mind."

But none of these pleasant experiences proved any lasting source of comfort. At the other end of a long drive by chaise lay the magnificent Kingsborough mansion. Mary Wollstonecraft entered its great gates "with the same kind of feeling as I should have if I was going to the Bastille."

CHAPTER V

Irish Crossing (1786–87)

CENTURIES OF ATTEMPTED conquest and subjugation had left Ireland in abysmal poverty and turmoil from which the country was enjoying a brief respite of peace (but not prosperity) when Mary Wollstonecraft spent ten months there in 1786 and 1787. Religious conflict had exacerbated the situation; the English had attempted to stamp out Catholicism so as to remove any possibility of foreign invasion from the Continent by using Ireland as a base. What Elizabethan violence had begun, Cromwellian atrocity had completed; the result was a backward, hungry, and intractably hostile Catholic peasantry, a Protestant gentry largely English in origin, imported to control and exploit the country, and government from London.

In the 1780's a change had gradually taken place. Because of the long war centering on the revolt of the American colonies and their loss, the British government had made some concessions to Ireland in trade and agriculture and in 1782 permitted the establishment of a Parliament in Dublin which was to last eighteen years, until the upheaval and revolt of 1798 brought about Ireland's forced union with Great Britain and the loss of all self-government.

It was during the interlude under "Grattan's Parliament" that Mary saw Ireland from an unusual vantage point; her employer, Lord Kingsborough, was unique among Irish landowners. Although he and his wife were of Irish Protestant stock, he set himself the task of turning his enormous landholdings from a waste exploited by middlemen who rack-rented the unfortunate peasants and raised only minimum subsistence crops into a productive estate under enlightened management.

Mitchelstown, the center of the 100-square-mile family holdings (extending into three counties—Cork, Limerick, and Tipperary), had been described as having "a situation worthy of the proudest capital," sheltered on one side by the Galties, a mountain range which Mary saw from her window. The highest mountain of the range, Galtymore, had an elevation of only 3,000 feet but rose with dramatic suddenness from the plain, and the cluster of its six attendant peaks—Temple Hill, Knockateriff, Lyracappul, Carignabinnia, Slievecushnabinnia, and Knocknanuss—gave it an effectiveness out of all proportion to its height, especially since it was often cloud-capped.

The marriage of the Kingsboroughs in 1769 had taken place in order to reunite ancient family estates; Lady Kingsborough brought her husband immense wealth. The couple settled in Ireland in 1775 and found appalling conditions: Poverty was general, and the land, like all Ireland, had been stripped bare of trees, which had been exported to England or burned for firewood. But by the time Mary came to Mitchelstown it had already become a showplace.

In addition to the magnificent home he built for his family, Lord Kingsborough laid out spacious gardens and nurseries, built stone houses for many of his staff and substantial cabins for the lesser servants, developed a herd of cattle and horses, and made Mitchelstown a model town which even today retains many of the features he created: neat streets, trees, schools and shops, a church and library—an interesting example of early town planning and development. There was work for hundreds in building, in tending the land and stock, and in the elaborate household the Kingsboroughs maintained. What happened in the property nearest to the Kingsborough residence had impact throughout the 1,300-acre estate. Lord Kingsborough even established local industries to take up the slack of employment when the major part of the building would be complete; he had begun this process in 1786, and Mary wrote her sister Everina that he had "established a manufactory near Cork."

None of these aspects of the Kingsborough establishment came, properly speaking, within the province of a governess. The wonder—and tragedy—of Mary's stay in Ireland is that she apparently did not catch even a glimpse of what was taking place at Mitchelstown. If she used the handsome library or any of its contents, she did not record the fact in her letters.

These are filled, instead, with despairing accounts of her poor health and angry descriptions of the company in which she found herself. Worn out with the accumulated fatigue from years of struggle to save first her mother, then Eliza, then Fanny, then the school, Mary was in no condition, physically or mentally, to maintain her equilibrium in an establishment consisting of a large crowd of family, guests, and retainers, all in a constant frenetic state of activity, with the uproar made even worse by the presence of large numbers of dogs. Conversation in the female society to which she was largely restricted was the same empty foolishness which had revolted her in Bath and again during her short stay at Eton.

The first impressions she received of the family were unfavorable. The children seemed "wild Irish, unformed and not very pleasing." Lady Kingsborough was "shrewd, clever, a great talker . . . a clever woman and a well-meaning one, but not of the order of being I could love." Lord Kingsborough fared no better: "With his Lordship I have had little conversation, but his countenance does not promise more than good humor, and a little *fun* not refined." (So much for the most progressive landlord in the country!)

Not only was Mary in poor health, but the society in which she found herself was in appalling contrast with the people with whom she had associated, even if infrequently, at Newington Green:

Confined to the society of a set of silly females, I have no
social converse, and their boisterous spirits and unmeaning
laughter exhausts me, not forgetting hourly domestic bicker-
ings. The topics of matrimony and dress take their turn, not in
a very sentimental style—alas, poor sentiment! it has no residence here. I almost wish the girls were novel readers and
romantics; I declare false refinement is better than none at
all. . . . Lady K.'s passion for animals fills up the hours which are
not spent in dressing. All her children have been ill—very
disagreeable fevers. Her ladyship visited them in a formal
way, though their situation called forth my tenderness, and I
endeavored to amuse them, while she lavished awkward fondness on her dogs. I think now I hear her infantine lisp. She
rouges—and in short is a fine lady, without fancy or sensibility.
I am almost tormented to death by dogs. . . . Oh! my Everina
my heart is almost broken. . . . Life has lost its relish, all my
faculties languish—I am grown a poor melancholy wretch. . . .
I long for my eternal rest—my nerves are so injured I suffer
more than I suppose I should do. . . . I would not write this to
Eliza—she cannot discriminate; but to you I *cannot* be
reserved, and I hope the dreadful contagion will not affect
you. . . .[1]

In reading such letters—and there were many of them—one
might easily think Mary was unable to carry out her duties. This
was not the case. She made every effort to accommodate herself
to her uncongenial milieu:

I make allowances and adapt myself, talk of getting husbands
for the *ladies*—and the *dogs*, and am wonderfully entertaining;
and then I retire to my room, form figures in the fire, or view
the Galties, a fine range of mountains near us, and so does
time waste away in apathy or misery. . . .[2]

Moreover, while her letters do faithfully record her state of
mind and body when she wrote them, both could change very
rapidly. A letter to Everina, written at midnight, complains of
her overwhelming lassitude. The next day she writes in very different vein to her publisher, Joseph Johnson; she wished Johnson
to know that she was looking for a broader horizon than her
present one:

As I mentioned to you, previous to my departure, that I entered on my way of life with extreme regret—I am vain enough to imagine that you wish to hear how I like my situation. A state of dependence must ever be irksome to me, and I have *many* vexations to encounter, which some people would term trifling—I have most of the [illegible] comforts of life— yet when weighed with liberty they are of little value. . . .[3]

Despite her many complaints, there is evidence that she was extremely successful in her main responsibility, the education of the Kingsborough girls. Yet here, too, was a cause of frustration, as she found herself severely limited in what she was permitted or able to accomplish. She wrote Johnson:

Confined almost entirely to the society of children, I am anxiously solicitous for their future welfare, and mortified beyond measure, when counteracted in my endeavors to improve them—I feel all a mother's fears for the swarm of little ones which surround me, and observe disorders, without having power to apply the proper remedies.[4]

Nevertheless, Mary was able to accomplish a great deal. In a very short time she had made a place for herself in the children's affections. When Margaret, the oldest of the girls and her favorite and most responsive pupil, became seriously ill, the burden of the nursing fell on Mary. Margaret would hardly let her governess out of her sight. And while her actual responsibility was limited to three girls, all the children loved her.

I go to the nursery, something like maternal fondness fills my bosom. The children cluster about me—one catches a kiss, another lisps my long name—while a sweet little boy who is conscious that he is a favorite, calls himself my Tom. At the sight of their mother they tremble and run to me for protection—this renders them dear to me—and I discover the kind of happiness I was formed to enjoy.[5]

The fact that the Kingsborough children were afraid of their mother was another reason Mary disliked her employer. Her ladyship had a hot and ungovernable temper which she vented on all comers; it aroused in Mary the same reactions as had her father's temper and that of Meridith Bishop. She could not express her own anger, but in an effort to make some kind of compensation to the Kingsborough children she lavished affection on them. She was their champion and defender, and in the end this was the cause of her departure from the Kingsborough household.

A governess with a different background might have been able to dismiss Lady Kingsborough's tantrums, for certainly Mary's situation was not without amenities. While the family were still in Mitchelstown, she was granted a few days' leave and paid a visit to a family in Tipperary who were cousins of the Bloods. When the Kingsborough household removed to Dublin in February for the social season there, Mary went ahead with the girls and enjoyed the respite from adult trivialities and tempers. During her stay in Dublin she had more comfortable quarters, with her own living room where she could entertain callers. She enjoyed seeing Betty Delane and George Blood. At least one member of the Kingsboroughs' acquaintances commanded her respect —George Ogle, a poet, Member of Parliament, and in some respects a man of advanced liberal views; Mary liked both him and his wife. There is also some basis for thinking that she had as a caller the young clergyman Henry Gabell, whose employer, John O'Neill, represented County Antrim in the Irish Parliament, and that she had at least a passing sentimental interest in him. One letter to him reflects a considerable degree of intimacy, or perhaps a wish for such intimacy:

> . . . be it known to thee—I am both sick and sleepy—it being past the witching time of night—and I have been thinking how "stale, flat and unprofitable" this world is grown to me—you'll say I am always running on in this strain, and perhaps tell me as a friend once before did, alluding to music, that I mistook a *flat* for a natural. . . . Good night—or good morning. . . .

Underneath her signature, she scrawled "Friday morning, two o'clock."[6]

We can perhaps speculate that some of the depression that hung over her was caused by the fact that Gabell did not reciprocate her interest and that she was once again suffering, not just the pangs of unrequited affection, which are always painful, but the whole traumatic pattern of rejection which overwhelmed her at the slightest excuse. There are obscure half-ironic hints in her letters to Everina that she was interested in someone: "I am like a *lilly* [*sic*] drooping—is it not a sad pity that so sweet a flower should waste its sweetness on the Desart—Dublin—air. . . ."[7] Another letter to her sister ends on a similar note: "An organ underneath my window has been playing for *tenderness formed* [*sic*]—and well a day my *poor heart*—my spectacles *are dim*."

Unfortunately Everina was an erratic correspondent. Mary found her letters too infrequent and unsatisfactory when they did arrive. She complained bitterly:

> You write so seldom, our separation is really *like death*—I wish to hear every *minute* particular concerning you—but you put it off from time to time, and then in a *hurry* to write, take up a *small* sheet of paper—and then have done with it—it is a disagreeable task—is it not so?—I know you are sometimes not well—but you have oftener not resolution to exert yourself —the most trifling amusement (I use your own words) will take up your attention and detach your thoughts from our situation—and yet your affections are not sufficiently warm or lasting to keep up a regular correspondence which would *improve* you, afford me *great* comfort, and turn your thoughts away from the present scene. "The deeds of kindness show the heart."—Can I suppose that I am loved when I am not *remembered*? I am not angry, but *hurt* and disappointed. . . .[8]

Some of Mary's criticisms could hardly endear her to a younger sister who was already feeling the weight of constant censure from her elders. When Everina still failed to write and the gap in her letters prolonged into weeks, Mary grew both angry and cruel: "I am a little surprised and disappointed at not receiving an answer to my last two or three letters—but I ought not to have expected from *you* that kind of affection which only can gratify *my* heart. . . ."[9]

But what of Everina? She was barely twenty-one, fully as unhappy as Mary and with fewer resources of escape and distraction. She loathed living with her brother—Mary's letters allude

repeatedly to Edward's unkindness to his youngest sister and to
the need for Everina to find a position which would enable her to
leave his home. Eventually Everina must have lashed out in self-
defense, for there is a letter from Mary ending with the cryptic
words: "I shall never mention your writing again. Adieu."[10] She
kept her word.

Although Mrs. Burgh had enabled Mary to pay off her other
creditors before leaving Newington Green, she felt keenly her
obligation to her generous friend. The best hope of repaying her
at an early date and of assisting both her sisters further appeared
to be a suit which Edward was conducting against a man named
Roebuck, for money owed, not to himself, but to the family estate.
The most likely basis for such a suit would seem to be Roebuck's
misappropriation of rentals collected from the Primrose Street
houses as Edward John Wollstonecraft's agent. Mary's legitimate
claim to a share in the money arose from the fact that her father
had appropriated part of her inheritance, but it was a claim Edward apparently chose to ignore. "Surely Edward will not attempt
to keep the money?"[11] Mary wrote Everina—but he did, probably because he felt that he too had a claim on it in view of his
father's mismanagement—or misappropriation—of *his* share of
his grandfather's estate.

Next, Edward made serious charges—we do not know their exact nature—against Everina for improper behavior. Mary was infuriated and temporarily forgot all her irritation with her younger
sister. She refused to believe the story and instead saw it as an
excuse for Edward's trying to remove Everina from his household:

> I am persuaded this motive made him invent the shameful
> story you mention—I am really full of indignation. The reputa-
> tion of a young person is not to be trifled with. . . . I very much
> approve your intention to leave his house and shall wait with
> impatience your next letter.[12]

A month later Everina still had not found a refuge, and Mary was
writing: "I shall be glad to hear you are out of Ned's house—let
you go where you will." To give Everina a change of scene,
Mary sent her money for the fare to spend a holiday near Eliza

(in Leicestershire). She was still deeply concerned about Eliza who despised her position, and Charles, then living with Edward to whom he had been articled for the study of law.

Dublin at the time of Mary's stay there was a capital, enjoying a social and cultural renaissance, however brief and illusory. There was more of the artificial social intercourse, the fashion, and the round of calling which Mary disliked, but there were also plays and opera and costume balls—to all of which Lady Kingsborough took her governess. Mary enjoyed *Macbeth* and other plays and a two-day commemoration of Handel's music. There were concerts at evening gatherings at the Rotunda, and on one occasion at least Mary wore a domino at a masked ball. "The lights, the novelty of the scene, and everything together contributed to make me *more* than half mad. I gave full scope to a satirical vein."[13]

Yet she continued to be critical of her employer and rebellious at the treatment she received. She acknowledged Lady Kingsborough's kindness in taking her into society, her attempts to be civil and concerned with Mary's welfare (to the point of trying vainly to make her see a doctor), her efforts to find positions for the Wollstonecraft sisters, her charity to her tenants. But Mary also continued to complain of her ladyship's temper, her neglect of her children, her frivolity, and even of her jealousy of Mary herself, not only in the matter of winning the children's affection, but in her own drawing room, to which Mary was occasionally invited—or summoned. There lay the rub. Mary's position was at best an inferior one, and the amenities she enjoyed were privileges which her employer accorded her. Having invited her into the drawing room, she could also—as Mary reported on one occasion—send her away again before the gentlemen joined the ladies and demonstrate pique at George Ogle's attentions to her governess. While she certainly made considerable efforts—and compromises—to keep her unusual employee happy, she could not achieve the impossible. Mary Wollstonecraft was the last woman to be a successful governess. Much the same was true of Charlotte Brontë, who also tried to make her living that way and was just as unhappy as Mary. In her case we are fortunate in having a description of her by a cousin of the children Miss Brontë was caring for, which applies in every respect to Mary:

> "If she was invited to walk to church with [the family], she thought she was being ordered about like a slave; if she was not invited, she imagined she was being excluded from the family circle . . ." clearly a prickly and difficult person to have in the house, miserably lacking in that serviceable outer skin with which the more resilient extrovert is provided.[14]

In a more bitter vein, George Eliot described the kind of person such a position required: "Everything looked blooming and joyous except Miss Morgan, who was brown, dull and resigned, and altogether, as Mrs. Vincy said, just the sort of person for a governess."[15]

Mary's rebellion expressed itself in her letters and in endless physical symptoms and psychological depression. At one time or another she complained of stomach spasms, headaches, faintness, and trembling fits. She wrote of efforts to accept her tribulations with religious fortitude. In reality she was storing up the ammunition for a devastating attack on the society of which she was an unwilling part, what it did to human beings and most especially women. The months she spent at the Kingsboroughs' would provide the impetus for whole sections of *A Vindication of the Rights of Woman* in which Mary pilloried the *haut monde* of the eighteenth century and its fashionable ladies in particular:

> You cannot conceive my dear Girl [she wrote to Everina] the dissipated lives the women of quality lead. . . . In many respects the *Great* and little vulgar resemble, and in none more than the motives which induce them to marry. They look not for a companion, and are seldom alone together but in bed —the husband, perhaps, drunk and the wife's head full of the *pretty* compliments that some creature, that Nature designed for a Man—paid her at the card table. . . . I see Ladies put on rouge without any mauvais honte—and make up their faces for the day—five hours, and who could do it in less—do many, I assure you, spend in dressing, including preparations for bed, washing with Milk of roses, etc., etc.[16]

Only Caroline Fitzgerald, Countess Kingsborough, could have sat for the portrait Mary would later draw in vitriol:

And she who takes her dogs to bed, and nurses them with a parade of sensibility when sick, will suffer her babes to grow up crooked in a nursery. . . . The woman I allude to was handsome, reckoned very handsome, by those who do not miss the mind when the face is plump and fair; but her understanding had not been led from female duties by literature nor her innocence debauched with knowledge. No, she was quite feminine, according to the masculine acceptation of the word; and, so far from loving these spoiled brutes that filled the place which her children ought to have occupied, she only lisped out a pretty mixture of French and English nonsense, to please the men who flocked round her. The wife, mother, and human creature were all swallowed up by the factitious character which an improper education and the selfish vanity of beauty had produced.[17]

What saved Mary from utter despair in so hated an environment was the fact that she could do so much more than just hate. She could also love, and she poured out the warmth of an unusually loving nature on the Kingsborough children, who responded in kind. She became particularly attached to the oldest Kingsborough girl, on whom, in the space of a few months, she had an amazing and lifelong impact. Tall and blue-eyed Margaret King (later Viscountess Mount Cashell), who was self-conscious about her height and craved love, and the governess who needed an outlet for her feelings developed a close relationship, although at first Mary had not been hopeful:

> I have committed to my care three girls, the eldest fourteen, by no means handsome, yet a sweet girl. She has a wonderful capacity, but she has such a multitude of employments it has not room to expand itself, and in all probability will be lost in a heap of rubbish, miscalled accomplishments. I am grieved at being obliged to continue so wrong a system. She is very much afraid of her mother—that such a creature should be ruled with a rod of iron when tenderness would lead her anywhere! She is to be always with me. I have just promised to send her love to my sister, so pray receive it. . . .[18]

In addition to overburdening her daughters with too much to learn, Lady Kingsborough had laid a ban on their reading any novels. Considering the level of most of the fiction available, there might have been some sense to the restriction under normal circumstances. But Mary, reasoning that the prohibition simply led to clandestine reading because the girls' affections and emotions had been starved, decided that even sentimental trash would be good for them and lifted the ban.

She had to struggle with Margaret's temper, undoubtedly inherited from her mother. If we accept the character of "Mary" in *Original Stories* as a portrait of Margaret, she was also clever at ridiculing and at mimicking the unpleasant characteristics of others.

It has been argued that because both Mary and her pupil later became ardent republicans, the pupil must have imbibed the seeds of such beliefs from her governess. There is no evidence, however, of incipient liberalism in Mary Wollstonecraft's thinking during her year in Ireland. The French Revolution, which was to shock many thinking minds into radicalism, was still two years away.

What Mary did store up in Ireland were impressions, which she would later remember and put to use. But it would be wrong to identify as political her rebellion against the milieu in which she now found herself. Mary's dislike of repression in any form, her habit of independent action, her intelligence—all conditioned her to political radicalism; these qualities she could not transmit to Margaret King, but only arouse and stimulate them if they were present in the responsive child.

CHAPTER VI

In the Shadow of St. Paul's (1787–88)

SOMETIME DURING THE SUMMER of 1787 the Kingsboroughs established their household at Bristol Hot Wells, another fashionable watering spot not far from Bath. From Mary's point of view, the choice could hardly have been worse. It was almost ten years since she had first arrived in Bath; nothing in her experience since then had made the frivolous atmosphere of a watering place more congenial to her.

Thrown back on her own resources while not employed with the younger Kingsboroughs, she turned once more to writing.

> My nerves grow daily worse and worse [she wrote to Eliza from the spa] yet I strive to occupy my mind when duty does not force me to it—in a trifling way I net two purses and intend having two smart ones to present to you and Everina—and when I have more strength I read philosophy—and write—I *hope* you have not forgot that I am an Author. . . .[1]

What she wrote was a short novel—fewer than 200 small pages —which she entitled *Mary, A Fiction*, containing many autobiographical details and characters and others difficult to distinguish between fact and fiction. There is Ann, the image of the dead Fanny, a father and mother palpably her own, a man whose array of noble qualities depict the kind of being with whom she wished to share her life; finally, there is Mary herself, endowed with all the virtues and in circumstances (as Professor Wardle has pointed out) totally unlike the distasteful circumstances which harassed her in real life—poverty, debts, and the occupations which she despised.

In Portugal, where "Mary" has taken "Ann" in search of health but where instead Ann dies, she meets and falls in love with a man named Henry, about whom we learn little except that he plays the violin and converses with the greatest felicity. He too sickens and dies, but not until he and "Mary" have celebrated a symbolic marriage through receiving the sacrament of communion together. "Mary" had previously been married to a young man to unite family estates (after the manner of the Kingsborough couple). Exalted by Henry's love, she now finds the strength to accept her marriage and to live in the country promoting the good of the people on her estates (again patterned on the Kingsboroughs).

It has been suggested that *Mary* is a cut above the general literary level of the time,[2] but the story is so totally lacking in any display of the ordinary skills involved in writing fiction—characterization, suspense, dialogue, or comic byplay—that no one would have hazarded such a judgment if its author had not been someone with the claim to fame of a Mary Wollstonecraft. Its only possible interest for us lies in seeing it as a seedbed wherein we can find, if we look closely, some suggestion of Mary's later development.

In the preface or "advertisement" of the book, which in all likelihood Mary wrote herself, she stated her purpose, headed by a quotation from Rousseau: *"L'exercice des plus sublimes vertus élève et nourrit le génie"*:*

In an artless tale, without episodes, the mind of a woman who has thinking powers, is displayed. The female organs have

* "The exercise of the most sublime virtues elevates and nourishes genius."

been thought too weak for this arduous employment; and experience seems to have justified the assertion. Without arguing *physically* about *possibilities*—in a fiction, such a being might be allowed to exist; whose grandeur is derived from the operation of its own faculties, not subjugation to opinion; but drawn by the individual from the original sources.

Mary had already proposed the importance of women being thinking beings in *Thoughts on the Education of Daughters* ("Let them be taught how to think"). In fact, the idea that women not only can but should become thinking human beings is one of Mary Wollstonecraft's greatest contributions. It is true, there had been forerunners who had suggested such a possibility—women like Mrs. Makin, Mary Astell, and "Sophia."[3] Among Mary's contemporaries were writers like Hannah More and Mrs. Barbauld and the whole coterie of Bluestockings. But the general inclination was to consider all such as unfeminine.

Mary Wollstonecraft's vision at this stage in her development was limited; it is doubtful whether she believed that "thinking women" could develop outside the upper and middle classes. But plainly she thought that such women should become far more general than they were. The character of "Mary" is an unusual woman. She has means and an established social position in life. The author suggests that as such she has the *responsibility* of being a thinking woman. If this idea could become accepted among the upper and middle classes, it would constitute a long step ahead of existing prejudices. In her novel, Mary Wollstonecraft pledged her commitment to this goal, using it as a means of forwarding her aim, because "in a fiction such a being may be allowed to exist."

Her attempt to create a character that would embody her idea failed, not only because Mary showed no gift for writing fiction or creating characters, but because creating a highly intellectual woman character has baffled more talented novelists—witness the failure of George Meredith in *Diana of the Crossways*. In the case of *Mary*, the attempt was too bound up with the author's efforts to exorcise her own past. Self-portrayal in fiction requires not only a degree of skill far beyond Mary Wollstonecraft's, but a sense of humor, which Mary patently lacked. Consider her attempt at self-analysis:

> She ["Mary"] had a wonderful quickness in discerning distinction and combining ideas, that at first glance did not appear to be similar . . . her quickness of penetration enabled her soon to enter into the characters of those she conversed with; and her sensibility made her desirous of pleasing every human creature. . . . She had not any prejudices, for every opinion was examined before it was adopted. . . . The exercise of her various virtues gave vigour to her genius, and dignity to her mind; she was sometimes inconsiderate, and violent, but never mean or cunning.[4]

We may feel a twinge of compassion for Lady Kingsborough, who must have found her governess both priggish and self-righteous.

What did Mary mean when she wrote Henry Gabell that her book was "drawn from Nature"? Was the "Henry" in her story modeled on Gabell himself? She might have had a passing sentimental interest in Gabell, who was now engaged to Ann Gage, whom he married three years later. Was *Mary* a kind of sublimated flirtation with a man the author knew was beyond her reach?[5]

It has been suggested that *Mary* was a useful piece of self-therapy which enabled Mary Wollstonecraft to rid herself of her past and of her habit of morbid introspection.[6] If so, it was hardly successful; she remained the frequent victim of neurasthenia and depression, as her letters to George Blood and her sisters continued to show—except during the periods when she was at the peak of busyness and success. Once she had settled in London, as her acquaintances grew and her writings multiplied, she achieved a fair degree of emotional stability—but never for very long. For her, as for many others, activity, new faces, fame proved therapeutic—but only for as long as they lasted. When they were withdrawn, when she was denied a relationship on which she had fixed her love and her hopes, the old pattern quickly reasserted itself.

The novel *Mary* made almost no impression when it was published and was never reprinted. Mary herself came to think of it as a piece of juvenilia, and it indeed was, although its author was twenty-eight years old when she wrote it.[7]

A fragment of another novel, *The Cave of Fancy, or Sagesta*, belongs to this same period, although it was not published until after Mary's death. Once again Mary tried to tackle the theme of service to others as the sole worthy motive of human life: "Only he who formed the human soul, can fill it, and the chief happiness of an immortal being must arise from the same source as its existence. Earthly love leads to heavenly, and prepares us for a more exalted state. . . ."

While *The Cave of Fancy* heralds what would be a frequent theme in her life and writings, it also demonstrates that at the age of twenty-eight, its author was still relying heavily on her own life as the source of her fiction:

> My mother was a most respectable character, but she was yoked to a man whose follies and vices made her ever feel the weight of her chains. The first sensation I recollect was pity; for I have seen her weep over me and the rest of her babes, lamenting that the extravagance of a father would throw us destitute on the world. . . .[8]

Mary was still dragging her past life behind her as she stood at the threshold of an extraordinary spurt forward to creativity, which would develop at astounding speed once she found herself in a congenial and forcing environment. Very little in that past would foretell the woman Mary would now become.

During the summer at Bristol Hot Wells, the possibility arose of a gift of money which would enable Mary to discharge all her indebtedness. She wrote to Eliza, for whom she always reserved the best, most encouraging news:

> I have *every* reason to think I shall be able to pay my debts before I again leave the Kingdom. A *friend* whose name I am not permitted to mention has insisted on lending me the money. I shall certainly borrow it, and as I shall reckon myself rich, I hope to contrive for yourself and Everina to spend the winter-vacation together, as the only alleviation I can devise to render your confinement tolerable. With respect to this money matter, you must not enquire, or expect any other explanation.[9]

The recent discovery of four letters from Mary Wollstonecraft to Henry Gabell underlines how little we still know about her personal relationships at certain periods of her life. We can only speculate about the identity of the friend who may have made Mary this timely "loan." The only people of means in Ireland of whom she spoke with any warmth were Mrs. Fitzgerald, Lady Kingsborough's stepmother, and George Ogle. Then again there may have been someone else of whose existence we are not even aware or whom Mary knew later but whose connection with her during this brief interim is obscure.

Perhaps the money came from Joseph Johnson, who was already interested in her literary talents and independence of spirit and may have wished to make it possible for her to leave the Kingsboroughs. Certainly such an act of kindness would go far to explain Mary's later trust in him.

There is also a strong possibility that despite the seeming certainty of this windfall, Mary never received the money. Months later she wrote Everina that she "could not pay Sowerby, after all," or bring Eliza to London after the holidays. Or perhaps the money had to be spent on Mary's own living expenses over a period of several months. For, sometime in August, Lady Kingsborough summarily dismissed her governess.

Mary had asked for a few days' leave to visit her sister, and her request was granted. The prospect of her absence for even so brief a period aroused such a storm of grief among her pupils, especially Margaret, that Lady Kingsborough was infuriated. She was convinced that her daughters had grown to love their governess more than their mother, which in Margaret's case was certainly true. The action came as no surprise to Mary, who had long been expecting it; she knew that Lady Kingsborough must be jealous of her hold on the girls' affections.

With the wages paid her by her employer, Mary went straight to London, to the home and shop of Joseph Johnson at 72 St. Paul's Churchyard, the street of houses which circled Wren's great cathedral.[10] While they discussed how Mary could earn her living, he gave her lodgings under his own roof, where—like the heroine of Charlotte Brontë's *Villette*, who also faced an uncertain future—she could hear the cathedral bells:

I had just extinguished my candle and lain down, when a deep, low, mighty tone swung through the night. At first I knew it not; but it was uttered twelve times, and at the twelfth colossal and trembling knell, I said: "I lie in the shadow of St. Paul's."[11]

The prospect before Mary was both intoxicating and terrifying. However unhappy she had been until now, she had always been part of a family domicile with its own steady rhythm. When she had taken Eliza away from her husband, she had had the support and companionship of her sisters and Fanny Blood. Now she was launching out alone, and she needed practical help, as well as encouragement. It is doubtful whether she would have been successful without the support Joseph Johnson gave her.

What kind of man was Johnson, to befriend Mary Wollstonecraft as he did? Clearly he was widely beloved, as well as respected, free of any trace of censure or suspicion of motive for such acts as lodging Mary or other women (Mrs. Barbauld stayed under his roof when she visited London on holiday, while her husband remained at the school they conducted together).

Joseph Johnson was born in 1738, in the village of Everton, near Liverpool, the younger of two sons of a family of farmers "of the dissenting baptist persuasion."[12] He served his apprenticeship as printer in London and subsequently launched his own shop in Fish Hill Street because it was near the hospitals and he could catch the trade of the medical students (all his life he remained interested in medicine and its practitioners and published many medical works).

Next, he moved to Paternoster Row, the center of the English publishing business. He was twice in partnership; in 1770 he suffered a disastrous fire, losing his entire stock of books, after which he moved to St. Paul's Churchyard, where he lived until his death in 1809.

Miss E. L. Nicholes has pointed out the seminal role Johnson played as a publisher for more than a quarter of a century: "His imprints show a remarkable range: novels, translations, poetry, textbooks, medical, scientific and political works . . . books and pamphlets supporting the cause of the American colonists and the

French Revolution; the political emancipation of women, Dissenters and Catholics; the abolition of the slave trade."[13]

John Nichols, the contemporary editor of the *Gentleman's Magazine*, has called attention to an interesting aspect of Johnson's work as a publisher—his preference for simple and inexpensive formats to luxurious and therefore expensive printing. "On this principle he usually consulted cheapness rather than appearances in his own publications; and if authors were sometimes mortified by this preference, the purpose of extensive circulation was better served." His primary concern was always, in the words of another authority, "the best interest of his species"; in pursuit of this goal he bought the manuscripts of needy writers, although he had no intention of issuing them, and published others he thought worthwhile, even if he did not expect a return on them for a long time, if ever.

His kindness and generosity were proverbial. "Perhaps few men of his means and condition have done more substantial service to persons whose merits and necessities recommended them to his notice" was the verdict of John Nichols. A confirmed bachelor without family responsibilities, Johnson made of his friends, his authors, and indeed of all needy scribblers, his family, over whom he watched with "friendly benevolence." He possessed that rarest of gifts, the ability to listen; he himself wrote of his relationship with Mary Wollstonecraft: "When harassed, as was very often the case, she was relieved by unbosoming herself, and generally returned home calm, frequently in spirits."

Yet Johnson could also be shrewdly admonitory. He reprimanded Mary and other young writers for their weaknesses. He never roused false hopes in his authors—Nichols says he was known rather for his pessimism—but when a work did succeed beyond his expectations, he could be extraordinarily generous, paying the author over and beyond what his contract entitled him to, what Johnson would insist was a just reward, as was the case with Cowper's poem *The Task*, for which the poet received 1,000 pounds which the publisher was under no obligation to pay him. In other ways Johnson's treatment of that afflicted man was discerning and sensitive. When Cowper's work, in Johnson's opinion, needed revision, he tactfully made helpful suggestions, which Cowper deeply appreciated:

> I never knew with certainty till now [he wrote Johnson] that the marginal strictures I found on the *Task* proofs were yours. The justness of them, and the benefit I derived from them, are fresh in my memory, and I doubt not their utility will be the same in the present instance.[14]

When Cowper's translation of Homer proved inadequate, Johnson, relying on his long-standing friendship with the artist Henry Fuseli, who was also an accomplished classicist, called on the latter for help; Fuseli went over the entire work, a labor of love for which Cowper was grateful.

Not that his authors did not occasionally complain of Johnson—usually about his dilatoriness. It sometimes took him a long time to get his books into print: Mrs. Barbauld, Cowper, and Maria Edgeworth suffered from the same problem. But Johnson's positive qualities far outweighed his shortcomings. None of his clients owed him more than Mary, as her feeling for him testified. "You would love him if you knew with what tenderness and humanity he has behaved to me," she wrote Everina. Elsewhere she referred to him as the only real father or brother she had ever had.[15] Certainly Mary would never have successfully launched herself into London literary life without his active and practical help, nor would she have achieved anything beyond mere sur-·vival as its first woman "hack" writer without the friendships and contacts Johnson opened to her.

He was not a man of striking appearance. "Little Johnson," Mary once called him, and she described his manner on first meeting as sometimes conveying "an impression of formality, or rather stiffness of manners . . . to his disadvantage." Nichols also thought his manner "somewhat cold and indifferent." Yet the impression Johnson made on the clergyman James Hurdis was just the opposite: "How d'ye do, sir? I dine at three,"[16] was his spontaneous, even instantaneous invitation to one of his deservedly famous dinners, famous not so much for the cuisine as the conversation.

It is recorded that "neither importunity nor ingratitude affected his equable disposition."[17] Yet Johnson was a lifelong victim of asthma. His portrait shows unmistakable traces of suffering and luminous, compelling eyes.

We may indeed wonder what it was in Mary Wollstonecraft that drew even as kindhearted a man as Johnson to such lengths of helpfulness as he displayed on her behalf. He not only gave her lodging for some weeks at this critical time of her life, but found her more permanent quarters. Later he undertook to help her with the management of Edward John Wollstonecraft's chaotic affairs, which involved (as he admitted) "no little trouble to both of us."[18]

We have random descriptions of Mary from the very last years of her life when she was Godwin's wife and winning the hearts of such men as the poet Robert Southey, the portrait painter John Opie, and enthusiastic admirers like George Dyson and Mary Hays. But what was she like now, at the age of twenty-eight, standing fearfully and yet intrepidly on the threshold of London life? It is maddening to know so little and be forced to hypothesize so much. The best we can do is recall the description Miss Hays wrote after Mary's death:

> Her person was above the middle height, and well-proportioned; her form full; her hair and eyes brown; her features pleasing; her countenance changing and impressive; her voice soft, and though without great compass, capable of modulation. . . . When unbending in familiar and confidential conversation, her manners had a charm that subdued the heart.[19]

Take away ten years, and we can see Mary as slender, perhaps even thin—she was often in poor health—with manners that might have lacked the poise of later years and perhaps a shriller voice. Over the brown eyes, the color of the hair would be concealed under the powder which was the fashion even among the middle class until the French Revolution put it into disrepute.

Of the two portraits painted by Opie, the one most frequently cited is the least helpful, for it has the conventional features to be found in all his fashionable portraits—same nose, same lips, same modeling of the cheeks and chin. It is the earlier portrait, undated but clearly painted before 1790 (because of the telltale powdered hair), that gives us a glimpse of the real Mary, with haunting eyes and a determined chin that sits oddly with the still-childlike cheeks and brow. This must have been very like Mary as she first confronted Joseph Johnson and enlisted his compassion and help.

Even before she came to London, Mary could hold her own conversationally in society, especially when her interest was challenged by intelligence, as her experience in Ireland and at Newington Green had shown. Later she would draw around her people from the most educated and polished circles, who would rate her highly as companion and friend. Johnson was only the first to fall under her spell.

Two other factors would have contributed to his interest in Mary. One was her extreme need, the other her resolution. The fact that these were combined in a woman and that he always showed himself sensitive to the plight of the neediest special groups—as his publishing list attests—made him Mary's staunch supporter and adherent for the remainder of her life.

Mary did not take her sisters into her confidence after she left the Kingsboroughs. During September, while Johnson was inquiring for a place where she could live, she visited them both, but she did not tell either of them her plans, and apparently she did not even mention the fact that she had already left the Kingsboroughs. To Johnson she wrote from Everina's school in Henley, near London: "Have you heard of a habitation for me? I often think of my new plan of life; and lest my sister should try to prevail on me to alter it, I have avoided mentioning it to her. I am determined!"

From Henley Mary returned to London and then traveled north to Leicestershire to see Eliza. Johnson himself put her in the coach, for she reported to him when she had reached her destination:

> You left me with three opulent tradesmen; their conversation was not calculated to beguile the way, when the sabled curtains concealed the beauties of nature. . . . I do not intend to enter on the *old* topic, yet hope to hear from you.[20]

Just where her sisters thought she was staying, after she left them both, and where they wrote to her, or what they made of her long silence, are puzzles. One person who knew she was no longer at the Kingsboroughs was Henry Gabell, to whom she wrote two letters, one from Johnson's and the other from Henley, begging him to help her find another position for Everina—

preferably as a companion—since she was most unhappy in the "vulgar school" where she was teaching. Mary said that she was "still on the ramble," and gave Johnson's bookshop as her address, adding, "I mentioned before that I had been disappointed in several attempts which wore [an] aspect more promising than the present, indeed it is so wild it looks like the *forlorn* hope. . . ."[21]

By Michaelmas (September 29) Mary was established in her own house in London, but she did not break her silence to her sisters for another month. We can only speculate that she was going through an emotional or a physical upheaval and did not feel equal to debating her new course with them. The house Johnson found for her was at 49 George (later Dolben) Street, south of the Thames and running off Blackfriars Road, only a short distance from the bridge of the same name. It was still standing until recently, one in a uniform row of three-storied buildings, dark with soot and grime, but then a pleasant yellow color since it had only recently been erected. There Mary lived alone except for a servant, but within walking distance of St. Paul's and Johnson's home and shop. From George Street she finally wrote to Everina of her whereabouts and her new way of life:

> Mr. Johnson, whose uncommon kindness, I believe, has saved me from despair and vexation . . . assures me that if I exert my talents in writing, I may support myself in a comfortable way. I am then going to be the first in a new genus; I tremble at the attempt, yet if I fall *I* only will suffer, and should I succeed my dear girls will ever in sickness have a home, and a refuge where for a few months in the year they may forget the cares that disturb the rest. . . . I must be independent. . . . And freedom, even uncertain freedom, is dear. . . . This project has long floated in my mind. You know I am not born to tread the beaten track, the peculiar bent of my nature pushes me on. . . .

In another letter to Everina she wrote that she had given Johnson the finished manuscript of *Mary* and that:

> . . . before your vacation I shall finish another book for young people which I think has some merit. I live alone. I mean I

have only a servant, a relation of Mr. Johnson's, sent to me out
of the country. All this will appear to you like a dream; whenever I am tired of solitude I go to Mr. Johnson's and there I
[meet] the kind of company I find most pleasure in. . . .[22]

How or when Eliza heard of the new developments, we do not
know, but she cannot have found them more gratifying than
Everina. It was not merely the chanciness of the venture which
would have disturbed them, since Mary's ability to earn a living
had been for years the one certain feature in their lives. What
was more shattering, especially to Eliza, was that Mary was putting her sisters on notice that from now on she expected to live
alone. "Her dear girls" could look forward to a haven for their
vacations or in time of illness, but it would only be temporary—
"for a few months in the year." Behind the sugarcoating ("seas
will not now divide us, nor years elapse before we see each other,"
Mary wrote, and again, that she wished "to be a mother to you
both"), the message was unmistakable. She loved them, she
was concerned for them, she would do all she could to help them;
but from now on she was going to follow her own destiny independent of theirs, and she would not make a home for them.

The blow must have been particularly harsh for Eliza, who
could not forget that this sister had taken her away from her husband with the promise that she would care for her. Nor can it
have been very palatable for Everina, who hated teaching no less
than Eliza and also looked forward longingly to the day when
Mary could make a home for the three of them.

But if it was hard for the sisters to accept, it was harder for
Mary to make the decision. Responsibility is more difficult to
surrender than security because it involves the conscience, and
Mary's sense of responsibility for her brothers and sisters had been
abnormally developed since childhood. No wonder that weeks
passed before she wrote her sisters of her whereabouts, weeks
during which she fought out the battle, perhaps with Johnson's
help, but mostly with herself—and knowing Mary, in prayer—of
which was the right course to pursue. She could only make her
way, unencumbered by two women with completely different
mentalities from hers. And so she cut the cords which had bound

the three of them so closely together. She continued to make efforts to help Everina and Eliza find better positions; she helped them financially; there are repeated references to holidays with her and the two younger boys staying with her—but always as an interim arrangement. It was *her* home, for which she was paying by her writing; her family came as guests, and there was a term to their stay with her.

Very slowly but unmistakably, the emphasis in Mary's letters—and in her life—now begins to shift from concern for those to whom she felt in duty and honor bound to protect and care for, to other goals and aspirations. What actually happened in the house on George Street, was that the twenty-eight-year-old "girl" named Mary Wollstonecraft took a long stride toward becoming a woman.

CHAPTER VII

Johnson's Circle (1788–90)

IN NOVEMBER, 1787, Mary gave Johnson another completed manuscript, which he published as *Original Stories from Real Life* sometime during the first half of 1788. It dealt with two girls, twelve and fourteen, easily recognizable as the two oldest Kingsborough girls except for the fact that at their mother's death, the father puts them in the care of a Mrs. Mason. The book is a loosely structured series of episodes in which Mrs. Mason uses incidents or homilies to instruct her charges and improve their characters and manners.

Although Mary referred to her book as one for children, it is obviously written for parents. In this connection, Johnson got a taste of Mary's stubbornness in adhering to what she considered essential values. In the Preface she had spoken out with considerable acerbity:

> Good habits, imperceptibly fixed, are far preferable to the precepts of reason, but, as this task requires more judgment than generally falls to the lot of parents, substitutes must be sought

for, and medicines given, when regimen would have answered the purpose much better . . . to wish that parents themselves would mould the ductile passions, is a chimerical wish, for the present generation has their own passions to contend with, and fastidious pleasures to pursue, neglecting those pointed out by nature.[1]

Johnson had qualms about how parents would receive such strictures and apparently suggested eliminating at least a part of them. Novice writer though she was, Mary refused:

Though your remarks are generally judicious [she wrote to Johnson]—I cannot *now* concur with you, I mean with respect to the preface, and have not altered it . . . believe me, the few judicious parents who peruse my book, will not feel themselves hurt—and the weak are too vain to mind what is said in a book intended for children.

In a postscript she added bitterly: "If parents attended to their children, I would not have written the stories; for what are books,—compared to conversations which affection enforces?"[2]

Whether it was the children or the parents who read and approved it, *Original Stories* sold so well that, as Professor Wardle has pointed out, it ran through three editions before 1800 and three more English editions in the early nineteenth century, in addition to three in Dublin and a German translation.[3] Yet modern critics have low-rated the book, largely because of the character of Mrs. Mason. Regarded as a character of fiction, she has all the weaknesses of Mary's writings in this genre; she is simply not believable as the human being Mary describes her, "a woman of tenderness and discernment." But if we abandon the attempt to measure Mrs. Mason as the creation of a novelist, we will find a great deal of interest in the book.

Mrs. Mason's pupils have been neglected, but also spoiled; Mrs. Mason confronts them with poverty and suffering and their individual responsibility to allay both, to the extent of their ability. In other words, she tries to teach them to be charitable. (In 1787, the philosophy of social change was still unborn.)

But Mrs. Mason introduces the girls to the poor not just in the role of Lady Bountiful; she recounts the circumstances that have resulted in their poverty. The story of the landlord who has caused the imprisonment of the needy old farmer's son for poaching, while underpaying his own laborers and insisting that "the fish they catch they must bring first to him, or they would not be allowed to walk over his grounds to catch them; and he will give them what he pleases for the most valuable part of their panier," is straight out of eighteenth-century rural England. So are the stories of Peggy and her impoverished father ("he had a sharp, famished look") and the woman who had lost her sailor-husband "and lost his wages also, as she could not prove his death." The incident of the shopkeeper's son who began drinking while he was in jail for debt, until all the money his mother sent him in prison went for drink, is reminiscent of Dickens' *Barnaby Rudge*, but Dickens wrote his novel more than half a century later.

There is the family Mrs. Mason takes Mary and Caroline to visit, whose husband has been out of work for a long time:

> They ascended the dark stairs, scarcely able to bear the smells that flew from every part of a small house, that contained in each room a family, occupied in such an anxious manner to obtain the necessaries of life, that its comforts never engaged their thoughts. The precarious meal was snatched, and the stomach did not turn, though the cloth on which it was laid was died [sic] with dirt. . . .

The visitors follow one of the tenants, a woman:

> [into] a low garret that was never visited by the chearful [sic] rays of the sun. A man with a sallow complexion and a long beard, sat shivering over a few cinders in the bottom of a broken grate, and two more children on the ground, half naked, near him, breathing the same noxious air. The gaiety natural to their age did not animate their eyes, half sunk in their sockets; and instead of smiles, premature wrinkles had found a place in their lengthened visages . . . they seemed to come into the world only to crawl half-formed—to suffer, and to die.

There is the story of "poor Robin." His wife and children die, of hunger. His dog is the only living creature who remains to him —and is shot, the final anguish that pushes Robin over the verge of sanity into madness. The story inspired one of William Blake's earliest and most terrible etchings when Johnson added illustrations to the second edition.

The book is not all darkness, though. Just as striking as the detailed observations which document the indictment of injustice are the lovely passages describing the English countryside, whose lyric simplicity Mary Wollstonecraft did not achieve again for many years. The pictures of birds and insects hark back to the memories of the young girl who roamed the Westwood common in her early teens, cherishing and marveling at all the living things she found—nestlings, spiders, even caterpillars.

These positive values in *Original Stories* are, of course, obscured for the modern reader by the frequent hortatory passages. But one suspects that what has most repelled Mary's biographers and critics from *Original Stories* is the author's emphasis on religion and her reiterated insistence that all things and events are related to a divine plan. The book reminds us once again that at this stage of her life Mary was a deeply believing Christian. But she did not teach a "stern religion," in which life was a "vale of tears." The whole point of the stories Mrs. Mason tells her pupils and the things she shows them is that these evils result from the wrong which human beings do one another; they are not the punishment of an angry, Calvinistic deity. On the contrary, Mary Wollstonecraft, speaking through Mrs. Mason, has no doubt whatever of a supreme and omnipotent God's love for each and every one of His creatures, of His essential goodness, and of the consoling hereafter beyond our worldly sufferings.

The portrait Mary drew of the curate's wife, Mrs. Trueman, is of great interest; this was her ideal (as of the year 1787):

> Her voice is sweet, her manner not only easy but elegant . . . her little ones hang on to her hands, and cling to her clothes, they are so fond of her. If anything terrifies them, they run under her apron, and she looks like a hen taking care of her young brood. . . . Her husband, a man of taste and learning, reads to her while she makes clothes for her children, whom she teaches in the tenderest and most persuasive manner. . . .[4]

This was the kind of mother she had in mind when she wrote Johnson that if parents would look out for their children, she would not have needed to write her book. A home founded on love, concern, and security would have been sufficient; certainly it was not the kind of home Mary had known in her own childhood, or at the Bloods', or at the Kingsboroughs'.

Mrs. Trueman is presented to Mrs. Mason's young charges in contrast with Lady Sly, who has a beautiful house and garden and fine horses, but "a little soul"; she is the product of the society Mary hated so bitterly. Mary Wollstonecraft would make the juxtaposition between Mrs. Trueman and Lady Sly again in the future; her disciples remembered Lady Sly but forgot Mrs. Trueman.

In 1787 England was enjoying a brief interlude of peace. At the time, there was still no hint in London of the revolution impending in France (and little enough in France except to a few perceptive minds). London itself was changing, with the beginnings of street illumination and sidewalks and some attempt at sewage control and disposal.

In literature there was a pause. The Augustan Age had come to an end with Samuel Johnson's death in 1784. The author of the great dictionary which had for the first time imposed self-consciousness on the written language was the last of the galaxy of writers—Fielding, Swift, Richardson, Defoe, Smollett, Goldsmith—who had given that era its greatness. The new generation of Wordsworth and Coleridge, of Jane Austen and Walter Scott was still mostly at its schoolbooks; although Maria Edgeworth was by then twenty, she did not write *Castle Rackrent* until 1800.

Literary London, which Mary Wollstonecraft was now confronting, was therefore not an arena of great personalities. It was in a period of transition. Yet thanks to the advent of the bookseller and publisher and to a growing middle class which combined literacy, leisure, and the means to satisfy both, there was a market for books. The most popular species were fiction, travel, theology, moral and philosophical speculation, and the controversial pamphlet—quick to write, quick to print, cheap, and easy to sell.

When Mary Wollstonecraft had tired of writing in her solitary little house on George Street, she had, for the first time in her life, an attractive alternative. Up to this time, work itself had been a refuge and a pleasure. Now, if she was lonely or low-spirited or jaded, she had a place to go where she was welcome and no fresh responsibilities awaited her, where she could find not only relaxation and amusement, but fresh stimulus.

It was only a mile or so from her house to Johnson's home and shop in St. Paul's Churchyard. Being poor, she must have walked it rather than take a horse-drawn chaise. A short block down George Street, she came out on Blackfriars Road, a main artery of traffic from the south into London. Crossing Blackfriars Bridge, she saw the vivid life of the river, still one of London's main throughfares, less congested than the streets and free of the hazards of mud, ruts, and passing horses and coaches. From the bridge she could see London Bridge to the east (the houses which had lined it were removed in 1758) and beyond it the outlines of the Tower of London. To the west, the new impressive bulk of Somerset House marked a curve of the Thames. Ahead on the left, as she picked her way cautiously through the filth underfoot, across the bridge, and through the narrow streets that led to Ludgate Hill, lay the oldest of the Inns of Court, the traditional lawyers' quarters—the Temple, the Law Courts, Lincoln's Inn, and, farther yet, Gray's Inn. The other buildings which stood out above the clutter of low dwellings and an occasional aristocratic residence were the innumerable churches, many built by Christopher Wren who had set his new St. Paul's Cathedral on the hill from which it commanded the entire city. She would have seen St. Mary-le-Strand, St. Clement Danes, St. Bride's to the west, St. Mary-le-Bow, St. Nicholas Cole Abbey, St. Mary Aldermary to the east—more than thirty of them in all—and heard their bells chiming the hour or ringing for evensong above the street cries and the rumble of wagons and coaches. Today their sound is smothered by the roar of the traffic.

Much that Mary Wollstonecraft saw on this route was dirty, sordid, and pitiful: prostitutes, press gangs searching for manpower for the Royal Navy, pickpockets, cripples and beggars, roving homeless children dragging their chimney sweeps, carriers of night soil carting their noisome load out of the houses, slops thrown from upper windows and running down the cobbled streets. A London lady no matter how modestly dressed had to watch her step, and the passersby, every foot of her way.

But street life was varied and had its lively, even gay aspect. Trade was brisk. Gentry, soldiers, literary lights, tradesmen, farmers from the country mixed with the mass of London poor coming or going from market and the shops, for this was London, already the heart of England and its most rapidly growing city.

If Mary climbed directly up Ludgate Hill, she had a fine view of Wren's masterpiece, ringed by the old houses of "the Churchyard," before she reached Johnson's house, with its "quaintly shaped upstairs room . . . walls not at right angles, where his guests must have been somewhat straitened for space," and where Johnson's table provided a "plain and hospitable dinner" and lively conversation.[5]

The company at Johnson's was varied, but almost entirely masculine. Paradoxically, this may have been because of its strongly liberal, even radical tinge. There were women in London capable of intellectual talk—Fanny Burney, Hannah More, the Bluestockings—but they were mostly conservative in outlook. At a later time the American Ruth Barlow came to Johnson's with her husband, Joel; an earlier visitor had been the writer Anna Letitia Barbauld; Thomas Christie, a close associate of Johnson's, met his future wife, a Miss Newell, at Johnson's, "about tea-time"; but women were nevertheless infrequent guests.

"Johnson's circle," as it became known, had a shifting membership. Curiously Godwin's *Memoirs* mentions only four as frequently present during the years 1789 to 1792: the painter Fuseli; the mathematician John Bonnycastle; George Anderson, "accountant to the board of control"; and the physician George Fordyce.[6] Because he was writing in 1797–98, during the period of repression which was a reaction to the French Revolution, Godwin omitted every name in the group associated with radical political or philosophical thought. We know, however, that many radicals frequented Johnson's and that Mary knew them. Although not all were first-rate intellects, they created a forcing climate in which the young woman who had written *Mary, A Fiction* and one book with some unconventional ideas on education developed within two years into an angry, articulate writer able to challenge one of England's leading statesmen on the explosive issue of social revolution and—only one year later—all views accepted by society on the position of women.

The most important figure in the group—and the most talkative —was the Swiss painter Henry Fuseli.[7] Born in 1741, he was also one of the oldest in the circle, eighteen years older than Mary, on whose life he was to have great impact. He had been destined for the clergy and ordained in 1761, but under the influence of Voltaire, Rousseau, and other radical writers who were unsettling contemporary thought, he had come into conflict with church and secular authority and left both his hometown and the church shortly after his ordination.

After Fuseli arrived in England in 1763, he wavered for a time between literature and art and experienced real hardship. A friend described his circumstances:

> . . . he is . . . disposed to all possible economy; but to be de-cently lodged and fed in a decent family cannot be for less than 3 sh. a day, which he pays. He might, to Millar's wish, live a little cheaper: but then he would have been lodged in some garrett [sic] where nobody could have found their way, and must have been thrown into ale houses and eating houses, with com-pany in every way unsuitable or indeed insupportable for a stranger of any taste. . . .[8]

For a while he earned his living by translating from French, Italian, and German and wrote a critique of Rousseau entitled *Remarks on the Writings and Conduct of J. J. Rousseau*, which Johnson published anonymously in 1767. But the great portrait painter Sir Joshua Reynolds encouraged him to paint; from 1770 to 1778 he studied the old masters in Rome. He tried tutoring but abandoned it for the same reasons that Mary rejected being a governess; he could not, he wrote to a friend, say yes when he meant no, and he could not live among courtiers.

In 1788, at the age of forty-seven, he married Sophia Rawlins. His first picture to attract attention, "The Nightmare," was hung at the Royal Academy the following year, followed by his Shake-speare illustrations in similar vein, notably "The Witches" and "Lady Macbeth," paintings in which he struck a completely new and sensational note. Today we might compare them to the work of surrealists like Dali. His influence on modern art has been great, and Fuseli is now belatedly receiving the recognition which forerunners are habitually denied. To an extraordinary degree in his paintings and drawings Fuseli heralded the discoveries of Freud, by plumbing the repressed depths of the human subconscious and the role of dreams. He speaks to modern artists not only by his choice of subject matter, but by the sense of impending crisis and anxiety which pervade his work and which arose from the social upheaval taking place, first in America and then in France.

His contemporaries are unanimous in their accounts of Fuseli's conversational powers. His interests were varied; his knowledge was vast; he was challenging, witty—often brutally so—impetuous, and effervescent. Despite the fact that he never mastered the English accent or distinguished between *v* and *f* or *t* and *th,* he spoke in a flood, and he would not tolerate interruptions: "I will now introduce you to a most ingenious foreigner," Johnson told Bonnycastle, another of his friends, as Fuseli was heard coming up the stairs, "but if you wish to enjoy his conversation, you will not attempt to stop the torrent of his conversation by contradicting him."[9]

If we bear in mind that he was deeply versed in the English classics—he devoted most of his later years to vast projects illustrating the work of Shakespeare and Milton—and was also an accomplished classicist, we get some understanding of his impact on the group assembled around Johnson's table, and in particular on Mary Wollstonecraft—intellectually eager but still immature. Up to now the best mind to which she had been exposed had been that of Richard Price. But Price had come into Mary's life before she was ready and while her mind was occupied elsewhere, and Price, moreover, had nothing of Fuseli's gift for projecting his highly theatrical personality.

Fuseli was a friend and admirer of William Blake. Their relationship began the same year that Mary came to London and was lifelong. There are strong resemblances between the two men's styles: the long, flowing line; the dynamism and violent motion; the emphasis on the unreal or what the public would consider unreal, though to both of them it was the essence of reality. When Blake first appeared at Johnson's dinners, also in 1787, he was at the beginning of his career as painter, engraver, illustrator—and poet. The sculptor John Flaxman had introduced Blake earlier to another circle of writers and artists who met in the parlor of the Reverend Henry Mathews and his wife, to whom Blake read some of his poems, occasionally singing them to tunes he had composed himself.

A friend (perhaps one of the Mathews) provided the money that enabled Blake to bring out a private printing of his first book of poems, *Poetical Sketches*, in 1783. The following year he began to exhibit his paintings at the Royal Academy. However friendly the reception accorded him at the Mathews', Blake apparently found Johnson's circle more to his taste. Although Johnson never published any of his poems, he gave him work as an engraver; Blake provided the striking engravings to the second edition of Mary's *Original Stories* in 1791. We may speculate whether he read any of his poems at Johnson's or expounded the intricate symbolic system, already taking shape from his Swedenborgian beliefs, which became his fantastic *Books of Prophecy*—and if he did, what did Mary make of them?

Another close friend of Fuseli's at Johnson's was the mathematician John Bonnycastle, who was later to be of great assistance to Mary with her brother James. Leigh Hunt's somewhat cruel description is of the man in even later years: "tall, gaunt, long-headed, with large features and spectacles, and a deep internal voice with a twang of rusticity in it; and he goggled over his plate like a horse . . . a bag of corn would have hung well on him. His laugh was equine, and his teeth showed upwards at the sides."[10] Gaunt and large-featured Bonnycastle may have been even in his late thirties, and he still had his rustic twang, for he came from a tiny Buckinghamshire village and was largely self-educated. Yet his gifts were such that despite this handicap, he became a professor of mathematics at the Royal Military Academy at Woolwich.

George Anderson, also born in an obscure Buckinghamshire village, was one of the younger members of the group. Bonnycastle heard of him through a letter Anderson sent to the *London Magazine*, with solutions to a series of mathematical problems it had published. When he sought Anderson out, he found a seventeen-year-old boy threshing in a barn whose walls were covered with mathematical diagrams of triangles and parallelograms. The

entire village became interested in the prodigy, the local rector
undertook to round out his education, and presently young
Anderson went up to Oxford and took his MA degree at Wadham
College in 1784, a privilege Bonnycastle never enjoyed. He found
a post with the Board of Control, a governmental financial
agency, and became adjutant general. He was therefore a well-
placed civil servant dealing with budgets and accounting when
Mary knew him.[11]

Dr. George Fordyce was the oldest member of the circle, and
—in his field of medicine—one of the most distinguished. A
graduate of the University of Edinburgh, he had been recognized
by election as a licentiate to the Royal College of Physicians in
1765 (and later a fellow), and as Fellow of the Royal Society, the
highest scientific honor then as now. (He was called to Mary's
bedside at the birth of her second child, despite the fact that he
was not an obstetrician, and his advice would have tragic consequences.)

There were others who frequented Johnson's table during
Mary's first years in London—John Aikin, the brother of Mrs.
Barbauld, another medical man, but an author as well, who had
collaborated with his sister on an early collection of essays before
her marriage; the Anglican clergyman James Hurdis; John
Hewlett, who had first introduced Mary to her publisher; the
Catholic Biblical scholar Alexander Geddes, whose radical views
had alienated him from the hierarchy of his church. Thomas
Christie was also a frequent guest by the spring of 1788, if not
before, when he and Joseph Johnson jointly launched their
new periodical, the *Analytical Review*.

Of all the omissions in Godwin's account of this period in
Mary's life, that of Thomas Christie is the most striking. A youth
of so many gifts that he had difficulty making up his mind
whether to pursue science, literature, or business, one wonders
why, because unlike some of the other radicals whom Mary knew,
his name does appear elsewhere in the *Memoirs*, including mention of his presence in Paris when Christie was representing an
English firm in dealings with the French revolutionary government.[12] Two years younger than Mary, he was born in the High-
land port of Montrose, far up the northeast coast of Scotland. He
was well educated, then placed in his father's "counting house"

(bank). Very early he displayed the extraordinary range of interests which led him to study at one time or another botany, medicine, theology, and general literature and to amass a first-hand knowledge, unique in his day, of Continental periodical literature.

He first came to London in the autumn of 1784, but he was still undecided between "medicine and merchandising" and returned north to study medicine at the University of Edinburgh for a year and a half. In 1787 he toured England, combining visits to hospitals, dispensaries, and medical men with calls on intellectual and literary figures. We have a description of him at this time from Anna Seward, who "trembled for his health, appearing as he does to have outgrown his strength; for he is very tall, and thin almost to transparency. . . . Mr. Christie's sprightly wit, scientific acquirements, ingenuous manners and literary ardour, exceed anything I have met of early excellence since I first knew Major André in his eighteenth year. . . ." (Actually Christie was then twenty-five; Miss Seward was comparing him to the brilliant young British officer hanged as a spy during the American Revolution.[13])

After his tour, Christie continued his medical studies for only a few more months; then his literary bent won out, temporarily. He would have liked to become the literary partner of John Nichols, editor of the *Gentlemen's Magazine*, according to Nichols, but instead, he launched the *Analytical Review* with Johnson, based in large measure on his own far-ranging tastes and reading. Nichols has testified that:

> . . . his mind ran constantly on topics of classical theological and philosophical Literature. He had carefully perused the best of the foreign literary Journals, and would refer with ease to their contents. . . . More than one of his intimate friends, some of them much senior in years, and not wholly inattentive to such pursuits, had often occasion to be surprised at the extent of his acquirements.[14]

He must have been at Johnson's often, looking for possible contributors. We can spare a thought to what might have been the outcome if he and Mary had been attracted to each other!

It would not have been easy for Mary to have made her way into that circle of men, all better educated than she was, with broader horizons, and already distinguished by their achievement. They would not be unduly impressed with either *Mary* or *Original Stories* and would consider her the equal of a Mrs. Barbauld or Mrs. Trimmer, rather than Catharine Macaulay (whose *History of England* under the Stuarts was highly regarded). Whether or not Mary even had much to say at first we cannot know, but we can be reasonably sure that the impact on her reading must have been immediate. At Johnson's she would have encountered not only the stimulus, but the means to gratify her aroused curiosity. She would also find a new source of information and ideas available to few women then—the newspapers, which most men read in the coffeehouses or the clubs they frequented. So, for the first time on a regular basis she had access to current events and—whether by word of mouth or in print—to the lively exchange of opinion between people to whom such events and the social trends behind them were of profound importance.

Her work did not immediately reflect these changes. For the next three years she wrote no original book of her own. Most of what she produced would have been considered by a more educated or sophisticated person as hack work, sheer drudgery. But Mary derived from it financial independence and a whole new way of life. Moreover, it was exactly the right kind of work for her at this time, giving her constant practice in self-expression and helping her to gain confidence in her own judgment and abilities, as well as sharpen her wits.

The bulk of Mary's work was translating, occasionally adapting as she translated, from French or German, books which Johnson was interested in publishing. (Beginning in the spring of 1788, she also wrote short reviews for the *Analytical Review*.)

Mary's ability to translate is somewhat puzzling, for today we make great demands on a translator—requiring a high degree of knowledge of the language, as well as a creative gift beyond word-for-word rendition. Mary's knowledge of French was largely self-acquired—she had been worried about its inadequacy at the Kingsboroughs' and periodically in her letters referred to her efforts to improve it. Yet early in 1778 she was already considering an ambitious project, the translation of a ponderous work on religious thought (popular reading in those days) by the French financier and statesman Jacques Necker.

She wrote to Everina, whom she had finally succeeded in placing with a French family in Paris in order to improve *her* French:

> . . . enquire of the *literary* man about some particulars relative to M. Necker, the late Minister. . . . He has written a book entitled *De l'Importance des opinions Religieuses*. It pleases me, and I want to know the character of the man in domestic life and public estimation &c and the opinion the French have of his literary abilities.[15]

She enclosed a letter for Everina to deliver to Necker, presumably after making preliminary inquiries. He must have passed muster in consequence of Everina's report, for Mary was soon launched on the book, which Johnson published late in the year.

Godwin tells us that she was also studying Italian and German at this time but she does not appear to have done any translating from Italian, although Johnson was willing to let her. When he gave her a manuscript to try her hand on, she refused it:

> I return you the Italian MS—but do not hastily imagine that I am indolent. I would not spare any labour to do my duty— and, after the most laborious day, that single thought would solace me more than any pleasures the sense could enjoy. I find I could not translate the MS. well. If it was not a MS. I should not be so easily intimidated; but the hand, and the errors in orthography, or abbreviations, are a stumbling block at the first setting out.—I cannot bear to do anything that I cannot do well—and I should lose time in the vain attempt.[16]

Although later on she asked Johnson for a German grammar, she only did one major piece of work from the German, Salzmann's *Elements of Morality* (see below, Chapter XI). In addition to the Necker, she made one other translation from French, *Young Grandison* (the book was originally written in Dutch), a collection of short episodes designed to edify as well as amuse children, like her own *Original Stories*; she also worked on versions of Lavater's *Physiognomie* and Campe's *New Robinson Crusoe,* but these were abandoned when other translations appeared in print.

In such a new environment, with new friends, congenial work, and the distinct possibility that she might eventually be able to free herself of debt, Mary's letters show some improvement in both her health and her spirits.

In January, 1788, after living less than three months in her house on George Street, she could write George Blood that she was "in better health than I have enjoyed in some years," that she had hopes of finding another situation for her "sister Bishop," that she was also preparing to send Everina to France. Everina stayed there for a year or more, while Eliza eventually moved to Mrs. Bregantz's school in Putney, outside London. Her brothers also benefited from Mary's new circle. Both Charles and James stayed with her for considerable periods. James needed further schooling in mathematics to be able to take an examination for first lieutenant and receive a commission, and he got it from John Bonnycastle. While James was studying under Bonnycastle, he lived with Mary and applied himself so energetically that she could write Eliza that this brother at least was rising in her estimation. Presumably after having been a care and an aggravation, James was settling down, and it was certainly high time; he was over twenty. In April, 1790, he sat for his examination for lieutenant, but he did not receive a commission at this time.[17]

Charles, the youngest of the family, had stayed the longest with his father and showed unmistakable signs of the latter's traits: charm, liveliness, and a tendency to become a rolling stone which caused Mary endless anxiety. In the hope that his eldest brother could help him, she articled Charles to Edward for schooling in the law, but Edward fell out with his father and insisted that Charles' indenture be transferred to another attorney. When he failed to give satisfaction in his new situation, Charles was soon back on Mary's hands.

Mary's feelings about her brother ran the gamut from affection to dismay. At times, when "his warm youthful blood paints joy in his cheeks and dances in his eyes," Mary was hopeful; but then he committed some youthful folly, and in the hope that George Blood (who had himself been a problem in earlier days) would have a good influence on him, she dispatched him to Ireland, with a letter which shows how fearful she was that he would follow the path of his father:

> I shall expect from you [a] faithful account of him—I would fain have made him a virtuous character and have improved his character at the same time. . . . I beg of you if you have any love for me try to make him exert himself—try to fix him in a situation or heaven knows into what vices he may sink! You may tell him that I feel more sorrow than resentment—say that I forgive him yet think he must be devoid of feeling if he can forgive himself. I know he will plunge into pleasure while he has a farthing left—for God's sake try to save him from [illegible] by employing him.

Mary's anxiety was intense because she had right before her the fate of George's sister Caroline:

> Mrs. Burgh wrote to me [from Newington Green] to inform me that the parish officers of Islington had been with her to inquire where her father resided that they might *pass* Caroline to him. She was taken up in a dreadful situation—and they now permit her to remain in the work-house, on conditions *I* pay them half a crown a week, "till I write to her father." What is to be done, my dear boy? I cannot allow them again to turn her out—nor will I see her. If she knew where I lived, she would come to me, and be a burden I could *not* bear.[18]

A fortnight later Mary proposed that she board Caroline "at the workhouse, and buy a few clothes to cover her," but she also asked, for the first time, that the Bloods assume the financial responsibility and that George's father, now adequately employed, send her 10 pounds.

By the spring of 1788 Mary was looking forward with a buoyancy that was entirely new to her. It was with George that she shared her optimism, as she had her deepest despondency:

> I have lately being [*sic*] very busy translating a work of some importance and have made a very advantageous contract for

another—besides I have had a variety of other employment—in short, my dear Boy, I succeed beyond my most sanguine hopes, and really believe I shall clear above two hundred pounds this year, which will supply amply all *my* wants and enable me to defray the expenses of Everina's journey and let her remain at Paris longer than I first intended. . . . I daily earn more money with less trouble.[19]

One source of Mary's increased income was the new *Analytical Review*. Its first issue appeared in May, 1788, pitting it against a number of established and not dissimilar reviews. The "abstract-essay" with a dash of critical opinion thrown in was already a familiar device for acquainting the public with what was appearing in the field of literature. A successful example was the *Monthly Review*, founded in 1749, with a liberal and dissenting viewpoint. Its principal rival was the *Critical Review*, which dated from 1756; conservative in tone, it was edited for many years by the novelist Tobias Smollett and had numbered Goldsmith and Johnson among its contributors. Lastly, there was the *English Review*, which had been in existence only five years and which was to merge with the *Analytical* at a later date.

The six-page announcement, "To the Public," which opened the first issue of the *Analytical* and which is credited to Christie declared that existing publications failed, either in objectivity or in the scope of their coverage. It announced that it would present comprehensive coverage of foreign publications ("The accounts of foreign Literature in our Journals has been censured, we think with some reason, as being defective"), a plan based largely on Christie's unique familiarity with the European journals; correspondence was invited, "either in Latin, French, Italian, Spanish or German."[20]

The *Analytical* was to reflect the sympathies of the group which gathered in Johnson's rooms, in theology, science, and politics, and to encourage the romantic trend in fiction and poetry. A good deal of the contents was ponderous and long-winded; some reviews carried over from one issue to the next—that of Gibbon's *Decline and Fall of the Roman Empire* ran for six issues.

It is difficult to reach any hard conclusions about the number or quality of Mary's contributions to the *Analytical*, since no names were signed to the reviews, and the initials are not always easy to identify. Many reviews signed M. and W. concerned books dealing with children and with women, which might very well have been by Mary, and it seems likely that she was also assigned miscellaneous fiction and poetry. (See Appendix D.) The only manuscript of an *Analytical* review by Mary which has come to light is a brief criticism of a novel, *Albert de Nordenshild*.[21] Concerning a review of some sermons by Dr. Johnson, she wrote her publisher with the same tart stubbornness she had displayed on previous occasions:

> I send you all the books I had to review except Dr. J——'s Sermons, which I have just begun. If you wish me to look over any more trash this month—you must send it to me directly. . . . If you do not like the manner in which I reviewed Dr. J——'s [sermon] on his wife, be it known to you—I *will* not do it any other way. . . .[22]

In general, what was important about Mary's work for the *Analytical* was its professionalism. She had assignments and deadlines to meet, and her subsistence depended on her doing the work, whether she wanted to or not. She also faced the kind of competition offered by other established and more experienced hacks who would be watching her work for judgment, style, and literacy. She was adding to her general stock of information and writing more easily and fluently. She was demonstrating to herself and to others that she had the necessary intelligence, ambition, and energy to meet the incessant challenge and strain of such work. The *Analytical Review*, together with the group she met at Johnson's, provided the climate in which Mary Wollstonecraft attained intellectual maturity in an astonishingly short span of time.

The first fruits of this growth was her translation of Necker's book, which Johnson published in the autumn of 1788; it was reviewed in the January, 1789, issue of the *Analytical*. Knowing that Mary was self-educated in the fields of philosophy and religion, one can marvel that she was able to make sense of Necker's abstruse arguments. It is in no way derogatory of her achievement to wonder whether any of Johnson's circle gave her help, either with the translation, as Fuseli did for Cowper, or with broader metaphysical or theological knowledge (as Alexander Geddes might have done).

Necker saw no conflict between reason and religion, holding that reason was a divine gift to man, a thought Mary was to develop in *A Vindication of the Rights of Woman*. It was perhaps also in his book that she first found the idea that man's highest attributes are a divine harbinger of his immortality. Necker found such "intimations" in the human ability to love and in the magnificent capacity for thought with which human beings are endowed:

> The grandeur of the human mind is indeed a vast subject of reflexion. This marvellous constitution seems to remind us perpetually of a design proportioned to such a noble conception. It seems almost unnecessary that God should have endowed the soul with such noble facilities for such a short life as ours, to fulfil its limited plan and trivial pursuits. Thus everything authorizes us to carry our views further. Were I to see such men as Columbus, Vesputius [sic], Vasco de Gama, in a ship, I should not suppose they were mere coasters. . . .[23]

The translation reads like Mary's style at its infrequent best, unencumbered by floweriness or undue digressions; she might have learned some much-needed lessons from Necker's beautifully ordered exposition, each chapter dealing with his thought in logical sequence and leading without repetition into the next. In the advertisement which prefaced her translation, Mary stated that she had taken "some liberties" with Necker's text, adding that these seemed necessary "to preserve the spirit of the original." There are times, however, when her changes do the opposite.

Mary later turned against both Necker and his book. She did not scruple to attack it in print, dismissing it as "a large book [of] various metaphysical shreds of arguments, which he had collected from the conversations of men, fond of ingenious subtleties; and the style, excepting some declamatory passages, was as inflated and diffused as the thoughts were far-fetched and unconnected."[24] She did not mention the fact that she herself had been happy to present the book to English readers, and her criticism seems particularly gratuitous because she herself so often sinned by a diffuse and disjointed style.

Anyone who could handle Necker's prose and thought could read most of the literature of the day. By now Mary was undoubtedly reading political and religious tracts, Rousseau (in French), parliamentary speeches, and travelers' accounts of the United States. What she did not have time to read she heard discussed, often heatedly; a placid, objective argument was hardly possible with personalities like Fuseli, Geddes, and eventually more active radicals involved.

Mary never again published anything which could properly be called a translation; instead, she turned out "adaptations" in which there would be some new material aimed at English readers. The only other book she worked on during 1788 which was published was an anthology entitled *The Female Reader*; what little we know of its contents is due to the *Analytical*, since no copy has yet been found. It was reviewed in the June, 1789, issue, and described in the catalogue of books and pamphlets published semiannually at the back of the magazine: *"The Female Reader; or Miscellaneous Pieces in Prose and Verse*, selected from the best writers and disposed under the proper heads for the improvement of young women; to which is prefixed a Preface containing some hints on Female education."[25] Its interest for us would lie in the Preface which might throw light on the development of Mary's thinking since she first demanded that girls learn how to think.

During 1789 Mary continued to review miscellaneous "trash," as she had called it, for the *Analytical*: such titles as *Infancy, or the Management of Children*, by Hugh Downman, MD (in verse); travel commentaries by Mrs. Piozzi; and another book of travel in South Wales, where Mary had lived briefly as a girl. In July, it is true, she wrote on Madame de Staël's *Letters on the Works and Character of Jean-Jacques Rousseau*, and in August she dealt with an account of the notorious private life of Guillaume Cardinal Dubois, commenting on the failings of the French nobility and absolute government in France. But despite their timeliness, Mary was still serving her professional apprenticeship when the storm broke across the Channel in 1789. She could have had no inkling of the impact it would have on her own life. Indeed very few read the signs of the shock which would end by jarring the social and political order of the Western world into new forms.

CHAPTER VIII

A Vindication of the Rights of Men (1791)

ON MAY 5, 1789, THE ESTATES-GENERAL of France met for the first time in more than 150 years, at the summons of Louis XVI, to deal with the imminent bankruptcy of the realm. Few foresaw Louis' inept stubbornness or the equal but far more gifted stubbornness of the people's representatives, and few had plumbed the acute need in both French cities and rural areas.

Instead, on July 11 the king dismissed his minister Necker (whose book Mary had lately translated); he had been trying to hold the dike against financial collapse on the one hand and popular discontent on the other. On July 14 the people of Paris attacked and captured the Bastille. (It is significant that Mary could have had firsthand reports of the stirring event from two of her friends who witnessed it: Henry Gabell[1] and the American Joel Barlow.[2])

As the news reached England, it found a changed group meeting at Johnson's. By November, 1789, Thomas Christie had severed his connection with the *Analytical* and was in Paris, where he wrote to Joseph Banks, the wealthy botanist who was president of the Royal Society:

[Medicine] was the line of life I should have preferred to any other, but my father being deeply engaged in commerce, and all my friends here also, I have been insensibly led on in the same track, in so much, that I now find it important to extricate myself without doing violence to the wishes of my friends and relinquishing prospects very flattering to one who is a beginner in life—I have therefore resolved to conform to circumstances, and have come here, not to study medicine, but to acquire the French language, and to attain all the information possible respecting the Commerce of France, in which I am likely to be materially interested.[3]

According to one source, Christie was acting as agent for Turnbull Forbes, London grain merchants, a connection Christie maintained for several years. However, he did not pursue the role of detached businessman. He was an ardent and articulate sympathizer with the Revolution, and in 1790 he wrote his first work on it, *A Sketch of the New Constitution in France*.[4] Mary's increasing responsibility for editorial assignments and as a kind of assistant editor to the magazine seems to date from his departure.

There were other changes in the group. William Blake was no longer the unknown lyricist of 1787. He had brought out his *Songs of Innocence* and two of his strange *Books of Prophecy*, *The Book of Thel* and *The Marriage of Heaven and Hell*, in 1790. He is reputed to have walked the streets of London wearing the "bonnet rouge, the traditional red cap of the poor man who is a free citizen," although he removed it when the Revolution swung through its wide arc to violent excesses.

The most important addition to the group was Tom Paine. He was then in his fifties, with a varied life already behind him. When he left England for the American colonies to better his fortunes in 1774, it was at a crucial moment in their history. Turning from journalism to controversy, he wrote *Common Sense* and the *Crisis* papers (pamphlets aimed at raising the Continental Army's morale in a period of defeat) and became famous.

In 1787 he came back to Europe, having launched on a new career—the designing and construction of steel bridges. One of his bridges was being built at Rotherham, near the steel center of Sheffield. In London he knew not only the Johnson group, but all the leading political figures who had supported the American cause, including Edmund Burke. He was also a frequent visitor in Paris and sent back news as the Revolution accelerated.

Today it is difficult to put ourselves into the frame of mind of those who, hating tyranny and knowing nothing of later developments—the excesses and the reaction they produced, the necessity of treading the whole weary route against arbitrary government over and over again—thought that each act, each sign of progress in France was a step into an unclouded future.

> Bliss was it in that dawn to be alive
> But to be young was very Heaven![5]

Wordsworth, young and on the scene in the French provincial town of Orléans, summed up for all time the frame of mind of the youthful idealist and reformer. The older ones were also beguiled by the rush of events; when had Europe seen a successful revolution against absolute monarchy? Richard Price, sixty-six years old and long retired from the active ministry, was only a year and a half away from his death and already a sick man, but he was as exalted by events in France as any younger person. Price's eloquence and the depth of his convictions made it inevitable that when he spoke out on events in France, he lit the fuse for the explosion of British public opinion for and against the Revolution.

On November 4, 1789, he delivered a sermon before the annual gathering in London of the Society for Commemorating the Glorious Revolution of 1688. That occasion had marked the bloodless transfer of power from the Stuart absolutists (who ruled by divine right) to James II's daughter Mary and her Protestant husband, William of Orange, Stadholder of the Netherlands. The society met annually to celebrate the beginnings of religious freedom and modern parliamentary rule in Great Britain. Price, however, used the occasion not only to hail the Revolution in France, but to reevaluate that of 1688 in the light of current happenings.

> . . . But let us remember that we ought not to satisfy ourselves with Thanksgiving. . . . Let us, in particular, take care not to forget the principles of the Revolution. . . . I will only take notice of the three following:

First; The right to liberty of conscience in religious matters.
Secondly; The right to resist power when abused. And
Thirdly; The right to chuse [*sic*] our governors; to cashier
   them for misconduct; and to frame a government for
   ourselves.

Price pointed out to his audience that this work was far from
complete. Full religious liberty did not exist as long as Dissenters
were barred from civil and military office (so were Catholics, but
Price did not mention them); gross inequality and even, he
hinted ominously, corruption still existed in parliamentary representation.

When the representation is partial [said Price] a kingdom
possesses liberty only partially; and if extremely partial, it only
gives a *semblance* of liberty; but if not only extremely partial,
but corruptly chosen, and under corrupt influence after being
chosen, it becomes a *nuisance*, and produces the worst of all
forms of government—a government by corruption—a government carried on and supported by spreading venality and prof-
ligacy throughout a kingdom. . . . We are, at present, I hope,
at a great distance from it. But it cannot be pretended that
there are no advances towards it, or that there is no reason for
apprehension and alarm.[6]

The drift of Price's argument was unmistakable and caused
both offense and alarm among those unfriendly to the French
revolutionary cause. These sentiments were exacerbated by the
congratulatory resolution to the French National Assembly voted
by the society. Price's sermon and the resolution were published
together and, of course, widely sold and discussed.

Opinion in England was, at the outset, either partial to the
Revolution or neutral, since it was widely accepted that France
was governed by an outdated despotism such as England had
long since dispensed with. The leader in hardening majority
opinion against the Revolution, a process that took almost four
years, was Edmund Burke, England's foremost liberal statesman.

His *Reflections on the Revolution in France, and on the Proceedings of Certain Societies in London Relative to That Event*
was written when he was sixty-two years old and had already

served twenty-six years in the House of Commons.[7] He was always primarily the spokesman for moderation and common sense, rather than abstract liberal principles, for the pragmatic in politics, as opposed to the theoretical; in addition, his wide knowledge of history and law, as well as his practical political experience, led him to emphasize the positive values inherited from the past (what Mary Wollstonecraft was to brand "the rust of antiquity") not as the ultimate and perfect, but as the necessary foundation for change and progress.

Seen in this light, Burke's opposition to Lord North's repressive government of the American colonies would give little promise of sympathy or support for the French Revolution. He argued that the colonies, because of the circumstances in which they found themselves, especially that of distance, had developed institutions of their own, among them one similar to Parliament (the Continental Congress). Therefore, whatever British rights existed must be exercised with restraint and an awareness of the feelings of those "on whose account all authority exists, I mean, the people to be governed."

These feelings could hardly be surprising, in view of the British antecedents of so many of the colonists. Burke therefore argued that:

> If there be one fact in the world perfectly clear, it is this: "That the disposition of the people of America is wholly adverse to any other than a free government"; and if this is indication enough for any honest statesman, how he ought to adapt whatever power he finds in his hands, to their case. *If any ask me what a free government is,* I answer, that, for any practical purpose, it is what the people think so; and they, and not I, are the natural, lawful and competent judges in this matter.[8]

Having put forward so empirical a definition of free government, he outlined the manner in which reform might be instituted and the limits within which freedom should be validly exercised:

> . . . The *extreme* of liberty (which is its abstract perfection, but its real fault) obtains no where, nor ought to obtain any where. Because extremes, as we all know, in every point which

relates either to our duties or satisfactions in life, are destructive both to virtue and enjoyment. Liberty must be limited in order to be possessed. The degree of restraint it is impossible in any case to settle precisely. But it ought to be the constant aim of every wise, publick council, to find out by cautious experiments, and rational cool endeavours, with how little, not how much of this restraint, the community can subsist. For liberty is a thing to be improved, not an evil to be lessened.[9]

These were the eternal paradoxes of the liberal position: "Liberty must be limited in order to be possessed," yet within as few limits as possible; on the other hand, those limits were to be gauged by "cautious experiments" and "rational cool endeavours." It was a philosophy tailored to the Parliament where it had evolved, but it did not recommend itself to critics for whom that Parliament was an insufficient example of liberty. Understandably the man who held such opinions might remain neutral during the earliest stages of revolutionary development in France, as Burke did; he would have little sympathy with events once the uncontrollable Parisian populace became their motive force.

A natural antipathy to violence was reinforced by Burke's personal experiences during the Gordon Riots which shook England in 1780, touched off by Protestant demonstrations against any relaxation of legislation depriving Catholics of political rights. Burke went into the streets to face the drink-maddened crowds who had opened the prisons and were burning houses and raging out of control; he even made speeches censuring their violence. His actions showed principle and courage alike, but he never forgot the experience; it was vividly in his mind when he heard of the events he believed to be similar taking place in France.[10]

Burke's reply to Price's speech did not appear until a whole year had elapsed. He was preparing a careful and comprehensive analysis; meanwhile, his position continued to harden. On February 9, 1790, Burke spoke in the House of Commons attacking the Revolution for the first time: "The excesses of an irrational, proscribing, confiscating, plundering, ferocious, bloody and tyrannical democracy" and its attendant evil, atheism: "a foul, unnatural vice, foe to all the dignity and consolation of mankind."[11] His speech was published and widely discussed in the clubs and coffeehouses. To the friends of the new regime in France, it marked Burke as an inveterate enemy of the oppressed and of the brightest hope to dawn on Western Europe since the Reformation.

For the next nine months Mary and the rest of Johnson's circle waited for the blast they knew Burke, with his immense prestige and formidable arsenal of knowledge and experience, was preparing. It came early in November, 1790, and was an overnight best seller, hotly disputed and quickly reprinted. Burke's *Reflections on the French Revolution* ran to more than 150 pages. It is an exhaustive and often violently critical analysis of the shortcomings of the French National Assembly and its program and a passionate defense of English society and parliamentary government. It is not difficult for us to sympathize with the fears Burke expressed for the future in the light of subsequent events: the Terror and the antidemocratic reaction which dominated France for the next century. Much of his argument is unexceptionable today—and was then—to anyone who deprecates extremism as merely the substitution of one type of violence for another.

Yet Burke's evaluation of the situation was factually wrong on almost every point. He had a totally unrealistic picture of conditions in prerevolutionary France (he had visited that country for only a few weeks in 1773 and stayed mainly in Paris). Moreover, Burke failed completely to recognize that what might appear to him as abstract theories of freedom propounded by Voltaire, Rousseau, Condorcet, and others were not abstractions to Frenchmen living under the Bourbon regime. He was certainly blind to the onerous burden of taxation and requisitions which impoverished the peasantry and the popular hatred of a regime whose *lettres de cachet* (signed "It is our will: Louis") could send a man to life imprisonment or the gallows.

With Richard Price, Burke took violent issue not only with respect to the French Revolution, but with his evaluation of the "revolution" in England in 1688. That "revolution," said Burke, had not given the English people the right to choose and dismiss their rulers (the change of rulers in 1688 had been based on the principle of legitimate descent). He based his own position, once again, on tradition and gradual parliamentary development. He portrayed England as a Utopia: prosperous, satisfied with distinctions of rank, watchful for the interests of the needy, buttressed by a church which supplied its spiritual needs, and—one might almost think on reading Burke—lacking in nothing except to the jaundiced eyes of a Richard Price.

The dangers which threatened British liberties were, Burke thought, the overthrow of existing institutions by the ideas unleashed in France and the inherent dynamic that would eventually threaten to propel the revolution beyond French frontiers. Burke was appalled at the threat to an aristocracy which he considered not only benevolent, but constructive and useful, and to an established church which was a necessary prop to the institutions he revered. Although his book is most often remembered for his astonishing panegyric of Marie Antoinette, this was actually not a significant part of his argument; he would have been just as hostile to the Revolution if the queen had never existed. He saw in that upheaval only its dangers, nothing of either its promise or its inevitability.

Burke's *Reflections* appeared on the anniversary of Price's sermon of the previous year, and for months the *Analytical* carried reviews of "Replies to Mr. Burke." Mary Wollstonecraft's *Vindication of the Rights of Men* seems to have been among the earliest of these replies, if not the very first.[12]

It is obvious that Mary could have given Burke's extended work little considered study or even digested it properly. Her tract has the lack of organization and the headlong style which were becoming characteristic of her work. In the fashion of the day, it was set up by the printer as she delivered the manuscript pages; one suspects that Johnson was not averse to cashing in on public interest while it was at a high pitch and before too many other replies had glutted the market. Sympathetic and supportive when Mary needed it, he also knew her well enough by now to vary the treatment if the occasion demanded. Godwin (who gave so little notice to Mary's pamphlet in the *Memoirs* that he never even mentions it by its full title), recounts a revealing episode:

> When Mary had arrived at about the middle of her work, she was seized with a temporary fit of torpor and indolence, and began to repent of her undertaking. In this state of mind, she

called, one evening, as she was in the practice of doing, upon her publisher, for the purpose of relieving herself by an hour or two's conversation. Here, the habitual ingenuousness of her nature led her to describe what had just past in her thoughts. Mr. Johnson immediately, in a kind and friendly way, intreated her not to put any constraint upon her inclination, and to give herself no uneasiness about the sheets already printed, which he would cheerfully throw aside, if it would contribute to her happiness. Mary had wanted incentive. She had expected reproach, rather than to be encouraged, in what she well knew to be unreasonable. Her friend's ready falling in with her ill-humour, and seeming to expect that she would lay aside her undertaking, piqued her pride. She immediately went home, and proceeded to the end of her work, with no other interruptions but what were absolutely indispensable.[13]

Mary had reason to be grateful to Johnson for his acumen. Her pamphlet, published anonymously but with her name on an early second printing, was reviewed by all the critical periodicals with either approval or condemnation, depending on their political slant, and established her reputation as a publicist.

A Vindication of the Rights of Men was Mary's first success. Its merits, however, are uneven. She gave her opponent's arguments little consideration. One recent critic has remarked that she "accomplished the unlikely feat of writing an answer to Burke without treating at all either of the French Revolution or the English revolution of 1688,"[14] which is only partially true; she did attempt a few specific refutations. But in the main, Mary confined her attack to the issues of human rights and social justice—in England. She did not describe conditions in France. Instead, she wrote of what she knew best, either by hearsay or her own direct experiences—social conditions in England of her time. She also relied, to a surprising degree, on personal abuse of Burke himself.

At the outset, she defined the basic human right to liberty: "such a degree of liberty, civil and religious, as is compatible with the liberty of every other individual with whom he is united in a social compact, and the continued existence of that compact."[15]

Instead of going back to Burke's utterances during the American war to demonstrate the inconsistencies of his present position, Mary confined herself to drawing on his speeches during the debate on the proposed regency while George III was mentally deranged in 1788. She contrasted Burke's outrage at the treatment of the French royal family with his own arguments for dethroning the English king and accused him of romantic sentimentality, on the one hand, and self-seeking partisanship, on the other. She criticized his reverence for what he portrayed as the lawful, traditional antecedents of British parliamentary authority on historical grounds. That authority, she argued, had emerged from the struggle for power and money between such rulers as Edward III and Richard II and the nobles and commons who alone could supply the king with needed funds; the product of such rivalry could hardly be placed above criticism or the need for further reform.

But Mary stood on the most solid ground when she raised, with great eloquence, the question of what kind of society really existed in England. Was it the Utopia Burke had urged the French to draw on as their model? This, in withering detail, Mary denied. She pointed out the injustice, the oppression, and the poverty, on the one hand, and the privilege, immunity, and corruption, on the other, that distinguished the lives of the poor from those of the affluent. She attacked the press gangs that provided the manpower for the Royal Navy and the laws that, by protecting game, penalized the farmer or the poacher who sought a meal for his hungry family. She attacked the venality behind the façade of parliamentary representation, the restrictions of hereditary property and entail on a more general distribution of wealth, the injustice of an aristocratic class whose real talents bore no relation to the influence and position they occupied. She excoriated the absentee clergy and the established church whose wealth had not been conferred on it by popular will but had been accumulated by greed.

When Mary Wollstonecraft wrote of these things, she wrote eloquently because she was writing about things she really knew and understood—what she had witnessed, heard from contemporaries, or read in the press about the England of her time:

Security of property! Behold, in a few words, the definition of English liberty. . . . But softly—it is only the property of the rich that is secure; the man who lives by the sweat of his brow has no asylum from oppression; the strong man may enter— when was the castle of the poor sacred?—and the base informer steal him from the family that depend on his industry for subsistence. . . . I cannot avoid expressing my surprise that when you recommended our form of government as a model, you did not caution the French against the arbitrary custom of pressing men for the sea service. You should have hinted to them, that property in England is much more secure than liberty, and not have concealed that the liberty of an honest mechanic—his all— is often sacrificed to secure the property of the rich. For it is a farce to pretend that a man fights for *his country, his hearth, or his altars,* when he has neither liberty nor property. . . . Our penal laws punish with death the man who steals a few pounds; but to take by violence, or trepan a man, is no such heinous offence—For who shall dare complain of the venerable vestige of the law that rendered the life of a deer more sacred than that of a man? . . . Misery, to reach your heart, I perceive, must have its cap and bells; your tears are reserved, very *naturally* considering your character, for the declamations of the theatre, or for the downfall of queens, whose rank alters the nature of folly, and throws a graceful veil over vices that degrade humanity; whilst the distress of many industrious mothers, whose *helpmates* have been torn from them, and the hungry cry of helpless babes, were vulgar sorrows that could not move your commiseration, though they might extort an alms.[16]

But this excerpt also illustrates one of the outstanding weaknesses of Mary's rebuttal. Not content with her case against Burke's ability to pass over the sufferings of the common people while he lamented the fate of nobility and royalty, she fell back repeatedly on namecalling, innuendo, and, on occasion, even slander. She accused Burke of vanity, envy, ambition, "infantile sensibility," "wilful misrepresentation and wanton abuse." If he had lived in the time of Christ, she charged, he would have joined in the cry for His crucifixion; if opinion in England had attacked the Revolution, he would have defended it; the *Reflections* was nothing more than an attempt to recapture his fading success and popularity. "Personal pique and vanity" dictated the "bitter sarcasm and reiterated expressions of contempt" which recurred throughout his book, but which even a friendly critic can hardly compare with Mary's language and allegations:

> I beseech you to ask your own heart, when you call yourself a friend of liberty, whether it would not be more consistent to style yourself the champion of property, the adorer of the golden image which power has set up.—And, when you are examining your heart, if it would not be too much like mathematical drudgery, to which a fine imagination reluctantly stoops, enquire further, how it is consistent with the vulgar notions of honesty, and the foundation of morality—truth; for a man to boast of his virtue and independence, when he cannot forget that he is at the moment enjoying the wages of falsehood (see Mr. Burke's bills for economical reform); and that, in a skulking, unmanly way, he has secured himself a pension of fifteen hundred pounds per annum on the Irish establishment? Do honest men, Sir, for I am not rising to the refined principle of honour, ever receive the reward of their public services, or secret alliance, in the name of *another*?[17]

Even the reviewer for the *Analytical* felt obliged to remark that "we never before heard that Burke had a pension." (Actually Burke received no such award until he retired from Parliament in 1795.[18])

When she defended Richard Price against Burke, Mary was far more unmeasured than Burke had been against Price:

> In reprobating Dr. Price's opinions you might have spared the man; and if you had but half as much reverence for the grey hairs of virtue as for the accidental distinctions of rank, you would not have treated with such indecent familiarity and supercilious contempt, a member of the community whose talents and modest virtues place him high in the scale of moral excellence. . . . I could almost fancy that I now see this respectable old man, in his pulpit, with hands clasped, and eyes devoutly fixed, praying with all the simple energy of unaffected piety; or when more erect, inculcating the dignity of virtue, and enforcing the doctrines his whole life adorns; benevolence animated each feature, and persuasion attuned his accents. . . . Is

this the man you brand with so many opprobrious epithets? he whose private life will stand the test of the strictest enquiry— away with such unmanly sarcasm and puerile conceits. . . .[19]

Mary Wollstonecraft was apparently oblivious that she was berating a man only six years younger than Price and a man who —given any degree of fairness—might also have claimed the distinction of a few "grey hairs of virtue." Although political controversy on such a level was not unknown at the time, it is difficult to explain the tone of Mary's whole onslaught, unless we recall not only that she was a recent convert to liberal thought, but that she had brought to her new vocation of advocate for the oppressed the same volatile reactions that had impeded her emotional maturity since childhood. She was still "a good hater" (in Godwin's words), and she sprang to the defense of those she loved with passion rather than the reason she claimed as her light. Price, who had helped her when she was in desperate need and was the kind of man Mary would have wanted for a father—wise, judicious, and loving—had been attacked, and she went to his defense with the same instinctive loyalty and emotional fervor— buttressed by her intellectual convictions—that she had displayed in protecting Eliza Bishop. In both cases she had a large measure of moral conviction on her side; in both cases she was breaking new ground and demonstrating her fearlessness and initiative, however open to question her judgment might be.

A Vindication of the Rights of Men thus demonstrates Mary's limitations, as well as her gifts. It was one thing to take arguments from experience when that experience had been varied and deep, as she was to do in her next work. But here she was on uncertain ground, unable to develop a philosophy of history which might adequately challenge that of Burke. She had read some English history, perhaps that of David Hume, whose latest volume dealt with British history prior to the Tudors and would have provided her with the background she needed in citing Parliament's differences with Edward III and Richard II. Otherwise, she could weigh what she herself knew of contemporary England only against her belief that men's rights derive from their creator and are inalienable from the human condition.

However flawed, it must be borne in mind that *A Vindication of the Rights of Men* is among the earliest serious political polemics by a woman.[20] Women had written few serious works outside the fields of general literature and classical translations. They had stood apart from political controversy because they lacked the education to attempt it; society frowned on such activity because women were not thought to be formed for it, mentally or physically. No one expected intellectual effort or achievement from them, and consequently nothing was demanded of them in the way of performance.

This is at least a partial explanation of why *A Vindication of the Rights of Men* was at first issued anonymously and why it was not a better piece of work. Johnson was at times a critical and exacting publisher. He did not hesitate to make suggestions to a poet like Cowper, yet he did not have similar standards when it came to an anonymous pamphlet (or one signed by a woman when Mary's name went on the title page of the second edition). By then, even if he had had second thoughts about Mary's choice of language, he was not likely, knowing Mary, to suggest tempering it, although a few changes were made: Mary rewrote a passage on fashionable women—a subject she had already written on—and made another, which had implied criticism of her father's handling of his children's inheritance, less personally allusive. But none of her growing number of literary acquaintances seems to have assumed the role of critic of her work to help her strengthen and improve it, probably because it seemed so remarkable that she was writing at all. Not until Mary Wollstonecraft met Godwin did she encounter anyone with a mind as good as her own who was willing to discuss her work with her in detail.

Whatever merits her pamphlet had, it was soon lost in the flood of answers to the *Reflections* (the best known among them Paine's *Rights of Man*, which is the only one remembered today). A German scholar first gave it the consideration it merits in the body of Mary's work; an American republished it for the first time since 1790.[21]

CHAPTER IX

Seedtime (1791–92)

IT WAS NOT EASY for her sisters to accept Mary's newly acquired prestige. Everina had returned from France, and by now both she and Eliza were teaching at Mrs. Bregantz's school in Putney. As usual, both were bitterly dissatisfied with their situation. Overnight, it seemed, they had a sister who had written an ambitious political tract which was widely (and not always favorably) mentioned in the reviews, who was making new friends, and whose path seemed to be diverging drastically from theirs.

Her brothers continued to be a source of worry, and relations with them were also uneven. Charles had failed to find a position in Ireland, despite George Blood's efforts, and had gone back to his father's home in Wales. In spite of his taking the examination, James found that promotion in the Royal Navy was slow without influential connections, and he was not situated so that he could wait. He irritated Mary by spending some of her hard-earned money "to dance after preferment when the fleet last paraded at Portsmouth" but was eventually persuaded to look elsewhere for interim employment and took the command of a small trading ship, although to Mary's regret it was "a voyage of speculation."[1]

She had also fallen out with George Blood. She upbraided him for not keeping her informed of Charles' situation and accused him of neglecting her, "a friend who would fain have been a mother . . . but I will not repine, the ways of Heaven are dark; yet ever just." When George wrote—belatedly—pleading business difficulties and lack of time, Mary's tone became shrill; he was not shut up in the Bastille, he might have taken a half hour from sleep without jeopardizing his health, no excuse was valid:

> I cannot use my india rubber to obliterate the traces of sorrow and disappointed affection your behaviour has left in my memory. I sincerely wish you happy and shall be glad to hear that you have extricated yourself out of your pecuniary difficulties but I do not think it probable that I will ever again be able to trust and respect you as I habitually did some months ago— I loved you, because I gave you credit for more substantial virtues than I now think you possess.

The ensuing silence lasted for more than a year, and then the correspondence was only briefly resumed. Apparently George had been writing to Everina and had hinted at a marriage proposal. Mary replied in her sister's behalf that Everina was too used to thinking of him as a brother:

> . . . but accustomed to consider you in that light she cannot view you in any other—let us then be on the old footing—love us as we love you—but give your heart to some worthy girl. . . . Everina does not seem to think of marriage.[2]

Behind Mary's high-pitched irritation with George and her sisters was her continuing need for a close personal relationship, what she called "a particular affection." Sometime early in 1791 Mary took into her home a little girl whom she intended to bring up as her daughter. The child was named Ann, one more indication that her beloved Fanny was still very much in Mary's mind and heart, and her arrival showed Mary's awareness of her deep need for someone to cherish.[3] Since she had not succeeded in establishing a family by the usual means, she would do so by adopting a child. It soon became apparent that she had taken on more than she bargained for; the child was troublesome, and a

year later Eliza Bishop declared she could tell from Mary's letters
that she was bored with "her daughter." It must have been a
strain trying to work in the same small house with a youngster
who required guidance, admonition, the companionship of other
children—all difficult problems when money is short and for a
woman tackling them without a husband and father.

The child's presence was an added irritant to Mary's relations
with her sisters, underscoring the decreasing likelihood that they
would get long-term financial assistance from her. It was a particular source of anger for Eliza, for Mary now had, in a sense,
the daughter Eliza had lost at Mary's instigation. Small wonder
that Eliza grew bitter, and vented her unhappiness in waspish
comments at Mary's expense, when she wrote to Everina:

> I have received a letter from *our sister* dated *Bedford Square*.
> She says James left her last Friday. Her letter is quite matter of
> fact—I conclude from it that she is in good spirits, heartily
> tired of her daughter Ann, and brimful of her friend Fuseli and
> visible pleasure at her brother's departure is expressed.

Early in 1791 Everina left Putney for Ireland, to be a governess
in Waterford, County Cork. With her departure Eliza was even
more alone. By May, 1791, she too had abandoned teaching and
the proximity of London—and Mary—for a post as governess in
Wales, not far from Laugharne. After a visit to her father, she
sent Everina a grim account of his condition:

> I thought I should have sunk into the ground when I beheld
> his ghastly visage and body worn to a mere skeleton . . . [his]
> countenance is now I really think the most dreadful I ever
> beheld! It appears constantly *convulsed* by ill humour and every
> unamiable feeling that can be expressed. His face is quite *red*,
> his hair grey and dirty, his beard long, and the clothes he wears
> not worth sixpence. . . . The sight of my father's ghastly visage
> haunts me night and day; for he is really worn to a mere skeleton,
> and has a dreadful cough that makes my blood run cold when-
> ever I listen to it, and that is the greater part of the night, or
> else he groans most dreadfully . . . there cannot be a more
> melancholy sight than to see him, not able to walk ten yards
> without panting for breath, and continually falling; still he is
> able to ride ten miles every day and eat and *drink* very hearty.

Charles, now twenty-one years old, was in even more pitiable condition, lacking any underclothing and "half-naked." The financial situation at Laugharne was desperate, and Eliza had little to offer in the way of suggestions to a man who would not give up drinking and would be worse off any place else than he was in Wales:

> When I beg him to be more careful in money matters, he declares he will go to London, and force Ned; or when I tell him Mary has been distressed, in order to make him save in trifles, he is in a passion, and exhausts himself. . . .

She also paid the only tribute to Edward John Wollstonecraft's second wife we can find anywhere: "a truly well-meaning woman, and willing to do the little she can to lessen the debts."[4]

Apparently the older Wollstonecraft was still not aware that by this time Mary, not Edward, was managing his affairs. In an earlier undated letter Mary had written Eliza that "the man from Primrose Street never brought the rent, and I am afraid to be importunate." She wrote George Blood in February, 1791, that she was deeply involved in "the settlement of my father's affairs" and that they were a serious problem. As usual, she was aided by the loyal Johnson, who later dourly recorded for Godwin's benefit that it was a business "attended with no little trouble to both of us."[5] Yet we also know from the family letters that money did reach Mr. Wollstonecraft from "Ned," albeit with shocking irregularity, and that Eliza Bishop occasionally contributed from her own modest earnings when the Laugharne household was destitute. When Mary went to France and lost touch with her family, it was Johnson, acting through Ned, who supplied what little money reached them; some of it may have come from Mary's earnings, but the major portion must have been from the precious rentals.

Mary's next work for Johnson was the free adaptation of a large work by the German educator Salzmann, who conducted his own coeducational school near Gotha and many of whose views were akin to those which Mary was slowly developing. *Elements of Morality* appeared in three volumes, successively in October,

1790, and January and March, 1791. In the advertisement prefixed to the first volume, Mary made it clear that this was to be no
servile translation:

> I term it a translation, though I do not pretend to assert that
> it is a literal one; on the contrary, besides making it an English
> story, I have made some additions, and altered many parts of
> it, not only to give it the spirit of an original, but to avoid intro-
> ducing any German customs or local opinions. My reasons for
> naturalizing it must be obvious—I did not wish to puzzle chil-
> dren by pointing out modifications of manners, when the grand
> principles of morality were to be fixed on a broad basis.

(She might have added that by now she was convinced that she
was capable of deciding how such "grand principles" were to be
inculcated and of inventing incidents and characters best calculated to do so.)

The framework of the Salzmann book is much like that of
Young Grandison and *Original Stories*, a "domestic history"
whose episodes and conversations are designed to teach not only
children, but their parents as well. The range of topics is wide:
health, cleanliness, morals, faith in the compassion and justice of
God and the immortality of man; such shortcomings as anger,
tattling, and pride, but also contempt for the poor, rudeness to
servants and foreigners, and cruelty to animals.

Although *Elements of Morality* was printed a number of times
not only in England, but in the United States, its most significant
effect was elsewhere. Far from begrudging Mary the liberties she
took with his text, Salzmann was grateful for the success of the
book abroad and interested in his adaptor's ideas. When *A Vindication of the Rights of Woman* was translated into German, it
contained notes and a preface by Salzmann which helped gain for
the book respectful consideration by critics and the reading public.[6] (Later he also translated Godwin's *Memoirs*.)

Despite the amount of work she was now doing for Johnson,
Mary still had financial worries, and these were occasionally
aggravated by dragging illnesses which left her depressed and
made work difficult. She had to deny one of Eliza's requests for
money and was even driven to borrow from Johnson to pay her
creditors.

But there was another source of unhappiness, in addition to health problems or money cares, and it may well have been more basic than either of these since by now Mary knew that she could maintain her independence. Her biggest problem had become emotional frustration.

Mary herself was for a time unaware of this. In the late summer of 1790, she paid a visit of several weeks to Henry Gabell, recently married and now headmaster of the Lord Weymouth School, near Bath. Since Mary had known Gabell in Ireland, he had been in Paris, a witness of the taking of the Bastille, where the mob, "who needed linen to make bandages for the wounded, stripped the shirt from his back, and tore it into suitable pieces for their purpose, the while apologizing profusely to 'Monsieur l'étranger' for the liberty they were taking!"[7]

At first her visit seemed a welcome glimpse of the family happiness which Mary had so rarely experienced—except at the Clares', when she was still an adolescent, and in the home of her Beverley friend Jane Arden. But in her first letter from Warminster to Everina, there is already an undercurrent of uneasiness:

> . . . you can scarcely imagine *how much* happiness and innocent fondness constantly illumines the eyes of this good couple so that I am never disgusted by the frequent [illegible] display of it. They seem in short just to have sufficient refinement to make them happy without ever straying too far from common life and to wish for what life never affords—or only for a few moments.

Stripped of its eighteenth-century verbiage, Mary was saying that she found the physical expression of affection disturbing. She had had very little exposure to such intimacy except when associated with unhappiness and anger, and consequently she was afraid of it. She very soon rationalized her feelings by counterposing a more desirable way of life to that of the Gabells:

> . . . my die is cast! I would not now resign intellectual pursuits for domestic comforts—and yet I think I could form an idea of more *elegant* felicity—where mind chastened sensation, and rational converse gave a little dignity to fondness. . . .

Her last letter from the Gabells was reiterative; she could not find happiness in such a setting: "Tell me, does it arise from mistaken pride or conscious dignity which whispering [to?] me that my soul is immortal and should have a nobler ambition, leads me to cherish it?"[8]

But more was at work here than repressed emotions. Along with a distaste for conjugal demonstrativeness, Mary was challenging the kind of domestic happiness which did not give a woman scope for developing her fullest human potential. Such a woman needed more than kindness or love; she required "rational converse," the opportunity to develop her "immortal soul." In these letters to her sisters, Mary was already stating the theme of her *Vindication of the Rights of Woman*.

It would be more than two years before she developed it. Meanwhile, she continued her round of reviews for the *Analytical*, wrote her *Vindication of the Rights of Men*, and searched for a viable way of life which would enable her to reconcile feeling and intellect. Not long afterward she "adopted" Ann. At Michaelmas, 1791, she moved from her house on George Street to Store Street, to the vastly different neighborhood of Bedford Square, the handsomest square in London, which set a fashionable tone for the surrounding area. Mary's move to Store Street, only a block off the square, has been ascribed, following Godwin's lead, to a newly awakened interest not only in her own appearance but in less ascetic living. Her new apartment was "commodious"; she also:

> . . . added to the neatness and cleanliness which she had always scrupulously observed, a certain degree of elegance, and those temperate indulgences in furniture and accommodation, from which a sound and uncorrupted taste never fails to derive pleasure.[9]

Godwin failed to mention the salient reason why Mary had moved to Store Street from the other bank of the Thames. She was now only a few blocks away from Henry Fuseli, who lived at 72 Queen Anne Street East (now Foley Street). In the course of the past three years the lively and irascible artist had become the central focus of Mary's life. As early as the summer of 1790, she had written Everina:

> . . . the only friend who would exert himself to comfort me is so circumstanced that he cannot—and he too is rich—yet I know while he lives I shall not want a warm indulgent friend—but his society I cannot enjoy.

Now, living only a few blocks away, she could see him more often and more easily. Only a month after she had settled in Store Street, Eliza wrote to Everina that their sister was "brimful of her friend Fuseli."[10]

The man with whom Mary had become infatuated was a complex personality. In 1790 Fuseli stood at the peak of his career. He was sophisticated, widely traveled, and well read, a brilliant conversationalist. Behind his façade modern critics have found evidence of a highly emotional and somewhat unbalanced nature, "a quivering emotional vulnerability (which) underlay the devil-may-care porcupinish insolence which Fuseli chose to present to the world."[11] His exquisite line drawings of demimondaines made during the 1780's show him as both sensuous and cynical. Though his reputation does not seem to have been that of a rake and he was considered to enjoy domestic felicity, he certainly also enjoyed the company of women: "I have heard," wrote the biographer Allen Cunningham, after Fuseli's death, "he was handsome when young, and with women (when gratified by their attentions), no man could be more gentle." He was not above flattering a woman with little regard for her feelings. The diarist Joseph Farington recorded that "Fuseli being in spirits had after tea paid much attention to Miss Archibald, and we laughed very much at our return at his sudden and extravagant admiration of her, as she is a very plain woman."[12]

He was a man of formidable intellectual gifts. His frequent, almost monthly reviews in the *Analytical* dealt with works of art, history, travel, the classics, religion, and science; unlike Mary's reviews, each one was "an essay in itself." Evidence has been found from his paintings alone that he studied the Greek and Latin classics, Dante, Ben Jonson, Spenser, and Shakespeare. Small wonder that Mary enjoyed his companionship. His biographer, Knowles, recorded that she told someone—perhaps his wife—that "I always catch something from the rich torrent of his conversation, worth treasuring up in my memory, to exercise my understanding." Godwin wrote that:

> . . . painting and subjects closely connected with painting, were their almost constant subjects of conversation; and they found them inexhaustible. . . . [Fuseli] amused, delighted and instructed her. . . . As a painter, it was impossible that she should not wish to see his works, and consequently to frequent his house. She visited him; her visits were returned.[13]

Yet there are puzzling aspects to this relationship and Mary's involvement in it. Fuseli's manner in general could hardly be described as affable. Everyone who has written about him dwells on his temper; his anger was unpredictable, frequent, and violent, his wit caustic, his allusions sometimes indecent. Why and how was Mary, who had been so deeply conditioned to dread and even abhor anger and violence, drawn to him? How did she react to the weird, even evil images of his Shakespearian and classical studies? How did his paintings and drawings strike a woman as unawakened sexually as she was at this time, who shrank from the demonstrativeness of a young husband and wife? What did she make of "The Nightmare" or "Titania and Bottom," of his innumerable drawings of women, all of them charged in some degree with eroticism, sometimes veiled, sometimes blatant?[14]

One would hardly expect Mary to be anything but repelled by the unabashed sexuality of so much of Fuseli's work. It seems inconceivable that she did not recognize it for what it was. The best explanation of why she was not, obviously, repelled is that she was able to accept it and suppress whatever attraction or anxiety might have been aroused in her, because the man himself was so unlikely a source of attraction. In the first place, Fuseli was already married, and therefore, any sexual interest in him was, by Mary's standards, inadmissible. He was, furthermore, physically unprepossessing, being shorter than herself (five feet two), broad-shouldered, with a prominent forehead, a large somewhat aquiline nose, and a rather wide mouth. (His eyes however were "large, blue, and peculiarly expressive and penetrating . . . his countenance in the highest degree intelligent and energetic.")

Last, Fuseli was old enough to be Mary's father. He was also violent, as her father had been, but easily placated. His critics agree that his anger could be almost instantly appeased, by a word or even a look of kindness. Here, then, was an approachable father, whose esteem and affection could be won, a father who could be honored for his accomplishments and loved for his interest and kindness. Here is also the key to Mary's reiterated insistence that there was nothing wrong or improper in her feelings for Fuseli, even when he himself at a later date tried to point out to her the ambiguity of her feeling for him and the difficulties arising from her ever-growing need for his presence and companionship. She was blinded even then to any logic because of her intense need for a viable relationship with a father which she had never outgrown because she had never experienced it.

That her feelings would eventually assume a sexual aspect and confront her with an insoluble problem was for the time being hidden to her. Whatever problems it eventually engendered, Mary's friendship with Fuseli was one of the most formative of her life. She had already grown rapidly in stature in the congenial climate of Johnson's circle; Fuseli was the principal agent responsible for her major work.

Frequent association with him was a wholly novel experience previously unknown to Mary and denied to most women—a friendship on terms of mutuality and respect, with a first-class mind. This experience, combined with her earlier interest in the inadequate education of women and the paucity of opportunity open to herself and her sisters and Fanny, led her to think further and more deeply along these lines. Nor can we overlook the likelihood that she was also spurred to a major effort by the desire to win Fuseli's approbation and applause, to demonstrate to him what she was capable of, what *a woman* was capable of. Possibly he encouraged her in her undertaking; in their many meetings Mary may have discussed some of her ideas with him.

Of Fuseli's feelings we know very little. A good deal of what Knowles wrote much later must be discounted as hindsight many years after the event, hindsight, moreover, of an old man who would like to forget, or make sure that the world forgot, how much he saw of Mary and rid himself of any imputation that he was in any way responsible for her infatuation. Knowles (and Fuseli himself) would have us believe that Mary, in appearance at least, embodied what the artist most disliked in women, that she looked like "a philosophical sloven; her usual dress being a habit of coarse cloth, such as is now worn by milk-women, black worsted stockings, and a beaver hat, with her hair hanging lank about her shoulders. . . ."

Perhaps Mary did look like this when she first came to Johnson's. But she could not have looked so and aroused Fuseli's interest—he who was not interested in "plain women." Knowles himself wrote that as Mary's feelings for Fuseli changed, so did her appearance. His account of her complaints that Fuseli neglected her and carried unopened letters from her in his pocket for days belongs to the latter part of their relationship. Whether or not Browning was right, that Mary never

> . . . quickened his pulse one beat.
> Fixed a moment's fancy, bitter or sweet[15]

it is clear at least that for several years Fuseli enjoyed Mary's company, either because her devotion flattered him or because he found her mind challenging and her personality attractive.

During the year 1791 Mary made a number of new and varied acquaintances. One of them was William Godwin, who came to dinner at Johnson's on a November evening, where he had requested the opportunity of meeting Tom Paine. Godwin at thirty-five was still unknown but was at work on *An Enquiry Concerning the Principles of Political Justice*, which would establish him as the outstanding radical thinker of his time when it appeared in 1793. He wished to talk with Paine because the latter's *Rights of Man*, Part I, had just been published, but his hopes of a mutually rewarding evening with the famous revolutionary thinker were dashed by Paine's disinclination to assert himself and Mary Wollstonecraft's insistence on doing so: "I heard her," wrote Godwin with ironic hindsight, "very frequently, when I wished to hear Paine." Moreover, Mary was derogatory in her comments on various people, and her opinions, to Godwin's way of thinking, were disappointingly superficial. Nevertheless, he carried away the impression of Mary as "a person of active and independent thinking."

Mary was more fortunate in being introduced by Fuseli to William Roscoe of Liverpool, and a friendship quickly developed. Roscoe was an attorney and businessman, who loved painting and literature, helped Fuseli sell his work, and wrote biographies of the Medici, Lorenzo the Magnificent and Pope Leo X.[16] In addition, he was a reformer and one of the earliest supporters of abolition of the slave trade. He gave Mary advice on business problems connected with the management of her father's affairs and tried to find a position for her brother Charles.

The closest friend Mary made during this period was Ruth Barlow, the wife of the American businessman Joel Barlow. The Barlows were from New England; their attraction for Mary lay in their embodiment of that new, young country, its energy, its optimism and equality of opportunity. When Joel went abroad at the age of thirty-four, he had already published a newspaper, run a store, and made his mark in literature. A member of a group called the Hartford Wits, he had published an ambitious narrative and philosophical poem, *The Vision of Columbus*. He first visited France, where as agent of the highly speculative Scioto Company he tried to sell land to French settlers in the Ohio Valley. When it collapsed, leaving him and Ruth stranded in Paris, he took to political journalism and pamphleteering. Barlow was able and ambitious, always resourceful despite or because of his changing fortunes, and boundlessly brash, an early version of the Yankee self-promoter. Even before *The Vision of Columbus* had been published in the United States, he had written Richard Price asking that elderly philosopher to find him an English publisher and had even forwarded an assignment of the copyright to Price:

As the King of France has condescended to patronize the work, I beg leave to suggest to you whether there would be an impropriety in causing a copy of it to be presented to the Emperor of Germany and another to the Emperor of Russia, as I have attempted to do honor to both their names in the course of the Poem. . . .[17]

Price presumably approved of the sentiments of *The Vision of Columbus*, whatever he may have thought of the author's idea of promoting it through the absolute monarchs of Europe. In any case, the poem appeared in London, and Barlow was already well-known there when he arrived in the summer of 1791 bearing a letter of introduction to Price from Thomas Jefferson. When he and Ruth settled there, they knew not only Price and Tom Paine, but Johnson, Godwin, and a host of others, including Mary Wollstonecraft.

Mary never really liked Joel; she grew to distrust his easy promises and to detest the commercial ventures with which he later supplemented his literary and political career. But her dislike does not seem to have materially affected her affection for his wife, and this is surprising, for Mary did not make friends easily with women. (When she did, she was highly critical, and her letters contain innumerable carping or patronizing remarks about them.) There was never a successor to her beloved Fanny, but Ruth Barlow came closer to being an intimate friend than any other woman.

Ruth was the daughter of a Connecticut blacksmith, but such a man had a very different social position from the one he would have occupied in an English village. While Ruth would not have received more than the rudimentary education afforded colonial girls, she was able by her intelligence and conversation to attract the intellectually eager Barlow and win his lifelong devotion. She was different from the women Mary had known or knew in London, more independent and self-reliant—qualities that would be attractive to a woman who had made her way as Mary had done. Her relationship with Joel was unique in Mary's experience. She was his companion; she went out with him, she knew his friends, she shared his business and political concerns, and she was informed about public affairs. Joel respected her, and his fidelity was unquestioned. More surprisingly still, he loved her.

When Ruth shared with Mary his expression of his love in his letters, Mary found the experience as distasteful as she had the Gabells' display of conjugal affection.

Mrs. B. has a very benevolent, affectionate heart [Mary wrote Everina] and a tolerable understanding, a little warped by romance . . . delighted with her husband's letters, she has exultingly shewn them to me; and, though I take care not to let her see it, I am almost disgusted with the *tender* passages which afforded her so much satisfaction. . . .[18]

Yet while Mary could write her sister in a manner so suggestive of sour grapes, she knew better. Whatever Joel Barlow's ups and downs, his endlessly peripatetic career, his continually broken promises that he would return the following week or month or that they would both shortly be going home, it was clear to Mary that a bond existed between the Barlows which was lacking in most of the marriages she had witnessed. Its origin, she gradually realized, sprang from the mutual recognition that the wife, as well as the husband, was a person of dignity and worth.

It was a new experience for Mary to encounter and become close friends with a woman whose potential qualities had not been largely atrophied or deformed. She could see in Ruth Barlow a sketch of what a woman could and should be (although Ruth lacked some of the independence and ability that Mary herself had been compelled, by force of circumstance, to develop). The friendship nourished Mary's need for companionship and affection, at the same time that it fed the book slowly taking shape in her mind.

In the *Memoirs,* Godwin wrote that "as far down as the year 1787 [Mary] regularly frequented public worship, for the most part according to the forms of the Church of England. After that period her attendance became less constant, and in no long time was wholly discontinued." But for an accurate appraisal of Mary's beliefs, we must go beyond Godwin. Our best source is Mary herself. The picture we can assemble from letters and her own writings makes it clear that her religion had always been a very individual one. Whatever religious education she had received had been Anglican, but there had not been much of it. Even if she had been well schooled, there would have been a patchwork aspect to these teachings, for Anglican doctrine after several hundred years' assault from Protestants of many colors—Socinianists, Arians, Arminians, deists, and theists—was considerably diminished from the creed spelled out in Cranmer's prayerbook. The general level of spirituality was low; baptism, marriage, and burial were not so much religious observances as part of the accepted social order.

Matters could hardly be otherwise with a clergy which was absentee more often than not. Innumerable clergymen held a plurality of benefices or livings (Henry Gabell had no less than four while he was also headmaster of Winchester).

Mary Wollstonecraft had little use or respect for the institutional church—she attacked it bitterly in *A Vindication of the Rights of Men.* Nor is there any evidence that she was ever influenced by "the methodies" or that she encountered the influence of the Evangelical reform, which had only just begun to ferment within the Anglican Church.

She might have found a harbor with the Dissenters, but that way was barred by her sweeping rejection of any kind of punishment after death. The reason is not far to seek: She found life so painful that the idea of anything worse in the hereafter was unthinkable. God was loving and merciful, and that love would extend itself to all his children no matter what their wrongdoing.

Of other Christian dogmas there is little sign in her thinking, although she knew the Bible and quoted liberally from both Old and New Testaments. "The account of the atonement that has been made, gives a rational ground for resting in hope until the toil of virtue is over," she wrote in her first book.[19] Otherwise, she does not dwell on the redemptive role of Christ, which is central to both the Anglican and Dissenting confessions, or on doctrines such as the Incarnation and the Trinity. Actually Mary's beliefs were on the verge of what we today would call Unitarianism, and this much she must have described to Godwin, who wrote that:

> . . . her religion was, in reality, little allied to any system of forms, . . . and was founded rather on taste, than in the niceties of polemical discussion. Her mind constitutionally attached itself to the sublime and the amiable. She found an inexpressible delight in the beauties of nature, and in the splendid reveries of the imagination. But nature itself, she thought, would be no better than a vast blank, if the mind of the observer did not supply it with an animating soul. When she walked amidst

the wonders of nature, she was accustomed to converse with her God. To her mind he was pictured as no less amiable, generous and kind, than great, wise and exalted.[20]

But no deist or theist felt a personal relationship with God. While Mary shows their influence in her frequent use of such terms as "Great Spirit" and "Supreme Being" and in her insistence on the importance of reason, she also believed in the loving providence of a Father in whose divine plan suffering made sense. She reverenced God, loved and trusted Him, and she believed that "the main purpose of our lives is to learn to be virtuous," because only such lives could make us fit for a happier hereafter. This faith alone made the present bearable.

Because Mary was first and foremost a teacher, she saw life as a school, "training us up for immortal bliss." Suffering was not so much reparation as the rod without whose use the child will be spoiled:

> Good must ultimately arise from everything, to those who look beyond this infancy of their being. . . . It is true, tribulation produces anguish, and we would fain avoid the bitter cup, though convinced its effects would be salutary. The Almighty is then the kind parent, who chastens and educates, and indulges not when it would tend to our hurt. He is compassion itself, and never wounds but to heal, when the ends of correction are answered.[21]

But as her own mind grew, this view of the educational process as primarily one of submission became too restricted and too passive. Room must be made in the divine plan for the intellect whose development so greatly concerned her, particularly where women were concerned. As early as 1787, she wrote a letter to Henry Gabell which showed the importance she assigned to the mind in religious faith:

> Why have we implanted in us an irresistible desire to think— if thinking is not in some measure necessary to make us wise unto salvation. Indeed, intellectual and moral improvement seem to me so connected—I cannot, even in thought, separate them. Employing the understanding purifies the heart, gives dignity to the affections, by allowing the mind to analyze them—

and they who can assign a reason for loving their fellow-creatures
—will endeavor to serve the Great Spirit *rationally*—they will
see the *beauty* of holiness, and be drawn by cords of love. How
can the mind govern the body if it is not exercised? . . . It is
true our reasonings are often fallacious—and our knowledge
mostly conjectural—yet these flights into an obscure region open
the faculties of the soul. St. Paul says "we see through a glass
darkly"—but he does not assert that we are *blind*.[22]

Here again are seeds of a great deal of *A Vindication of the
Rights of Woman*. For if "thinking is . . . necessary to make us
wise unto salvation," it is just as crucial for women to learn how
to use their minds as it is for men. Here Mary asserts what she was
to say repeatedly, that mind and faith go together and enlighten
each other. Like John Locke and Richard Price, she believed that
reason, no less than faith, comes from God and that they do not
conflict. Reason is not necessarily the agent of destruction for
religious belief, as many philosophers of the Enlightenment believed—and hoped. It is, in Mary Wollstonecraft's beautiful
phrase, "the heaven-lighted lamp in man."[23] The term "man" here
is generic; she did not visualize the gift of reason as being limited
to one sex. The *Vindication of the Rights of Woman* would be an
eloquent plea to recognize the presence of reason in women, as
well as men, and to tend it, because it was a divine gift.

CHAPTER X

A Vindication of the Rights of Woman (1792)

In october, 1791, having settled into her new quarters in Store Street, Mary wrote her friend Roscoe that she was launched on a new project:

> Be it known to you, my dear Sir, that I am actually sitting for the picture and that it will shortly be *forthcoming*. I do not imagine that it will be a very striking likeness, but if you do not find me in it, I will send you a more faithful likeness—a book that I am now writing in which *I* myself, for I cannot yet attain to Woman's dignity, shall certainly appear, hand and heart—but this between ourselves—pray respect a woman's secret![1]

The portrait (in the Tate Gallery in London) shows her with the cap and powdered hair then still in fashion, but due shortly to disappear. The face is that of Mary Wollstonecraft struggling with the work that was to be her enduring memorial.

Although Godwin declared that *A Vindication of the Rights of Woman* took her only six weeks to write, Mary worked at it for more than three months, and she had thought about it much longer.[2] When she finished it on January 3, 1792, she wrote Roscoe on the same day:

> I [have] been very much engrossed by writing and printing my *Vindication of the Rights of Woman*. . . . I shall give the last sheet to the printer today; and, I am dissatisfied with myself for not having done justice to the subject—Do not suspect me of false modesty—I mean to say, that had I allowed myself more time I could have written a better book, in every sense of the word, the length of the Errata vexes me. . . .

The fault, she implied, was Johnson's, who kept his "printer's devil" waiting on her doorstep while she wrote the final pages of the manuscript. Quite likely she herself had lagged because of the distraction of her usual family cares; whatever the reason, the *Vindication*, like most of her work, is a headlong production.

Some of the strands that went into it have been traced in the preceding chapter, but there remains the question of what led her to write the book at this particular time. The answer lies in the developments in France. Having curbed the royal power and abolished feudalism, the French Constituent Assembly proceeded next to abolish the church-directed and clerically staffed educational system, intending to replace it with one more suited to a democratic society. On September 10, 1791, it heard a report by Talleyrand, former Bishop of Autun, calling for free education but making no reference to the education of women.[3] Mary's first knowledge of his speech must have come from newspaper accounts, but she also read it later in pamphlet form and was shocked to find that the French Revolution, despite its goal of a new society in which all *men* would be free and equal, would not materially affect the position of women. With the intention of influencing developments in France, as well as stirring up controversy in England, Mary wrote her own prescription for women and dedicated the work to Talleyrand.

Few of her contemporaries shared her concern, and even those were probably unknown to her: Olympe de Gouges, the melodramatic actress and writer whose pamphlet *The Rights of Women* had appeared in September, 1791, and who died on the guillotine, not for her feminist sentiments, but because she offered to defend Louis XVI when he was tried for treason; the philosopher Condorcet, who had outlined his ideas for the education of women in "Letters to a Citizen of New-Haven." There is no reference in the *Vindication* to either of these or to those in the preceding 200 years, both in France and in England, who had argued on behalf of women's right to and need for better education: the French dramatist Marivaux; the obscure seventeenth-century cleric Poulain de la Barre, whose ideas were amazingly modern; and the English writers or women like Mary Astell and "Sophia" (mentioned earlier). We are forced to conclude, from the authorities she did cite in the *Vindication*, that most of these were unknown to Mary Wollstonecraft.[4]

A Vindication of the Rights of Woman is therefore not the outgrowth of previous social or philosophical thought, except insofar as it arose within the wide movement for social change in Western Europe and the United States. Broadening that movement to include a concern for women was Mary's unique contribution, and she made it, not so much because of what she had read or the thinkers she had listened to and argued with, but from her own personal experience and her reflections on those experiences. To distill as she did from her life (and the lives of other women she knew) the basic principles she put into the *Vindication* was an extraordinary imaginative feat, of a kind that does not take place very often.

It is worth noting in a class-conscious age such as ours that to read the *Vindication* and search for such a viewpoint will not be rewarding. Mary Wollstonecraft was not at this time interested in the economic exploitation of women (later she would begin to recognize it). She declared in the *Vindication* that women from the lower levels of society, provided they have some kind of livelihood, are better off than those who are affluent.

She *is* concerned with middle-class women and the ladies of the "gentry" because she believed that these classes set the tone and pattern for society as a whole. She is intent on removing the stigma attaching to woman—any and all women—as creatures of instinct and feeling, devoid of intellectual powers or the capacity for intellectual growth. Every page of the *Vindication* is charged with the excitement of this idea and with anger at the mutilation of mind and spirit—and body as well—inflicted on women by a society which reduces them primarily to the role of sexual beings —"the toy of man, his rattle, and it must jingle in his ears whenever, dismissing reason, he chooses to be amused."[5]

It seemed to Mary that at every point in her life she had seen women demeaned or belittled, either by men or by themselves. Her own experiences and those of her sisters added up to a drudging, ignoble livelihood at best. So did the endless and woefully unprofitable toil of the women in the Blood family and the final degradation of Caroline Blood in the parish workhouse as the sole alternative to prostitution. There was the bondage of Mary's own mother, tied to a man who had robbed her and her children of the inheritance that could have provided them with comfort and some degree of education.

By contrast, affluence was responsible for women like Mrs. Dawson or Lady Kingsborough—petty-minded tyrants who lived in a puppet world of fashion, artifice, and chicanery. There were exceptions, to be sure—Mary could hardly have forgotten Mrs. Clare or Mrs. Burgh, whose heads and lives were neither empty nor trivial. But such women were not rich, and they were mere accidents whose lives might also have been fuller, happier, more significant if they had not been lonely exceptions to the generality of mediocrity and waste.

The problems of economic insecurity and deprivation, on the one hand, and of empty triviality and low moral standards, on the other, were rooted in the same condition. Women suffered from a lack of education because their nature was assumed to be different from that of men: "man was made to reason, woman to feel." Men wanted women to be pleasing, and that was exactly what they got—women incapable of anything else, including either the rearing and education of their own children or the ability to support themselves. Instead, women had to be able to think, to reason, to bear responsibility. A woman in comfortable circumstances should have the capacity to manage her affairs in the event of her husband's death. During his lifetime, she should be his intellectual equal, a mature and educated being; otherwise, she was not his companion but his mistress. Furthermore, she had a role in society beyond her home—that of citizen. Without the proper attributes of a responsible reasoning being she exercised a corrupting influence on society, just as slavery corrupted the slaveholder, his wife and children.

Too many women of means lived an existence preoccupied with dress, lap dogs, gambling, and "red coats," each of them an affront to their creator, who had conceived not only man but woman in His own image and whose destiny for both was eventual unity with Him. Let society recognize a new role for such women, and the effects would soon spread to other strata, a belief in which the course of social history has profoundly justified her.

A few passages will establish the main lines of Mary's thinking:

> The grand source of female folly and vice has ever appeared to arise from narrowness of mind. . . . Pleasure is the business of woman's life, according to the present modifications of society; and while it continues to be so, little can be expected of such weak beings.
>
> It is time to effect a revolution in female manners—time to restore to them their lost dignity—and make them, as part of the human species, labour by reforming themselves, to reform the world.
>
> I throw down my gauntlet, and deny the existence of sexual virtues, not excepting modesty. For man and woman, truth, if I understand the meaning of the word, must be the same. . . . Women, I allow, have different duties to fulfil; but they are human duties, and the principles that should regulate them, I sturdily maintain, must be the same. To become respectable, the exercise of their understanding is necessary, there is no other foundation for independence of character; I mean explicitly to say that they must bow only to the authority of reason, instead of being the *modest* slaves of opinion.
>
> If woman be allowed to have an immortal soul, she must have, as the employment of a life, an understanding to improve . . . and when she is incited by present gratification to forget her grand destination, nature is counteracted, or she was born only to procreate and rot.
>
> Yet if love be the supreme good, let woman be only educated to inspire it, and let every charm be polished to intoxicate the

senses; but if they be moral beings, let them have a chance to become intelligent; and let love to man be only a part of that glowing flame of universal love, which, after encircling humanity, mounts in grateful incense to God.[6]

Mary posed a question to society that had not been asked before. What kind of people were women? Her answer was not pleasant. Women—most women—were trivial-minded, selfish, mean, petty, cunning, and, of all things, in a society that demanded from them virtue and modesty, they were immodest and immoral. The fault lay not primarily with themselves, but with the emphasis society placed on reputation, on show, and on virtue as applying only to one thing. A woman might gamble or neglect her children, but if she were not guilty of losing her honor ("as it is absurdly called"), she could neglect every other obligation with impunity.

"Women" says some author, I cannot recollect who, "mind not what Heaven sees." Why, indeed, should they? It is the eye of man they have been taught to dread—and if they can lull their Argus to sleep, they seldom think of Heaven, or themselves, because their reputation is safe; and it is reputation, not chastity and all its fair train, that they are employed to keep free from spot, not as a virtue, but to preserve their station in the world.[7]

Mary took to heart Pope's description of women—"every woman is at heart a rake." She asked why—and answered that until "women are led to exercise their understandings, they should not be satirized for their attachment to rakes; or even for being rakes at heart, when it appears to be the inevitable consequence of their education. They who live to please—must find their enjoyments, their happiness in pleasure." Character is shaped by employment and by one's thoughts; since women's thoughts revolved around their appearance, was it surprising that they regarded looks as more valuable than character or intelligence? Inevitably they also concluded that they could be effective only by exercising their charm—or exploiting their weakness: "From the tyranny of man, I firmly believe, the greater part of female follies proceed; and the cunning, which I allow makes at present a part of their character, . . . is produced by oppression."[8]

Such women made bad mothers, not just because their minds were not centered on their responsibilities, but because they had never been trained to control themselves, let alone their children.

> To be a good mother, a woman must have sense, and that independence of mind which few women possess who are taught to depend entirely on their husbands. Meek wives are, in general, foolish mothers. Unless the understanding of woman be enlarged, and her character rendered more firm, by being allowed to govern her own conduct, she will never have sufficient sense or command of temper to govern her children properly.[9]

Without the ability to think straight, with no intellectual discipline or fund of knowledge, women were also incapable of educating their children. As a result, they neglected them, or turned them over to the care of others, or spoiled them. The daughters would grow up in the mother's image, and the sons in that of the father (Mary had little more respect for most men than for her own sex).

Such women had a slim chance to maintain themselves (or their children) in decency and comfort, if the need arose. Whether they were single or widows left without adequate subsistence by a husband's unforeseen death, they were not prepared to manage for themselves. Not only were they unskilled and denied by society any but the few occupations which Mary had sampled, but they were totally unequipped to carry responsibility or make decisions. They were timid, vulnerable, and helpless.

Moreover, she pointed to the women who, having been fortunate enough to receive an education (usually from an educated father), nevertheless lacked any opportunity to lead useful and happy lives:

> How many women thus waste life away the prey of discontent, who might have practiced as physicians, regulated a farm, managed a shop, and stood erect, supported by their own industry, instead of hanging their heads surcharged with the dew of sensibility. . . . How much more respectable is the woman who earns her own bread by fulfilling her duty than the most accomplished beauty!

She suggested wider spheres for them:

> They might also study politics, and settle their benevolence
> on the broadest basis. . . . Business of various kinds, they might
> likewise pursue . . . the few employments open to women, so far
> from being liberal, are menial. . . .[10]

Women suffered other handicaps. The law denied them adequate protection if they were single; if married, they had no legal identity apart from their husbands, into whose persons they were incorporated by the doctrine of coverture. They lacked any representation in lawmaking bodies because they lacked the franchise; Mary's famous plea for women suffrage is limited to one sentence, but it is explicit. Women must become rational and useful citizens of their country, their love of country founded on knowledge, "because it is obvious that we are little interested about what we do not understand . . . private duties are never properly fulfilled unless the understanding enlarges the heart . . . and public virtue is only an aggregation of private." Not only physical and moral but civil freedom is needed before their characters can improve or society at large can benefit from that improvement. (This perspective Mary promised to explore further in another volume, which she never wrote.)[11]

When woman was not actually oppressed by being deprived of a livelihood or legal rights, she was corrupted by treatment as a privileged class, her existence a kind of gilded slavery. It was not only the woman who suffered from this state of affairs, or her children. Men, all men, were degraded, because irresponsible power is degrading. All class distinctions were therefore at fault—absolutism of any kind, even property rights in excess—and must be reformed. Correct such errors in the social fabric, and there would be no obstacle to the flowering of humanity; Mary Wollstonecraft is in the great tradition of her time in seeking the betterment of the whole human race. The reformers of the eighteenth century had not yet tasted the inherent limitations of reform; perfectibility was for them still a viable goal.

But Mary was not writing a tract on human perfectibility—that would be the work of William Godwin, who was even then working on his *Enquiry Concerning the Principles of Political Justice*. With respect to the needs of women and how these might be remedied, there was, in the main, only one remedy. Economic independence, sound parenthood, the virtues of modesty and purity were to be acquired by exercising and developing the faculties, through education:

> . . . not only the virtue but the *knowledge* of the two sexes should be the same in nature, if not in degree, and . . . women, considered not only as moral but as rational creatures, ought to endeavor to acquire human virtues (or perfections) by the *same* means as men, instead of being educated like a fanciful kind of *half* being—one of Rousseau's wild chimeras.[12]

Most of Mary's ideas about education were radical for her day. Because her primary concern was the education of girls, we tend to overlook the fact that she also advocated drastic changes in the education of boys, argued for a national system of education (since private efforts would always be inadequate), for coeducation, and the mixing of all classes, at least in the elementary schools. She opposed boarding schools for pupils of any age because she believed that they tended to foster laxity and vice (her visits to Eton and Warminster had left a deep impression on her). Moreover, living at home encouraged the mutual affection of parents and children, something Mary valued the more for having missed it. Forgetting the rapidly increasing population of the cities, she drew an idyllic picture of the country day school; here the children of all classes might learn, "by the jostlings of equality," to form a sound opinion of themselves and their surroundings.

Concrete proposals, however, occupy a relatively small space in her argument. She recommended that the government establish day schools for different age groups open to both girls and boys. The primary level (ages five to nine) would be a free school (an idea she took from Talleyrand) in which rich and poor would dress alike; there must be an open tract of land nearby for plentiful outdoor exercise.

The curriculum proposed for this age group is breathtaking even today: botany, mechanics, astronomy, reading, writing, arithmetic, natural history, and "some simple experiments in natural philosophy"—for children from five to nine. Presumably a good deal of this would be on the level of "the bees and the birds" while the astronomy would consist of stargazing. Perhaps, in suggesting that "the elements of religion, history, the history of man, and politics, might also be taught by conversations in the Socratic form," Mary was hoping to progress beyond the level of lisping baby talk, which she had abhorred at the Kingsboroughs', and was testifying to her belief that children could be taught more, at an earlier age than had hitherto been thought possible, a radical concept we are only now beginning to realize.

Her commitment to democratic education does not go beyond the age of nine. At that time:

> . . . girls and boys intended for domestic employment, or mechanical trades, ought to be removed to other schools, and receive instruction in some measure appropriate to the destination of each individual, the two sexes being still together in the morning; but in the afternoon the girls should attend a school, where plain work, mantua-making, millinery, etc., would be their employment.[13]

Mary Wollstonecraft has been favorably compared to Hannah More, the contemporary writer who was not only dourly anti-feminist, but wholeheartedly committed to a social outlook we would deplore. The poor should be kept in their place and taught little besides habits of piety and industry. "My plan for instructing the poor is very limited and strict. They learn of week days such coarse work as may fit them for servants. I allow of no writing," Miss More declared. "My object has not been to teach dogmas and opinions but to form the lower classes to habits of industry and virtue."[14]

While the curriculum Mary proposed for the primary schools is much more enlightened, she too drew the line against equal opportunity at a very early age. (This is merely to admit that while in some respects Mary was far ahead of her time, in others she was very much a part of it.) There is hope only for those who, whatever their circumstances, have shown unusual promise:

The young people of superior abilities, or fortune, might now be taught, in another school, the dead and living languages, the elements of science, and continue the study of history and politics, on a more extensive scale, which would not exclude polite literature. Girls and boys together?—I hear some readers say. Yes.

Mary could not repeat too often that the general moral improvement and happiness of all mankind depended on a formation of character grounded for both sexes in rational understanding. The only alternative was the prevailing double standard of morality and a relationship between men and women lacking not only refinement, but true companionship and moral responsibility:

> To render mankind more virtuous, and happier of course, both sexes must act from the same principle; but how can that be expected when only one is allowed to see the reasonableness of it? To render also the social compact truly equitable, and in order to spread those enlightened principles, which alone can ameliorate the fate of man, women must be allowed to found their virtue on knowledge, which is scarcely possible unless they have been educated by the same pursuits as men.

There are times when Mary was inconsistent, as when she applauded virtue in the poor, who had obviously not had the opportunity of developing their minds:

> With respect to virtue, to use the word in a comprehensive sense, I have seen most of it in low life. Many poor women maintain their children by the sweat of their brow, and keep together families that the vices of the fathers would have scattered abroad . . . the good sense I have met with, among the poor women who have had few advantages of education, and yet have acted heroically, strongly confirms me in the opinion that trifling employments have rendered woman a trifler.

It is also clear that she had still not made up her mind what was a woman's role. To be a "patient drudge, who fulfils her task like a blind horse in a mill," was not enough:

> It is plain from the history of all nations, that women cannot be confined to merely domestic pursuits, for they will not fulfil family duties, unless their minds take a wider range, and whilst they are kept in ignorance, they become in the same pro-

portion the slaves of pleasure as they are the slaves of man. Nor can they be shut out of great enterprises, though the narrowness of their minds often make them mar, what they are unable to comprehend.[15]

Nevertheless, she repeatedly insisted that a woman's family, specifically her maternal responsibilities, came first. "Whatever tends to incapacitate the maternal character, takes woman out of her sphere." It was not, she wrote, her intention to suggest that they be taken out of their families, "speaking of the majority"; she did, however, reserve a different option for a limited group: "Though I consider that women in the common walks of life are called to fulfil the duties of wives and mothers, by religion and reason, I cannot help lamenting that women of a superior cast have not a road open by which they can pursue more extensive plans of usefulness and independence. . . ."

Yet only a few pages earlier she had drawn a portrait (reminiscent of Mrs. Trueman in *Original Stories from Real Life*) of a very different woman:

I have then viewed with pleasure a woman nursing her children, and discharging the duties of her station with perhaps merely a servant-maid to take off her hands the servile part of the household business. I have seen her prepare herself and her children, with only the luxury of cleanliness, to receive her husband, who, returning weary home in the evening, found smiling babes and a clean hearth. . . . I have thought that a couple of this description, equally necessary and independent of each other, because each fulfilled the respective duties of their station, possessed all that life could give. Raised sufficiently above abject poverty not to be obliged to weigh the consequences of every farthing they spend, and having sufficient to prevent their attending to a frigid system of economy which narrows both heart and mind, I declare, so vulgar are my conceptions, that I know not what is wanted to render this the happiest as well as the most respectable situation in the world, but a taste for literature, to throw a little variety and interest into social converse, and some superfluous money to give to the poor and to buy books.[16]

We do not know in Mary's acquaintance a family which could be the prototype of this one, unless she reached back into her childhood to the Arden family. Was her ideal, then, this domestic woman who cultivated her mind so as to be her husband's companion and her children's tutor? Twice in her life Mary reached out for marital happiness and children, but each time she struggled to combine it with a continuing program of study and writing. In both cases this was required by economic necessity. Would it have been her choice otherwise? To this question her brief life has given us no certain answer.

We come now to an aspect of Mary Wollstonecraft's thinking which sets her apart from many radical reformers of her own time and from others who followed her, including most of the feminists: her stubborn insistence in *A Vindication of the Rights of Woman* that reason—the quality which sets human beings apart from the animals—is a gift from God. For Mary this is an axiom requiring no proof, but itself serving as proof that humanity has an immortal destiny. To deny woman the power of reason is to deny her what Christian faith has promised her. Reason cannot, therefore, be the property of one sex alone, and by its very nature it cannot be different in one sex from the other.

Even if her functions differ in some respects from those of man, woman, like him, is capable of and destined for godliness:

> The power of generalizing ideas, of drawing comprehensive conclusions from individual observations, is the only acquirement for an immortal being, that really deserves the name of knowledge. Merely to observe, without endeavoring to account for anything, may (in a very incomplete manner) serve as the common sense of life; but where is the store laid up that is to clothe the soul when it leaves the body? This power has not only been denied to women; but writers have insisted that it is inconsistent, with a few exceptions, with their sexual character. Let men prove this, and I shall grant that woman only exists for man.

Reason is a sign of an immortal quality in us, the evidence of our immortal nature present in a nascent state:

The stamen of immortality, if I may be allowed the phrase, is the perfectibility of human reason. . . . Every individual is in this respect a world in itself. More or less may be conspicuous in one being than in another; but the nature of reason must be the same in all, if it be an emanation of divinity, the tie that connects the creature with the Creator; for, can that soul be stamped with the heavenly image, that is not perfected by the exercise of its own reason?[17]

It is not only men who have been at fault and who are responsible for the degradation of women in both past and present society. Women themselves have been acquiescent and submissive, and Mary tries to rouse them from their lethargy by invoking their pride. A year earlier in her reply to Burke, she pointed out the rightful source of that pride in recognizing God's supremacy as creator:

I reverence the rights of men.—Sacred rights! for which I acquire a more profound respect, the more I look into my own mind . . . my heart is human, beats quick with human sympathies—and I FEAR God! I bend with awful reverence when I enquire on what my fear is built.—I fear that sublime power, whose motive for creating me must have been wise and good; and I submit to the moral laws which my reason deduces from this view of my dependence on him. . . . This fear of God makes me reverence myself.—Yes, Sir, the regard I have for honest fame, and the friendship of the virtuous, falls far short of the respect that I have for myself. . . .[18]

If woman, no less than man, is endowed by God with His own nature, if she is created for a transcendent destiny as the Christian Gospel proclaims, then she cannot be confined to the role bestowed on her by society and best described by Milton: "He for God only, she for God in him." In the last analysis, Mary rested her argument, not on appeals to justice, or logic—sheer reason itself—but on the basic principles of Christian faith:

Gracious Creator of the whole human race! Hast Thou created such a being as woman, who can trace Thy wisdom in Thy works, and feel that Thou alone art by Thy nature exalted far above her, for no better purpose? Can she believe that she

Mary Wollstonecraft, a portrait by John Opie
The Tate Gallery, London

Beverley minster

Westwood, Beverley

The publisher Joseph Johnson by Moses Haughton

Illustrations by William Blake for *Original Stories from Real Life*. At top, *"Indeed we are very happy."* Center: *"Economy and self-denial are necessary in every station to enable us to be generous."* Bottom: *"The Dog strove to attract his attention."*

Self-portrait by Henry Fuseli

Self-portrait of Henry Fuseli
dated May 23, 1792

Victoria and Albert Museum.
Crown copyright

"The Nightmare" by Henry Fuseli
Detroit Institute of Fine Arts

William Godwin, a portrait by John Opie

Mary Wollstonecraft Shelley, a portrait by R. Rothwell

The British Museum

Another portrait of Mary Wollstonecraft by John Opie

National Portrait Gallery, London

was only made to submit to man, her equal—a being who, like her, was sent into the world to acquire virtue? Can she consent to be occupied merely to please him—merely to adorn the earth—when her soul is capable of rising to Thee? And can she rest supinely dependent on man for reason, when she ought to mount with him the arduous steeps of knowledge?[19]

However, there is little metaphysical speculation, even of a religious nature, in the *Vindication*, and what there is of it is essentially positive, optimistic, free of Calvinist preoccupation with man's innate sinfulness and the election of a minority to divine grace, and of the Jansenist disenchantment with our corrupted state. Human beings *can* be regenerated—here Mary stands four-square with the ameliorists who believe that history moves in the direction of progress. But she differs from the majority of them in her insistence that it is God who has put the power of regeneration in our hands, if only we will exert ourselves to that end. It is He who has put the unique stamp of His own dignity and worth upon us all, man and woman alike.

Although Mary's ideas were usually essentially her own, we can find here and there the influence of others. A clear source of this last concept is *The Dignity of Human Nature* by James Burgh, the Newington schoolmaster and philosopher whom Mary never met but whose widow so staunchly befriended her. His book does not deal directly with women except for a brief section on the education of girls, but there are passages which would have confirmed Mary in her own thinking if they did not actually spark it:

> To exhibit a comprehensive idea of the true dignity of human nature [wrote Burgh in his Introduction], it will be necessary to consider what is fit for a human being who at present inhabits a perishing body, itself an immortal spirit. . . . To answer the Divine intention in furnishing him with rational faculties, it is evidently proper that he labour to improve those faculties with knowledge. . . .

Burgh recommended a broader education than that commonly afforded to girls, although it fell far short of Mary's recommendations in the *Vindication*. His immediate purpose was a more

limited one—he wished to improve women's conversational powers so that they might make more suitable companions for their
husbands—but his ultimate goal foreshadowed her own vision:

> What an advantage must it be for future states, to have begun
> the work here, that is to be carried on to eternity. . . . No doubt
> it is necessary in the nature of things that our minds in their
> present infant state (as this may very properly be called) be
> formed and disciplined, by custom and habit, to that temper
> and character, which is hereafter to be their glory, their per-
> fection and their happiness.[20]

In a more general sense than Burgh, Mary was influenced by
John Locke's philosophy of education and the moral philosophy
of Richard Price. But Mary's principal debt was to Catherine
Macaulay, whose *Letters on Education* had appeared in 1790.
Mrs. Macaulay also blamed women's weaknesses on the prevalent
social mores. She too believed that men and women were equal
before God and should therefore be equal in their earthly life:

> I have given similar rules for male and female education on
> the following grounds of reasoning. First, there is but one rule
> of right for all rational beings, consequently true virtue in one
> must be equally so in the other. . . . Lastly, that as on our first
> entrance into another world, our state of happiness may possibly
> depend on the degree of perfection we have attained in this, we
> cannot justly lessen, in one sex or the other the means by which
> perfection . . . is acquired.[21]

In reviewing the Macaulay book in the *Analytical*, Mary had
praised it and its author, whom she described as having superior
gifts and a wide fund of knowledge. Catharine Macaulay died
the following year, a fact Mary mentioned with regret in the
Vindication, saying that many of Mrs. Macaulay's opinions coincided with her own; yet the statement hardly constitutes adequate recognition of a work which antedated her own and passages of which are remarkably similar to some in the *Vindication*.

It is the only book, and its author the only writer, Mary cited
with respect. She gave the works of Madame de Genlis and Mrs.
Chapone a passing nod. The remainder, whether they dealt with
education or manners—Lord Chesterfield, Madame de Staël,

Mrs. Piozzi, and such currently popular works as Dr. Fordyce's *Sermons for Young Women* and Dr. Gregory's *A Father's Legacy to His Daughters*—she denounced as responsible in varying degrees for shaping women into the creatures Mary found such pitiful travesties of what human beings might be. She reserved the greatest portion of her denunciations for Rousseau's *Émile,* which incidentally is the only book of those she condemned still read by anyone but students of the period.

Jean Jacques Rousseau's was one of the great seminal minds of the eighteenth century. To the degree that his ideas helped undermine absolutism and orthodoxy whether in religion, education, or government, Mary Wollstonecraft recognized and admired them. But his thinking was not consistent, and when he exalted feeling and sentiment over rationality, she differed with him; his ideas about women outraged her. She devoted an entire section of fifteen pages in Chapter V of the *Vindication* to rebutting the theories he expounded in *Émile* on the nature of women and how they should be educated. She attacked his insistence on their innate weakness and the need for their submitting to men in all things. She regarded his advocacy of guile and coquetry as degrading.

Modesty, according to Rousseau, was a device with which to arouse and attract men. A woman should disguise her charms so cleverly that a man "would conclude that every part of her dress, simple as it seems, was only put in its proper order to be taken to pieces by the imagination." "Is this modesty?" asked Mary. "Is this a preparation for immortality?"

Although in so many respects Rousseau was in revolt against society, he shared its fundamental assumption about women: They had no minds and no capacity to develop them. They had, in fact, no role as human beings, apart from their relationship—a subservient one—to men:

> For this reason the education of women should always be relative to men. To please, to be useful to us, to make us love and esteem them, to educate us when young, and take care of us when grown up, to advise us, to console us, to render our lives easy and agreeable—these are the duties of women at all times, and what they should be taught in their infancy.[22]

Mary's own lack of a rounded education is obvious throughout her book. It is doubtful whether she actually read some of the authorities she referred to, such as Swedenborg (whose thinking she probably knew largely through Blake), Monboddo, Adam Smith, Bacon, and Leibnitz. She might have dipped into their works or read reviews in the literary journals, including the *Analytical* or heard them discussed at Johnson's, but she could not have crammed such studies into her four brief years in London before she wrote the *Vindication*, years already crowded with desperate scrabbling for a livelihood.

Her lack of education is also shown in her inability to organize material, to follow a consistent train of thought, or to avoid digressions when they are largely irrelevant and in her habit of loose generalization. She is incapable either of the coherent organization of ideas or of avoiding repetition. She makes the same points in the Introduction, the dedication, and almost all the thirteen chapters. And she never really substantiates her basic assumption, that all women, or even most women, are as she describes them: trivial, deceiving, pleasure-loving, and weak in character, morals, brain, and body. Even the exceptions she admits to this general rule—such intellectuals as the Bluestockings and other "notable" women—allow no place for some of the women she had known, such as Mrs. Clare, Mrs. Burgh, Jane Arden, and Fanny Blood.

The literary journals divided along predictably partisan lines in reviewing the *Vindication*, the general public usually likewise, but the book's weaknesses were responsible, at least in part, for some reactions. Many women shrank from its exaggerations; others refused to admit its truthfulness. Still others were antagonized for reasons having nothing to do with the book itself. One of the latter was Hannah More, whose reaction has been cited as a significant instance of how Mary's more intelligent women contemporaries felt about her strictures:

> I have been much pestered to read the *Rights of Woman* [she wrote to Horace Walpole] but am invincibly resolved not to do it. Of all jargon, I hate metaphysical jargon; beside, there is something fantastic and absurd in the very title. How many ways there are of being ridiculous! I am sure I have as much

liberty as I can make use of, now I am an old maid; and when I was a young one, I had, I dare say, more than was good for me. . . . To be unstable and capricious, I really think, is but too characteristic of our sex; and there is, perhaps, no animal so much indebted to subordination for its good behaviour as woman.[23]

Hannah More's prejudices were rooted partly in her innate conservatism and her more fortunate circumstances: She had been educated by a devoted father, and for many years she and her three sisters ran a successful school. But she was also a friend and warm admirer of Edmund Burke, who had represented her home city of Bristol in the House of Commons, and she would have been outraged at Mary's attack on Burke the previous year.

There were satirical "replies" to the *Vindication*, such as *A Sketch of the Rights of Boys and Girls*, by an author cloaked by the pseudonym of "Launcelot Light," and *A Vindication of the Rights of Brutes*, which may have been written by the neo-Platonist philosopher Thomas Taylor. But although Hannah More turned her back on Mary's book, another bluestocking, Anna Seward, was more appreciative, calling it "wonderful," even if she tempered her praise with criticism: "It has, by turns, pleased and displeased, startled and half-convinced me that its author is oftener right than wrong."[24]

The *Vindication* sold widely, and before the end of the year Johnson published a second edition; there were others in the United States and translations in France and Germany. While it did not continue to sell that well to succeeding generations of readers, we know that Mary Wollstonecraft wrote a classic whose seminal influence on the social history of women has no equal. It was read by all the woman leaders of stature throughout the nineteenth century and into our own and was often the decisive force in crystallizing their determination to struggle for education, and social and political freedom for their sex; in our own country Margaret Fuller, Lucretia Mott and Elizabeth Cady Stanton acknowledged their debt to Mary's book.

For whatever the defects of the *Vindication*—its turgidity, its repetitions, its exaggerations—basically Mary Wollstonecraft was right. If social consciousness was to move ahead, if human beings were to develop concern for their fellow creatures, then concern and progress could not be limited to men. (Today we are discovering belatedly that such concern cannot be limited by the color of people's skins.) Dignity, intelligence, moral responsibility know no sex; since Mary's book, this concept has become, however gradually, part of the democratic tradition and has spread in our time from the Western world into Africa and Asia.

CHAPTER XI

Revolution and Renewal (1793–94)

A Vindication of the Rights of Men had first established Mary Wollstonecraft as a writer of ability and prestige; her *Vindication of the Rights of Woman* brought fame. The book was a sensation, thrilling or scandalous, according to the reader's viewpoint. One sympathized or rejected it—or, like Horace Walpole, refused to read it at all, having taken its measure from the reviews or from other readers.

It made some money for Mary. Even more important, although it did not solve all her financial problems, it opened a way to future stability by guaranteeing her a reading public for anything that she wrote. She had promised the readers of the *Vindication* a sequel devoted to further problems of women, but she was not limited to this subject. Controversial writings, especially anything bearing on the rapidly developing situation in France, were selling almost as fast as they could be printed. Having challenged first an opponent of the stature of Edmund Burke and then all conventions with respect to women, Mary could now turn her lively mind to almost any topic. She might even have looked forward, as a possible future goal, to assuming more responsibility for editing the *Analytical Review*.

Instead, she did none of these things. Why not? Why, having achieved more than she could have imagined when she was still trapped in poverty and frustration six years earlier, did she not go on to further achievement and greater heights? Why was she not optimistic, creative, and happy?

On the surface her life appeared busy and full of interest. According to her brother Charles, she was making every effort to enhance her physical appearance and had grown "quite handsome." She saw a good deal of the Barlows and continued to see, and be seen with, Fuseli. On one occasion she attended a masked ball in the company of Fuseli and his wife, Sophia, and the Swiss writer Lavater (whose work on physiognomy Mary partially translated, although it was never published).

She entertained the French statesman Talleyrand, to whom she had dedicated her book on women, when he came to England on a diplomatic mission in the spring of 1792. The French government was urging a Franco-British alliance for a joint attack on Spanish colonies in the Americas. Talleyrand's mission was a failure, but it is interesting to note the presence in London at this time of several men, who were to figure in a later plan to transfer the Spanish colonies to France, with the help of the United States, which would have a bearing on Mary's life; they included Joel Barlow, and his shadowy aide Mark Leavenworth—both known to Mary—and possibly an American ex-soldier named Gilbert Imlay. Mary might therefore have met Imlay in the course of 1792 although we have so far no direct evidence to that effect.

Predictably, Mary's new contacts and her improving situation did not make for closer or warmer relations with her sisters. She thought them "tolerably well settled" (a notion far from the truth) and wrote them less frequently; at one time Eliza complained to Everina that she had not heard from Mary for three months and on another occasion declared that "I never think of our sister but in the light of one who has died." Mary's letters could be even more embittering than her failure to write, as when she wrote Everina of a marriage offer which she had rejected:

Be it known to you that my book, etc., etc. has afforded me an opportunity of settling *very* advantageously in the matrimonial line with a new acquaintance; but entre nous—a handsome house and a proper man did not tempt me; yet I may well appear before you with the feather stuck in my cap. . . .[1]

This was hardly the most tactful vein in which to write a letter to one lonely sister, still a governess in Ireland, who would inevitably pass along its contents to an even more lonely and embittered sister, suffering as a governess in an isolated Welsh castle. In her dealings with Everina and Eliza, Mary always showed a high degree of concern, but very little perception that their situation still closely resembled her own before she had extricated herself from the Kingsboroughs and begun to make her own way under Joseph Johnson's protective tutelage. Imaginativeness in her relations with others was not one of Mary's gifts.

It was also lacking in her relationship with her adopted daughter. Little Ann was no longer a source of satisfaction. She stole sugar out of the closet ("constantly"), and although she impressed visitors as "a fine girl," Mary was discovering other limitations, as she wrote Everina in the same letter:

She will never be the kind of child I should love with all my heart. She has great *animal* spirits, and quick feelings, but I shall be much mistaken if she have any considerable portion of sensibility when she grows up.

No one in those days knew the connection between the lack of affection and the need for lesser but instant satisfaction such as that furnished by sweets, but Mary might have remembered that she too had needed love before dismissing a child as incapable of much "sensibility."

She also continued to concern herself with her brothers. James was an occasional visitor and needed further outfitting. His promotion had not materialized, but at least he was at sea. The real "blister" was and remained Charles, more like their father than any of the other Wollstonecrafts: charming, unstable, and lazy. Mary attempted vainly to get him an appointment with the East India Company. Then she wrote to William Roscoe of her difficulties, and he offered, with his customary helpfulness, to employ

Charles. Mary refused; she did not think Charles was adequately qualified. Perhaps she was afraid that Charles would not justify Roscoe's confidence and determined not to let him take advantage of Roscoe's friendship with her or jeopardize it by committing some act of folly.[2]

For a while she pinned her hopes for Charles on Joel Barlow, who had shown considerable interest in him. It was Barlow's idea that he and Ruth take Charles with them when they returned to the United States, where Charles could take up farming. Mary bought her brother a suitable wardrobe and sent him to a farm in Leatherhead, some twenty miles south of London, where he could get some practical experience. She wrote hopefully to Everina:

> [I] think Charles' prospect a promising one indeed. I shrewdly suspect that Mr. B. has some thoughts of keeping him in his own family; but he waits till he sees more of him before he avows his intention. The other day he clapped C. in his dry way on the knee and said—"as his wife and he could never contrive to make any boys they must try what they could do with one ready brought up to their hands."

But Charles wore out his clothes in Leatherhead to no avail. Barlow procrastinated and continued to pursue other more attractive schemes. Her brother was not dependent on her at the moment. But Mary was afraid that the vagaries of his character would upset the delicate balance of his affairs, and "in continual fear of having him thrown on me for his full support."[3]

She wrote in this vein to her old friend George Blood, but it is the last letter that we know she sent him. She was becoming more and more involved with new interests and new intimates and moving away from the associations of earlier and very different years. On June 10, Joel wrote his wife from Paris that he had reserved accommodations for "Madame Wollstonecraft and co—." (Mary had given herself the title of "Mrs." in the fashion of the day for a single woman who had achieved a certain eminence.) The expedition was to include Johnson and the Fuselis. They were to leave London sometime during the first part of August and stay in Paris six weeks; Mary promised she would find a position for Eliza where she could improve her French, similar to the one Everina had held earlier.

Her promises did not impress Eliza, who wrote sardonically to her younger sister:

> So the author of The Rights of Women [*sic*] is going to France, I dare say her chief motive is to promote her poor Bess's comfort. Or thine my girl or at least I *think* she will thus reason. Well in spite of Reason I think when she reaches the Continent she will be but a woman. I cannot help painting her at the height of all her wishes, at the very summit of happiness for will not ambition fill every chink of her Great Soul (for such I really think hers) that is not occupied by Love! And after having drawn this sketch you can hardly suppose me so sanguine as to expect my pretty face will be thought of when matters of state are in agitation . . . you actually have the vanity to imagine that in the National Assembly personages like M and F will bestow a thought on two females whom nature meant "to suckle fools and chronicle small beer?"[4]

Mary herself looked forward to the trip with high hopes. She would be visiting France as a woman of prestige, in stimulating company, and as they would be traveling together and staying at the same lodgings, she would see Fuseli daily; he would show her the art treasures of Paris. Sophia Fuseli's presence offered no problem, since Mary still believed that her own feelings were simply those of friendship. They would share a carefree holiday and view the making of history in France at firsthand.

Matters turned out otherwise; the party got under way but went no farther than Dover. We do not know precisely why they turned back, but there were several possible reasons. Barlow had already written his wife that "you will hear frightful stories about the riot at the Tuileries on the 20th [of June]—you must believe but little," and the party of travelers had therefore adhered to their plans, despite alarmist stories in the London newspapers, and left the city early in August. But on the night of August 10, before they crossed the Channel, an insurrection broke out in Paris, the Tuileries was again attacked, and this time 600 of the king's Swiss guards were slaughtered; it was the virtual end of the French monarchy.

News of the event may have reached Dover by courier while Mary's party waited to make the Channel crossing and could have been a decisive factor in their change of plans. But in addition, the travelers were an ill-assorted group. The perceptive Johnson must have realized that Mary's absorption in Fuseli, her dependence on his companionship, and her possessiveness were building up to an impossible situation. Riding together in the confined quarters of a traveling coach must have dramatized this fact for all concerned, including Mrs. Fuseli, perhaps at long last Mary herself.

After the party returned to London, Mary was absent from the city for a while; perhaps she made an effort to come to terms with herself. If so, she failed. The abortive expedition roused the gossips, some of whom theorized that Mary and Johnson were getting married.[5]

Johnson, however, knew the real source of Mary's problem and that Mary was doing almost no writing. "Her exertions were palsied, you know the cause," he wrote to Godwin in providing Mary's husband with the outline of the principal events of her life in London up to 1793. Both men did indeed know the cause. Early biographers like Mrs. Pennell and W. C. Durant denied Mary's infatuation with Fuseli because this revealing sentence in Johnson's memorandum was deliberately suppressed by Kegan Paul.[6]

The evidence of Mary's slackness is twofold: a sharp falling off of reviews that can in any way be identified as hers in the *Analytical* and failure to produce the promised sequel to *A Vindication of the Rights of Woman* or anything else, despite her continuing need for money.[7] After so many years of uninterrupted hard work, Mary might understandably have needed a breathing spell. But the evidence points rather to the fact that her feelings about Henry Fuseli had finally become unmanageable.

In her first book Mary Wollstonecraft had dealt in no uncertain terms with precisely those emotions which she could now no longer control:

Nothing can more destroy peace of mind than platonic attachments. They are begun in false refinement, and frequently end in sorrow. . . . If a woman's heart is disengaged, she should not give way to a pleasing delusion, and imagine she will be satisfied with the friendship of the man she admires and prefers to the rest of the world. The heart is very treacherous, and if we do not guard its first emotions, we shall not afterward be able to prevent its sighing for impossibilities. If there are any insuperable bars to a union in the common way, try to dismiss any dangerous tenderness, or it will undermine your comfort, and betray you into errors.[8]

This passage could serve as an accurate description of her plight seven years later.

Mary had even become completely absorbed in Fuseli's work to the exclusion of her own. She fancied herself a vital source of inspiration and support to the painter, who was staking everything on an ambitious new venture. Having won acclaim for his work in John Boydell's *Shakespeare Gallery*, a volume of reproductions from oils by leading painters to which Fuseli had contributed weird and vivid scenes illustrating *Macbeth*, *King Lear*, *Richard III*, and *A Midsummer Night's Dream*, he had now embarked on an ambitious solo venture—a series of canvases illustrating Milton's *Paradise Lost*.

Mary reported his progress—and problems—to Roscoe, incidentally revealing her own:

> Our friend Fuseli is going on with more than the usual spirit, like Milton he seems quite at home in hell. . . . I rather doubt whether he will produce an Eve to please me in any of the situations he has selected, unless it will be after the fall. . . .

Six weeks later she wrote with less coyness, and very real concern:

> Schemes for printing works *embellished* with prints have lately been started with *catch-penny* eagerness, and such an inundation, to borrow a fashional [*sic*] cant word, has damped my hopes with respect to our friend's. I love the man and admire the artist, and I'm sorry to find that subscriptions come in very slowly, this I mention to you in confidence and make light of it for him, for on this work the comfort of his life, in every sense of the word, seems to depend. . . . The first number will probably have considerable effect toward filling the subscription:

but till then I am sorry Mr. F. has not more encouragement for I should be vext to see his fancy brooding over disappointments.[9]

But it was no longer enough to offer Fuseli consolation and encouragement or to see him so often (by this time he may also have begun to discourage her frequent visits). She wrote him letters, which Fuseli sometimes carried around in his pockets for days, unread. Eventually, still convinced that she sought only an unexceptionable platonic relationship, Mary called on Sophia Fuseli and asked to join their family circle and live under the same roof with Sophia and her husband; she could no longer exist without "the satisfaction of seeing him and conversing with him daily."

Mrs. Fuseli apparently made no attempt to reason with Mary; she simply asked her to leave. When Mary appealed to Fuseli, he remonstrated with her. Her answer, if we are to believe Fuseli's biographer (and there is no other source), was: "If I thought my passion criminal I would conquer it, or die in the attempt. For immodesty, in my eyes, is ugliness; my soul turns with disgust from pleasure tricked out in charms which shun the light of heaven." Whether or not these were Mary's exact words, whether she said them to Fuseli or wrote them in a letter, essentially they ring true. She saw nothing wrong with what she described to William Roscoe as "a rational desire."

Mary was both mistaken and unconventional, but she was also intensely human. We do not need to go far even in literary history to find other such cases. But Fuseli never gave the slightest indication that he had any interest in jeopardizing his domestic situation. In November, 1792, faced with this fact and with her own continuing unhappiness, Mary made her decision: She would leave London and go abroad to Paris.

The qualities that Mary had inherited from her strangely dissimilar parents—her mother's stamina and instinct for survival, her father's uncalculating adventurousness—all dictated the decision, but her pride must have made it a difficult one. No one in the group around Johnson would be ignorant of the real reason for her departure. To Roscoe she wrote with a jauntiness that could hardly deceive him:

... I intend no longer to struggle with a rational desire, so have determined to set out for Paris in the course of a fortnight or three weeks, and I shall not now halt at Dover; for as I go alone, neck or nothing is the word. ... At Paris, indeed, I might take a husband for the time being, and get divorced when my truant heart longed again to nestle with its old friends; this speculation has not yet entered my plan.[10]

To her sisters, she justified her departure by the promise, once again, not to return from France before she had found a position for Eliza. The latter received these assurances with her usual sardonic skepticism but nevertheless promptly pinned all her hopes on Mary's promise.

Before leaving, Mary prepared for sweeping changes in her way of living. She parted with the adopted child, Ann. We do not know how she accomplished this, for there is one letter reproaching Everina (in Ireland) for not sending her news of the little girl and another, somewhat later from Paris, to Ruth Barlow in London, hoping that she had not failed "to employ little Ann."[11] The child may have been shunted between relatives in the Skeys family and the warmhearted, childless Ruth before finding a home. Mary never referred to Ann in her letters again. (It is strange that the woman who cared so lovingly for her own younger brothers and sisters, who was to become a devoted mother herself, and who had written with such emphasis about the rights of children to nurture and care could be so casual about a child she had taken into her home, just as she had been casual, if not arbitrary, about Mary Bishop, the offspring of the tragic Bishop marriage.)

She was able to unload another burden in somewhat happier fashion, providing Charles with passage for America. He sailed early in November from Liverpool, speeded on his way by the ever-friendly Roscoe. Now twenty-two years old, Charles would perform, not surprisingly, in a manner very reminiscent of his father, just as Mary had always feared. Letters to Eliza describing highly speculative ventures which would enable him to care for his sisters if they joined him alternated with long periods of silence, which augured poorly for the realization of his ambitions.

Even Eliza, frantically eager to get away from her lonely post in Wales, took little stock in his wild promises.

On the verge of leaving for revolutionary Paris, Mary worried far more about those she was leaving behind her than about the hazards of her journey. Indeed she worried a great deal, chiefly about her father, and the health of her friend Johnson, who seemed increasingly frail. She had always been apprehensive, but now there was another reason for fearfulness. A deep-seated change had taken place in her religious beliefs. Mary's loss of faith has been usually dated several years earlier, despite the frequent recurrence of the religious theme throughout the *Vindication*. Instead, her loss of faith appears to have taken place at the time of her break with Fuseli, and her disillusionment then seems to have been very nearly total, although occasional references do occur in her later writings.[12]

(It is worth noting, however, that Mary never attacked religion either in her published works or in her letters. She voiced no skeptical views, and she never regretted or denied anything that she had previously written or professed. In a letter to Johnson from Paris, she denied that she had become an atheist.[12])

But the evidence that she had become, if not an atheist, then at least agnostic is inescapable; so are its causes. She had found the burden placed on her by the God she loved and trusted—which is how she had always interpreted her trials up to the impasse with Fuseli—too heavy to bear, the outcome of her hopes and "rational desire" too unjust to accept. Like her earthly parents, her heavenly father had failed and rejected her. Henceforth she could count only on human beings and mostly on herself.

From the rationalist point of view this was, of course, an emancipation and should have freed Mary for new and even greater achievements. There was no obstacle now to her taking a place among the other leading figures of an era to which she had already made a unique contribution. Yet Mary made no such further contribution in the remaining five years of her life. They were taken up instead largely by personal tragedy far greater than that of her frustrated love for Fuseli. The circumstances of these years suggest that Mary had suffered loss rather than gain from her change of beliefs, a loss for which she was unable to compensate.

Moreover, Fuseli's rejection taught her nothing, brought her no new insights or emotional maturity, which continued to elude her even as she recovered her initiative and launched herself gallantly on a new path. Instead, she continued to search for an ideal human relationship which would give her the support and understanding she needed, because she had never experienced them. Mary went to Paris in December, 1792, still lacking in the wisdom needed to make any adult emotional relationship viable and enduring.

In her last letter to Roscoe before she left, Mary had exhorted him not to join those who were becoming disenchanted with the Revolution because of the violent outbreaks in France:

> . . . let me beg you not to mix with the shallow herd who throw an odium on immutable principles because some of the mere instrument [*sic*] of the revolution were too sharp—children of any growth will do mischief when they meddle with edged tools . . . but if the nations be educated by their governments it is vain to expect much reason till the system of education become more reasonable.[13]

Now she was to exchange the reading of newspaper reports or listening to travelers' accounts for actual experience. France was already at war with the absolute monarchies of Prussia and Austria, a war it had invited, and feeling was mounting that the mere existence of the king encouraged conspiracy and kept open the threat of attempted restoration. When Mary reached Paris late in December, the city was quiet, but tense, and preparing for Louis' trial.

On the day after Christmas, he rode in a coach past Mary's lodgings to the opening session. The streets were empty, and only the National Guard surrounded his carriage; there was no sound except for an occasional drum roll. Mary's overheated imagination caught fire:

> I have been alone ever since [she wrote Joseph Johnson that evening]; and though my mind is calm, I cannot dismiss the

lively images that have filled my imagination all the day. Nay, do not smile, but pity me; for once or twice, lifting my eyes from the paper, I have seen eyes glare through a glass door opposite my chair, and bloody hands shook at me. My apartments are remote from those of the servants, the only persons who sleep with me in an immense hotel, one folding-door opening after another. I wish I had even kept the cat with me! I want to see something alive, death, in so many frightful shapes, has taken hold of my fancy. I am going to bed, and for the first time in my life, I cannot put out the candle.[14]

The "immense hotel" where Mary was staying was at 22 Rue Meslée (now Meslay). The house, a substantial building as Mary described it, is still standing, only a few blocks from the grim prison of the Temple, the ancient stronghold of the Knights Templar which then housed the imprisoned royal family. The mansion was the home of Aline Fillietaz, the married daughter of the Madame Bregantz at whose school in Putney both Eliza and Everina had taught. The family was away from home when she wrote Johnson.

Mary was fortunate in having no acute financial worries. During her first half year in France we know that she drew on Johnson at least three times, for sums of 30, 20, and 23 pounds and some silver; there may have been other occasions as well.[15] Not all these drafts were against Mary's earnings from her books. Everina sent Johnson 20 pounds to cover part of one draft, and apparently Eliza also contributed.

Mary also had friends in the city—the Christies, Tom Paine, and Joel Barlow. She carried letters of introduction to "several agreeable families," one of them to Helen Maria Williams, a young English writer of lively reputation who was in Paris with her mother and sister and who took Mary into her social circle.

Mary Wollstonecraft was, by the time she came to Paris, a woman of reputation and prestige. *A Vindication of the Rights of Woman* had already been translated and published in France; in addition, she was known and respected for her defense of the Revolution against Edmund Burke. Already, in February, she wrote to Ruth Barlow that she was "almost overwhelmed with civility." As the political situation worsened and the position of aliens became critical, Mary stayed in Paris, not because she was trapped by circumstances, but by choice.

Nevertheless, she found the language a real difficulty, experiencing a period when she was "unable to utter a word, and was stunned by the flying sounds." It was exhausting to try, on top of mastering the language, "to form a just opinion of political affairs." She complained in her letters of her old lassitude and general poor health. Yet when war broke out between France and England on February 1 and Mary had the offer of a place in a gentleman's coach to return to England, she declined it, explaining that she was at last "turning the corner" and was at work "writing a plan of education for the Committee appointed to consider the subject."[16]

We can only guess how Mary became involved in such a project. Tom Paine was a friend of Condorcet, the liberal French philosopher who was a leading political figure. Both men were on the committee which drafted the new constitution, and Condorcet was also a member of the important Committee on Public Instruction. Condorcet himself was on record in favor of full educational and political rights for women (in his *Lettres à un Bourgeois de New-Haven* and his essay *Sur l'Admission des Femmes au Droit de Cité*). But in his long address to the Legislative Assembly in April, 1792, he had made no provision for the education of girls beyond the primary grades, postponing the matter to a later report, and had discussed the importance of educating them only in a memorandum submitted along with his report to the Assembly.

It seems likely that Mary undertook to work on a plan for French education in order to press for the inclusion of women at every level and also for coeducation, as she had discussed it in the *Vindication*. Unfortunately we do not know whether Mary completed her plan and presented it to the committee.[17]

At almost the same time, she was writing "A Letter on the Present Character of the French Nation." Apparently it was to be the first of a series recording her impressions of the people and events taking place in France. Unfortunately she recorded no events, and her impressions of the people are largely moralistic generalizations, committing in fact the very offense against which she had warned Roscoe, of following the "shallow herd" in judging the Revolution prematurely and without due consideration of all the factors involved. The French, she concluded after only a few weeks in their country, were the most superficial and sensual people "in the world"; the aristocracy of birth was being "levelled to the ground only to make room for that of riches." While acknowledging that the evils of "the old system" went far to explain the present bloodshed and violence, she saw little hope in "the principle of commerce which seems everywhere to be shoving aside the *point of honour* of the *noblesse*." The "Letter" ended on a note that was far from sanguine:

> You may think it too soon to form an opinion of the future government, yet it is impossible to avoid hazarding some conjectures, when everything whispers that names, not principles, are changed, and when I see that the turn of the tide has left the dregs of the old system to corrupt the new. For the same pride of office, the same desire of power, are still visible; with this aggravation, that, fearing to return to obscurity after having but just acquired a relish for distinction, each hero, or philosopher, for all are dubbed with these new titles, endeavours to make hay while the sun shines; and every petty municipal officer, become the idol, or rather the tyrant of the day, stalks like a cock on a dunghil [*sic*].[18]

Mary met a widely assorted group of people in Paris, but there seems to be no basis for Godwin's assertion that "she was personally acquainted with the majority of the leaders of the French Revolution." She probably knew at least one leading member of the Convention, Brissot de Warville, and some of his friends and colleagues, but was better acquainted among the Swiss and German émigrés whose republican sympathies had brought them to Paris. Among these, her most devoted admirer was Count Gustav von Schlabrendorf, a widely traveled, cultivated Silesian who had moved in the best Continental society and rejected it for the company of revolutionary sympathizers in Paris. His portrait of Mary, written in later life, is one of the most vivid we have of her: "A woman of sweetness and grace, with a face whose spiritual expression was more beautiful than any classic beauty. . . . There was magic in her look, her voice, her gestures. . . . One of the noblest, most modest and feminine human beings I ever knew!" However, Von Schlabrendorf was highly susceptible and in love with various women during his long life, although he never married. In 1793 he was engaged to marry a Jane Christie, probably Thomas Christie's sister. There are letters from Miss Christie to Von Schlabrendorf while he was in prison during the Terror which reveal she was willing, even anxious, to wait for his release and marry him. But Von Schlabrendorf lost interest in his Scottish fiancée and later in life realized that he had fallen in love with Mary Wollstonecraft and would have married her if she had accepted him.[19]

But although she liked Von Schlabrendorf and even visited him in prison during the Terror (which no one did lightly), she fell in love with a very different kind of man. In April, 1793, Joel Barlow wrote to his wife (still in London):

> Between you and me—you must not hint it to her or to J——n or to anyone else—I believe [Mary] has got a sweetheart, and that she will finish by going with him to A—a a wife. He is of Kentucky and a very sensible man.

Two weeks later he wrote again to "Ruthie": Mary's "sweetheart affair goes well. Don't say a word of it to any creature."[20]

Why such emphasis on secrecy? Barlow was never happier than when he was being mysterious, but he may also have been warned by Mary herself, who knew that if word of her attachment reached England, it would throw her family, especially Eliza, into a panic (as it eventually did). Or perhaps it had something to do with the ambitious project in which Mary's "sweetheart" was involved.

The "very sensible man . . . of Kentucky" was neither sensible nor from Kentucky. Today we know a great deal more about Gilbert Imlay than Mary ever did. He posed as a frontiersman, a useful role in Europe at that time, which permitted him to claim authority for two books which he published in London: *A Topographical Description of the Western Territory of North America* in 1792 and a novel, *The Emigrants*, the following year. It was as a frontiersman with a wide knowledge and long experience of the "Western Territory" that he maneuvered himself into an important position in the French scheme to attack the Spanish colonies of the Mississippi Valley and win them back for France, a project which would rely largely on the efforts of American Western settlers disaffected with the struggling young federal government in the East.

The plot was of vast proportions and has been discussed in detail elsewhere.[21] In American history books it appears as the episode involving "Citizen Genêt," the French envoy who did his unsuccessful best to embroil the United States in a war with the European colonial powers. Imlay was at the Paris end of the chain of events which Genêt tried to precipitate. The plan is of interest here only for the light it throws on the man with whom Mary Wollstonecraft fell in love.

For the Americans involved—in Paris Imlay, Barlow, and his shadowy aide, Mark Leavenworth, in the United States men of such standing as General James Wilkinson and General George Rogers Clark—it was a treasonable conspiracy. American policy at the time, for reasons of self-preservation, was to maintain peace and noninvolvement with neighboring colonial powers. The scheme aimed to reverse this policy by armed activity of the frontiersmen under French leadership (partially financed by France) which would drag the United States into war with Spain.

A memorandum Imlay presented to the Committee of Public Safety is explicit on this point and incidentally replete with loose generalizations based on his alleged familiarity with the territory in question. He estimated that the population of the Mississippi Valley was then 400,000, of whom 40,000 were capable of bearing arms; that on the lower Mississippi between New Orleans and Natchez the population numbered 50,000, all French or Americans with an armed Spanish force of only 1,500, many of whom were of French descent. He declared that "selfishness, that unhappy principle which too often influences the political policies of the United States, would undoubtedly lead it to promptly suppress any project undermining Spanish power, for fear of precipitating war with Spain, a policy which was rooted in the interests of the eastern seaboard and which was dishonorable, as well as cowardly," and he assured the committee that the investment of 750,000 pounds would assure success. Furthermore, if the committee balked at such expense, he, Imlay, was certain that there were men "in the west" who would finance the expedition at their own risk and expense, provided they could count on assistance from the French government and its colonials.

The leading French advocate of the plan was Brissot de Warville, a member of both the Committees of Public Defense and Foreign Affairs. Pierre Lebrun, Minister of Foreign Affairs, seems to have opposed the scheme or at least delayed its execution; on April 22, Brissot wrote an urgent note to Lebrun, to be presented by Imlay, complaining that "nothing had been done to ready the Mississippi expedition" which had to leave within fifteen days: "Please take decisive action. Money must not be a consideration at this point. Lose no time!"[22]

Time was indeed a crucial factor in the struggle for the leadership being played out between Brissot and the other Girondist deputies and the supporters of Robespierre, who would shortly triumph.

The important point where Mary Wollstonecraft is concerned is that according to Brissot's memorandum of April 22 to Lebrun, her newfound "sweetheart" was prepared to leave within two weeks on a secret military expedition to America which would involve him in wilderness fighting for some time. But in Barlow's letter of April 19 to his wife he had voiced the opinion that Mary might be going to America soon as Imlay's wife. How much did Mary know about the Louisiana scheme? The dream of settling in the United States with Imlay, which recurs in her letters to him (and to her sisters), was either a hope he had held out to her or one which she had manufactured and which had received some credence from him. Certainly it bore no relation to his real activities at this time. Far from having told her the truth, he seems to have completely deceived her.

Gilbert Imlay was an adventurer. Certainly he was no product of the American frontier. He was born in Monmouth County, New Jersey, and his home was probably in Imlaystown, the village which still bears the family name.[23] His family was in comfortable circumstances by the standards of the time; different members held considerable property, married into other prosperous families, and conducted businesses. At least two Imlays, an uncle and a grandfather of Gilbert's, were judges. Gilbert himself must have received an adequate education according to existing standards; he was able to be a surveyor, to write books, and to mix acceptably with cultivated society in France and England.

Imlay did serve in the American forces during the Revolutionary War, but only briefly; he was wounded, but in view of his later activities in the Western territories it is doubtful if he left the service because of disabilities. Though the records show his rank as lieutenant, in Europe he passed as "Captain" Imlay.

Daniel Boone's explorations had opened Kentucky to settlers, and land fever ran high. Imlay began buying land in 1783, and he continued to make such purchases on a speculative basis until 1786. In 1784 he was appointed a surveyor in Fayette County. He gave his bond for 1,000 pounds to Boone himself and then resold land to other speculators. As his holdings pyramided and involved him in more ambitious financial dealings, he became associated with General James Wilkinson, who later figured at the Kentucky end of the Mississippi Valley conspiracy.

Legal actions followed Imlay's land deal manipulations and continued to multiply, the charges varying from trespass to default on debts. Despite mounting court summonses, he continued to expand his activities; his last scheme was for the development of an ironworks. But even while he was taking out letters patent on new holdings, his creditors were taking further legal steps to obtain satisfaction on bonds he had given them. When the pace became too hot, Imlay left Kentucky and, at an unknown date, the United States. He was a fugitive from the Kentucky courts from 1786 to 1799, when the cases pending against him were finally closed in default of any possible recovery.

Nothing is yet known of Imlay's whereabouts or activities from 1786 to 1792. Since his *Topography of the Western Territory* was published in London in that year, it is quite likely that he was there at the time. Certainly toward the end of that year he was in Paris. Both the *Topography* and the later novel, *The Emigrants*, whatever their many shortcomings, contained liberal sentiments on such issues as slavery and divorce, which would have commended their author to Mary Wollstonecraft's attention.

He and Mary met at the Christies'; by August they were lovers. The relationship had been hastened by history. On June 2 Robespierre's leading opponents were arrested. A few escaped, but Brissot went to prison, along with others whom Mary knew. English citizens were suspect as citizens of a country at war with France, and those known to have close and active Girondist connections would be doubly in jeopardy. Mary could not risk endangering the Fillietaz family. She left Paris for the village of Neuilly, then still remote from the capital, and rented a small cottage.

There for a few weeks Mary lived an idyll unlike any other period in her life. The place belonged to an old man who kept a garden and delighted in giving Mary its produce, even grapes; in addition, he kept the place tidy for her. She had nothing to do but work on a new book, an account of the Revolution, and dream—and wait. There Imlay came to visit her, and there, if not before, their love became a complete commitment.

Soon there came further change. As a result of the capture of the Mediterranean port of Toulon by the British fleet, the French government ordered all British subjects imprisoned and their property confiscated. The Christies were back in London, but eventually Tom Paine, Helen Maria Williams, and Von Schlabrendorf all went to prison. For the first time Mary was now in direct danger. The English papers carried stories of her arrest. She was undoubtedly spared because Gilbert Imlay registered her at the American embassy in Paris as his wife and therefore an American citizen. It was the obvious, simple way for him to safeguard a woman with whom he was, for the time being, on intimate terms. Since neither of them considered marriage, except as a legal fiction to guarantee Mary's safety and freedom, Imlay had nothing to fear in the way of commitment and responsibility.

He had been attracted in the first place by Mary's fame and charm. Now he found her enchanting. With that mercurial rebound which characterized her recovery from despair, without responsibilities and with no one to find fault with her actions, Mary's emotions had flowered. The glowing woman who met him at the *barrière* (one of the customs gates which had replaced the gates of the old city walls of Paris) evoked both tenderness and protectiveness in a man temperamentally suited to casual encounters. The portrait Godwin drew of her at this time must owe its origin to someone who knew her:

> . . . her whole character seemed to change with a change of fortune. Her sorrows, the depression of her spirits, were forgotten, and she assumed all the simplicity of and the vivacity of a youthful mind. She was like a serpent upon a rock, that casts its slough, and appears again with the brilliancy, the sleekness, and the elastic activity of its happiest age. She was playful, full of confidence, kindness and sympathy. Her eyes assumed new lustre, and her cheeks new colour and smoothness. Her voice became cheerful, her temper overflowing with universal kindness; and that smile of bewitching tenderness from day to day illuminated her countenance, which all who knew her will so well recollect, and which won, both heart and soul, the affection of almost every one that beheld it.[24]

For Mary the experience of loving and being loved blotted out every other consideration—her family, her anguish over Fuseli, even immediate preoccupations with politics or the future. She believed she had found what she had been looking for: a relationship onto which she could throw her full weight, a love in which she could feel secure. For a few weeks the passionate joy of that discovery blinded her to any apprehension or doubt. If she had not needed love and security so deeply, her love for Imlay might have been less total and unquestioning. If she had not abandoned herself so completely to her love for him, she might have suffered less when the idyll began, in not too long a time, to fray.

CHAPTER XII

Disillusionment (1794-95)

MARY WOLLSTONECRAFT'S LOVE AFFAIR with Gilbert Imlay ran the first year of its course against the somber background of the French Revolution during its most violent period, from June, 1793, to July, 1794. In July, 1793, the guillotining of Marat's assassin, Charlotte Corday, began the stream of executions which climaxed in the Reign of Terror. Civil war had already broken out, and the government's repressive measures became ferocious. It was impossible to shut out the reverberations of these events even in Mary's Neuilly retreat. Once, visiting Paris during the day, she crossed the square where the dreaded guillotine stood and, looking down, saw the paving stones covered with fresh blood. Her indignation broke out, and she was saved from reprisals only because "a prudent bystander warned her of the danger, and intreated her to hasten and hide her discontents."

Since Imlay visited her only occasionally in Neuilly and since the extraordinary tensions of the time heightened Mary's chronic need for reassurance and support, she began to feel the need for other human relationships. She tried to keep in touch with

Ruth Barlow; one note to Ruth is an unusually human sidelight into the lives of two women in that stormy time:

> MY DEAR FRIEND:
>   A word or two which dropt from you, when I last saw you, for the circumstances scarcely allowed me to speak to you, have run in my head ever since—Why cannot we meet and breakfast together, *quite alone*, as in days of yore? I will tell you how—will you meet me at the Bath about 8 o'clock either monday or tuesday?—I will come on monday, unless it rain or you should write to forbid it.—We may then breakfast in your favorite place and chat as long as we please before we part to return to our respective homes, for I do not wish to spend a whole day in Paris for a little while to come and when I do I must visit Madame Schweizer.
>
>   Yours affectionately,
>   M. WOLLSTONECRAFT
>
> Remember the pills!
> and do not forget to ask Mrs. Stone what is become of Schla-brendorf. . . .[1]

Because Gilbert Imlay was known to have been connected with Brissot and the Louisiana conspiracy, he had to justify himself to the new regime as a loyal supporter of the Revolution. He was therefore actively promoting another career in Paris, and if Mary wanted to see him more frequently, she would have to return to the city. Since she was now known as his wife, there was no need to continue her relationship with him on an illicit basis. The logical thing for them to do was to set up a home together, and they did.

Mary's deepest longings should now have been satisfied. Yet almost from the outset there was doubt and friction between them. In one of her earliest letters to him, written just before she left Neuilly, there are already hints of a gap between expectation and reality:

> You can scarcely imagine with what pleasure I anticipate the day, when we are to begin almost to live together; and you would smile to hear how many plans of employment I have in my head, now that my heart has found peace in your bosom. Cherish

me with that dignified tenderness, which I have only found in you; and your own dear girl will try to keep under a quickness of feeling, that has sometimes given you pain. But good-night! God bless you! Sterne says that is equal to a kiss—yet I would rather give you the kiss into the bargain, glowing with gratitude to Heaven, and affection for you. I like the word affection, because it signifies something habitual, and we are soon to meet, to try whether we have mind enough to keep our hearts warm. I will be at the barrier a little after ten tomorrow.[2]

Gilbert Imlay was not the man to find anything "habitual" necessarily attractive. It seems clear in retrospect that he did not enter into a domestic relationship with the same perspective as Mary, and his actions indicate that he very soon rejected the shackles of family responsibility.

Together with Joel Barlow and a Swedish merchant, Imlay now launched a commercial enterprise which would provide the French government with such badly needed products as grain, iron, and soap. Elias Backman, an importer and exporter in Gothenburg, provided the capital and the merchandise. Barlow handled sales and orders out of Paris. Imlay took care of shipments in and out of the French channel port of Le Havre. In September he left Paris—and Mary—for his new base of operations.

He promised her that his absence would be brief, a manifest impossibility from the nature of his commitment to the joint venture. Also characteristically, he told Mary little about it, so that she could form no judgment of her own, and as weeks lengthened into months, he reiterated the promise that he would shortly return.

His letters were balm to her disquiet—when they came, which was infrequently. Her own were loving, but impatient and increasingly exigent, hardly calculated to reassure a man of Imlay's temperament. It became apparent to Mary quite soon that their natures were poorly adapted to each other:

I have found out that I have more mind than you, in one respect; because I can, without any violent effort of reason, find food for love in the same object, much longer than you can. The way to my senses is through my heart; but, forgive me! I think there is sometimes a shorter cut to yours. . . . I do not know how I fell into these reflections, except one thought produced it— that these continual separations were necessary to warm your affection. Of late we are always separating. Crack! crack! and away you go! . . .[3]

It was not just his absence that caused her unrest. She admitted that even when they were together, she had felt doubts; "I do not know why, but I have more confidence in your affection, when absent, than when present" (hardly an effective argument for his return). Already she saw him as two-sided, with "a money-getting face" and an "honest countenance" which could be "relaxed by tenderness; a little—little—wounded by my whims! and thy eyes glistening with sympathy."

It was not a promising combination: a heartsore woman of thirty-four who wanted a perpetual lover, always attentive, always concerned, and an adventurer, speculator, and—it should not be forgotten—a fugitive from justice. The insoluble conflict lay in the fact that the eternal lover would soon have bored Mary, yet a man who was active and ambitious wounded her each time he disengaged himself, while he became more and more irritated by her efforts to absorb him completely.

Events in Paris were not calculated to make life any easier for an insecure woman, deeply in love, lonely, and harassed by doubts about the man to whom she had committed herself. On October 17 Marie Antoinette followed her husband to the guillotine. At the end of October came the mass execution of twenty-one deputies, headed by Brissot, whom Mary had known personally. The news of their death caused her "one of the most intolerable sensations she had ever experienced," and she fell on the floor unconscious.[4] Nevertheless, such an extreme reaction as fainting was not in Mary's style and was probably related to an announcement she made to Imlay in November:

Ever since you last saw me inclined to faint, I have felt some gentle twitches, which make me begin to think that I am nourishing a creature which will soon be sensible of my care. This thought has not only produced an overflowing of tenderness to you, but made me very attentive to calm my mind and take exercise lest I destroy an object in whom we are to have a mutual interest, you know. Yesterday—do not smile—finding that I had hurt myself by lifting precipitately a large log of wood, I sat down in an agony, till I felt those said little twitches again.

Are you very busy?

Perhaps if Mary had fallen in love with a statesman or a writer (as she did later), his being "busy" would not have rankled, nor his absences been so shattering. But to Mary business was synonymous with materialism, trickery, and greed. Both Johnson and William Roscoe had been involved in business affairs, but that fact had been blunted for Mary by their intellectual pursuits. Imlay's affairs, however, were abhorrent to her not only because they kept him away from her (or so he made it appear) but from their very nature:

> I hate commerce. . . . You will tell me that exertions are necessary! I am weary of them! . . . anything but commerce, which debases the mind, and roots out affection from the heart . . . shall I talk about alum or soap? There is nothing picturesque about your present pursuits. . . .[5]

The relationship would not have lasted as long as it did, despite Mary's desperate clinging to Imlay, if the attraction had been wholly one-sided. But Imlay's feelings were extraordinarily ambivalent. He made promises and broke them, prevaricated, ran away, and often misled her; but he also reaffirmed his love for her on countless occasions, renewed his commitment, and declared that their lives were inextricably interrelated, and each time he did so, he revived her hopes and her faith in him. By a combination of intelligence, wit, charm, and tenderness, she had managed to do to Imlay exactly what she charged him with having done to her: "twisted yourself more artfully round my heart than I had supposed possible." In his own perverse way, despite every inclination and attribute that led him away from Mary, he loved her. There is no other explanation, not even congenital indecision or a desire to avoid scandal, for the fact that he never told her unequivocally that he was done with her or demanded that she should leave him in peace. There are even indications that Mary occasionally begged him to do so and that Imlay was incapable of it, that her hold over him was as deeply rooted and difficult to overcome as the grip he held on Mary.

Some of Imlay's appeal for Mary can be laid to the strange resemblance between the pattern of his actions and character and that of her father, the father who was easily angered, restless, and dissatisfied with his occupation and place in society, who wanted wealth and position but lacked the capacity to work slowly and steadily for the realization of his ambitions. Mary's letters to Imlay repeatedly argue that he was really a better man than he himself would admit or recognize and that only she believed in that finer self. In her long struggle to mold him into the man she badly needed, the steadfast, supportive protector, as well as lover, Mary Wollstonecraft was still trying to resolve the failures of past relationships, of daughter with father, and wife (her mother) with husband.

Later generations of feminists have hailed Mary's love affair with Imlay as the assertion of a woman's right to live as she saw fit, irrespective of conventional morality or traditional domestic responsibilities. They have ignored the full scope of Mary's thinking—and dilemma—by emphasizing her radical demands for education and broader opportunities for women, while they omitted or drastically deemphasized her longing for family life and happiness. Yet the author of *A Vindication of the Rights of Woman* wrote her lover that "the books sent to me are such as we may read together; so I shall not look into them till you return, when you shall read, whilst I mend my stockings" and was appeased, after one of their earliest quarrels, by Imlay's vision of their future together:

> What a picture you have sketched of our fireside! Yes, my love, my fancy was instantly at work, and I found my head on your shoulder, whilst our eyes were fixed on the little creatures that were clinging about your knees. I did not absolutely determine that there were six—if you have not set your heart on this round number. . . .[6]

Mary's conflict here was not solely her own and cannot be attributed to emotional immaturity. It has repeated itself in the situation of countless women from her day to ours, who have not been any more successful in resolving it than she was. It is *the* dilemma of modern woman, and how it can be resolved is still an open question for many women today.

Soon Mary began urging that she join him. At first he discouraged—or forbade—her coming, but the combination of her pregnancy, growing depression, and the appalling acceleration of daily executions led him to relent. In February she left Paris, writing ahead that she hoped

> . . . to tell you soon (on your lips) how glad I shall be to see you. I have just got my passport, so I do not foresee any impediement [*sic*] to my reaching Havre, to bid you good night next Friday in my new apartment, where I am to meet you and love, in spite of care, to smile me to sleep, for I have not caught much rest since we parted. You have, by your tenderness and worth, twisted yourself more artfully round my heart than I supposed possible. Let me indulge the thought that I have thrown out some tendrils to cling to the elm by which I wish to be supported. This is talking a new language for me! But, knowing that I am not a parasite-plant, I am willing to receive the proofs of affection, that every pulse replies to, when I think of being once more in the same house with you. God bless you!

For the next six months the couple lived at Le Havre in a house that Imlay bought and from which he was only occasionally absent for brief trips to Paris. Thanks to her preoccupation with her own work and the child she was carrying, Mary took these absences with tolerably good grace, even the first, which occurred very shortly after her arrival.

> We are such creatures of habit, my love, that, though I cannot say I was sorry, childishly so, for your going, when I knew you were to stay such a short time, and I had a plan of employment; yet I could not sleep. I turned to your side of the bed, and tried to make the most of the comfort of the pillow, which you used to tell me I was churlish about; but all would not do. . . .
>
> Do not call me stupid for leaving on the table the little bit of paper I was to inclose. This comes of being in love at the fag-end of a letter of business. You know, you say, they will not

chime together. I had got you by the fireside, with the *gigot* smoking on the board, to lard your bare ribs, and behold, I closed my letter without taking the paper up, that was directly under my eyes! What had I got in them to render me so blind? I give you leave to answer the question, if you will not scold. . . .

On May 14, 1794, a baby girl was born, whom Mary named Fanny, for the dead friend who still haunted her memories. She showed considerable independence in her program of aftercare, getting out of bed only one day after labor and taking a walk on the eighth, to the astonishment of her nurse. Fanny was reared with every encouragement for her playfulness, bodily vigor, and awakening faculties, and responded in kind. Even Imlay showed a new side to his nature by his pleasure in both mother and child. "I feel great pleasure in being a mother," Mary wrote to Ruth Barlow (with her customary insensitivity in such matters, for Ruth had been unable to bear children), "and the constant tenderness of my most affectionate companion makes me regard a fresh tie as a blessing. . . . My little girl begins to suck so MANFULLY that her father reckons saucily on her writing the second part of the R——ts of Woman."[7]

If Imlay displayed what was for him an unaccustomed degree of domesticity, Mary had also changed; under the influence of motherhood and of Imlay's continuing presence, her attitude toward his occupation mellowed. Now that he was providing for a family, she could better understand what had previously appeared to her as mere grubbing for wealth. She sympathized with his difficulties and blamed them for a spell of poor health and even a serious illness, which she attributed to the fact that he was "harass[ed] by continual disappointments. . . . Sh[ips] do not return, and the government is perpetually throwing impediments in the way of business. . . ."

Although she was now at a distance from the endless grim procession to the scaffold on the Place Louis Quinze, Mary was aware of what was taking place there and elsewhere in France and of the dangers threatening friends who were not in prison. She wrote to those in Paris only when she could rely on someone connected with Imlay and Barlow's business to carry her letters safely:

Of the state of things here, and the decrees against the English,
I will not speak.—The French carry all before them—but my
God! how many victims fall beneath the sword and the guillo-
tine! My blood runs cold, and I sicken at the thought of a
Revolution which costs so much blood and bitter tears. . . .[8]

Two months before the birth of her child, Mary had completed
the manuscript of the book she had begun while living in Neuilly,
*A Historical and Moral View of the Origins and Progress of the
French Revolution and the Effect It Has Produced.* It was
planned as "a considerable work," but as in the case of *A Vindication of the Rights of Woman,* no further volume was written.
Unlike the *Vindication,* however, this volume cannot stand by
itself. Despite the resounding title, it is the least interesting and
important of Mary's books.

It does speak for both her courage and stamina that she was
able to write it at all. She was faced with great practical difficulties, not the least being the lack of source materials. Then there
was the problem of writing a book highly critical of the course the
Revolution had taken at a time when denunciation as an enemy
of the state would have sent her to prison, if not to the guillotine,
in spite of her status as the wife of an American. "I have sent off
the great part of my Ms.," she wrote to Everina in March, "which
Miss Williams would fain have had me burn, following her example; and to tell you the truth, my life would not have been
worth much had it been found." (In the same letter she warned
against mentioning politics when writing to her; a letter she had
received from James would have had dire consequences for her if
it had been intercepted.)

Mary's account deals only with the first six months of the Revolution, from June, 1789, to the beginning of 1790, and covers
only a few of the events of that crucial period. One would never
know from reading it that the Revolution was taking place in a
city which Mary knew, that she had walked past the riding school
hall where the Estates-General met, had seen the face of the king
on his way to trial, that the churches, the river, the bridges,
squares, and streets through which the revolutionary mob ebbed
and flowed all were familiar to her. It is also incredible that the
author of *Original Stories* or *A Vindication of the Rights of*

Woman should have written such an unperceptive description of the women who marched on Versailles: ". . . mostly market women, and the lowest refuse of the streets, women who had thrown off the virtues of one sex without having power to assume more than the vices of the other. . . ." The reader is reminded of Mary's old antagonist Edmund Burke—and may legitimately wonder which of them wrote some of its passages. Although Mary did acknowledge the misgovernment and deep-seated injustices which had precipitated the Revolution, there is none of the anger and passion or the knowledge of abuses which lifted her *Vindication of the Rights of Men* to occasional eloquence, no description of the privileged classes in France which can compare with her devastatingly lifelike portrait of the English woman of fashion and leisure in *A Vindication of the Rights of Woman*. The heart of Mary's problem in this book was that she did not know France or French history or even the most recent political developments; therefore, her innate tendency to generalize, digress, and lapse into lengthy oratory and moral pronouncements went unchecked.

Only when she was describing Versailles—which she had visited and where she could record her impressions at first hand—did she achieve the fire and authority which mark her writing at its best:

> How silent is now Versailles!—The solitary foot, that mounts the sumptuous stair-case, rests on each landing-place whilst the eye traverses the void, almost expecting to see the strong images of fancy burst into life.—The train of the Louis, like the posterity of the Banquoes, pass in solemn sadness, pointing at the nothingness of grandeur, fading away on the cold canvas, which covers the nakedness of the spacious walls—whilst the gloominess of the atmosphere gives a deeper shade to the gigantic figures, that seem to be sinking into the embraces of death.
>
> Warily entering the endless apartments, half shut up, the fleeting shadow of the pensive wanderer, reflected in long glasses, that vainly gleam in every direction, slacken the nerves, without appalling the heart. . . . The very air is chill, seeming to clog the breath; and the wasting dampness of destruction appears to be stealing into the vast pile from every side. . . .[9]

That acerb Yankee John Adams kept a running commentary on the margins of his copy of Mary's book. He took her to task for her fine phrases ("There is more wit and point than Sense to this"; "very pretty"; etc.) and for her reliance on secondhand information of dubious accuracy. But most of his strictures dealt with her lack of knowledge of political affairs and her idealism, which continued to hope in the Revolution despite its excesses. The estimate of the man who was to succeed Washington in the American Presidency was not unflattering to Mary:

> This is a Lady of a masculine masterly understanding. Her Style is nervous and clear often elegant, though sometimes too verbose. With a little Experience in Public Affairs and the Reading and Reflection which would result from it, she would have produced a History without the Defects and Blemishes pointed out with too much Severity perhaps and too little gallantry in the Notes. . . .[10]

In August, 1794, Imlay left Le Havre for Paris. In September, he went to London, possibly returning to Le Havre before he left the country. Little Fanny, meanwhile, after a few months of sturdy good health, contracted smallpox and almost died of it. Mary believed that if she had followed the advice of the French doctor, she would have lost the child. "I however determined to follow the dictates of my own reason," she wrote to Everina, "and saved her much pain, probably her life, for she was very full, by putting her twice a-day into a warm bath."

Mary wrote to her sister from Paris, where she had gone to await Imlay's return. The Terrorist regime had been overthrown in July, and the long agony of executions had ended with the guillotining of its leaders. The journey from Le Havre had been perilous, Mary's carriage "overturning" four times (it probably landed on its side in the ditch).

With hindsight we can now say that Imlay had no intention of returning to Mary and their child; eight months of domesticity had been enough for him. But if he hoped that his departure would anger Mary into taking the initiative and breaking off their relationship, he handled his end of the matter with his customary ambiguity, which allowed her at first to accept his absence as a business necessity. She tried to veil her doubts in nostalgia, but her bitterness was evident:

There is nothing picturesque in your present pursuits; my imagination, then, rather chooses to ramble back to the barrier with you, or to see you coming to meet me, and my basket of grapes. With what pleasure do I recollect your looks and words, when I have been sitting on the window regarding the waving corn! . . . If you call these observations romantic, a phrase in this place which would be tantamount to nonsensical, I shall be apt to retort, that you are embruted by trade and the vulgar enjoyments of life. Bring me then back your barrier-face, or you shall have nothing to say to my barrier-girl; and I shall fly from you, to cherish the remembrances that will be ever dear to me. . . .[11]

But she did not fly, although for several reasons life in Paris was less than pleasant. Many friends were no longer there. The Christies had long since gone back to England. The Barlows, sickened by the bloodletting of the Terror, had left in the spring for Hamburg, where Joel carried on his commercial enterprises for more than a year.[12] Miss Williams was in Switzerland; she had been in prison only two months but had spent the winter of 1793–94 "with the knife of the guillotine suspended over my head by a frail thread"[13] and was glad to leave at the first opportunity. Paine was at first still in prison but was freed on November 4.

Mary probably saw something of Count von Schlabrendorf, who had been released at an unknown date, with undiminished faith in the Revolution despite his grim experience of it, and who stayed on in Paris. She also made a new friend, the Irish patriot Archibald Hamilton Rowan, who was in Paris as a refugee from the British authorities in Dublin, on his way to exile in the United States, and who left a vivid record of his friendship with Mary:

Mr.——, who was with me [Rowan wrote to his wife], joined a lady who spoke English, and who was followed by her maid with an infant in her arms, which I found belonged to the lady. Her manners were interesting, and her conversation spirited, but not out of the sex. He whispered to me that she was the author of the "Rights of Woman." I started! "What" said I within myself, "this is Miss Mary Wollstonecraft, parading about with a child at her heels, with as little ceremony as if it were a watch she had just bought at the jeweler's. So much for the rights of women" thought I. But upon further inquiry I found that she had, very fortunately for her, married an American gentleman a short time before. . . . My society was now most agreeably increased, and I got a dish of tea and an hour's rational conversation, whenever I called on her.[14]

As Imlay continued to postpone his return, pleading the exigencies of his business affairs in London, Mary slowly began to face the fact that he no longer loved her, that his suggestion that she join him in London was "merely dictated by honour," and that she could no longer live on his bounty.

> When I determined to live with you, I was only governed by affection. I would share poverty with you, but I turn with affright from the sea of trouble on which you are now entering. I have certain principles of action; I know what I look for to found my happiness on. It is not money. With you I wished for sufficient to procure the comforts of life, as it is, less will do. I can still exert myself to obtain the necessaries of life for my child, and she does not want more at present. I have two or three plans in my head to earn our subsistence; for do not suppose that, neglected by you, I will lie under obligations of a pecuniary kind to you! no; I would sooner submit to menial service. I wanted the support of your affection; that gone, all is over!

The following day she wrote again.

> . . . When you first entered into these plans you bounded your views to the gaining of a thousand pounds. It was sufficient to have procured a farm in America, which would have been an independence. You find now that you did not know yourself, and that a certain situation in life is more necessary to you than you imagined—more necessary than an uncorrupted heart. . . .[15]

Imlay has always been accused of having deserted Mary. It might have been better for her if he had. Given her resilient temperament and her drive for life and growth, she might have recovered more rapidly from the trauma of an actual separation. But Imlay did not desert her; he was incapable of so decisive an act. Instead, he suggested once again that Mary join him in England. At first she refused, arguing that it would only lead to further future intermittent separations and that she would be stranded in "a country that has not merely lost all charms for me, but for which I feel a repugnance that almost amounts to horror. . . . Why is it so necessary that I should return? Brought up here, my girl would be freer. . . ." There were other cogent arguments which she did not dwell on—her unwillingness to face her former friends, Fuseli in particular, in the event that she was stranded with a child by a man who had deserted her and the renewed burden of concern for her family. She had known for a long time that Eliza was once more in difficulties and her father's plight desperate, and she quailed at becoming once again involved in that bottomless bog of responsibility, when her own situation was so grim.

Nevertheless, six weeks later Mary was on her way to join Imlay in London, in response to a letter from him, which said in part: "Business alone has kept me from you.—Come to any port, and I will fly to my two dear girls with a heart all their own." She traveled with little Fanny, still less than a year old, and her devoted French maid Marguerite. While she waited for favorable winds to cross the Channel and despite her preoccupation, she wrote two letters to Archibald Rowan back in Paris, offering him the use of the house in Le Havre as a stopover on his way to the United States; she had "left a little store of provisions in a closet, and the girl who assisted in our kitchen, and who has been well paid, has promised to do everything for you." Her furniture had already been sold, and the house was for lease. (She wrote also of the faint hope that she might one day visit America and asked Rowan to take her affectionate remembrances to her brother Charles.[16]

To Imlay she wrote:

> Here I am at Havre, on the wing towards you. . . . I shall not attempt to give vent to the different emotions which agitate my heart. . . . I cannot indulge the very affectionate tenderness which glows in my bosom, without trembling, till I see, by your eyes, that it is mutual.

She was quickly disabused; it was not mutual. Imlay provided her with a furnished house at 26 Charlotte Street, and on occasion he did visit her. But it soon became apparent that he was conducting another affair (Godwin says with "a young actress from a strolling company of players"). Surprisingly, Mary at first accepted his support. Then, at the end of May, she tried to commit suicide.

Godwin is our only source of information, and he knew very little about what actually took place:

> I only know, that Mr. Imlay became acquainted with her purpose, at a moment when he was uncertain whether or not it was already executed, and that his feelings were aroused by the intelligence. It was perhaps owing to his activity and representations, that her life was, at this time, saved. She determined to continue to exist.[17]

Imlay then suggested a project which would give Mary a fresh incentive for living and at the same time offer a practical solution to how and where she might live for the next few months. He appointed her his representative or agent for a journey to Scandinavia in connection with his business dealings with Elias Backman in Gothenburg and a firm in Copenhagen. In a letter which was to serve as her authorization, he mentioned the recovery of money owed him by one Peter Elisson and the disposition of a cargo of goods in the hands of the Messrs. Myburg & Co. He described the bearer as "Mary Imlay, my best friend and wife," and gave her the broadest discretionary powers: "Thus, confiding in the talent, zeal, and earnestness of my dearly beloved friend and companion, I submit the management of these affairs entirely and implicitly to her discretion. Remaining most sincerely and affectionately hers, G. Imlay."[18] Dangling at the other end of the journey was the promise that he would join Mary in Hamburg for a holiday together in Switzerland. She accepted the proposal and arranged to leave at once.[19]

How can one explain this extraordinary reversal of roles on Mary's part? It was one thing for Imlay to resort to a device which would put her intelligence to use and at the same time get her out of his way for a while. (No doubt he safeguarded his interests with further explanatory letters to Messrs. Backman and Myburg explaining—and delimiting—the role of his "best friend and wife.") Mary's actions are less easy to understand. She, who abhorred "commerce," who felt it corrupted all those who engaged in it, that it was all of a piece—"a crooked business"—who demanded complete integrity in personal relationships and had repeatedly told Imlay she wanted nothing from him if he did not love her, was now launching herself on a long and difficult journey with a child only a year old, on behalf of a man whose fluctuating affections had just driven her to an attempt on her life.

The only explanation is sheer desperation. Mary could no longer make rational decisions or choices. She was living from day to day in the irrational hope that somehow she could tame this man and win him back despite the obvious fact that he no longer responded to her love and appeals.

On or about June 9, Mary, Fanny, and Marguerite left London for the North Sea port of Hull.

> Imlay, dear Imlay [she wrote before beginning her journey], am I always to be tossed about thus? How can you love to fly about continually, dropping down, as it were, in a new world—cold and strange—every other day? Why do you not attach those tender emotions round the idea of home, which even now dims my eyes? This alone is affection—everything else is only humanity, electrified by sympathy.[20]

The author of *A Vindication of the Rights of Woman* was begging for love and living on delusive hopes. She was only thirty-six years old, but the latter half of the year 1795 is the nadir of her life.

CHAPTER XIII

Dark Passage (1795-96)

ALONG WITH her growing alienation from Imlay, another tragic rift was developing between Mary and her two sisters; in the case of Eliza, the break would be lasting. Mary seemed incapable of admitting her real situation to either sister; far from giving them the truth, she actually misled them.

Eliza was still in Wales, with a family who were bitterly anti-French; the unhappy governess had the greatest difficulty in even getting newspapers to read. Meanwhile, she continued to hope that Mary would be able to find her a position in France. But in April, 1793, the British government forbade its nationals to travel to France, and Eliza had to face the fact that this way out of the trap in which she found herself was closed.

Then she received a letter from Mary dated June 13, 1793, which again raised her hopes, although Mary wrote with tantalizing vagueness:

> . . . I have been convinced that it is next to impossible to obtain a passport or a situation for you here until things have settled and peace [is] in view. But do not be discouraged. . . . I

cannot explain myself except just [illegible] that I have a plan
in my head, it may prove abortive, in which you and Everina
are included, if you find it good, that I contemplate with pleasure
as a means of bringing us all together again. . . .

A second letter in the same vein, dated June 24 and written in
case the first failed to reach its destination, referred to "a plan in
my head which promises to render the evening of your life more
comfortable." (Eliza was at this time all of thirty years old!)

There followed a long period of silence, grimly punctuated by
printed accounts in the British papers that Mary Wollstonecraft
had been arrested. "I hope to God she is safe," Eliza wrote
Everina from her father's in Laugharne, "yet the contrary idea
haunts me and makes me forget her few faults; I am truly glad
we sent the money." Meanwhile, Mr. Wollstonecraft had been
near death from a leg condition, and Eliza derived a certain grim
satisfaction from her father's sufferings, since they took place in
his eldest son's home:

> The money that was spent would have paid all his debts. He
> was near four months at his son's who has promised to be punc-
> tual . . . he fairly tortured the money from him after deranging
> the whole house . . . Ned and his Mrs. were truly frightened,
> and he lived wonderfully well. . . . I spent rather a pleasant
> week at Laugharne, my father was a lamb. . . .[1]

Not until March did the sisters hear from Mary again. She
asked for news of her family, having had only one letter months
ago, from Eliza, who she presumed to be in Ireland, and reiterated that she still had "in my mind some place for her future
comfort." At long last she also told them something of her personal situation (she insisted that she had written them earlier,
but that the letters had gone astray):

> . . . I am safe, through the protection of an American, a most
> worthy man, who joins to an uncommon tenderness of heart
> and quickness of feeling, a soundness of understanding and
> reasonableness of temper rarely to be met with. Having been
> brought up in the interior parts of America, he is a most natural,
> unaffected creature. I am with him now at Havre, and shall
> remain there, till circumstances point out what is necessary for
> me to do.

If this seems a reasonably clear suggestion that Mary was living with Imlay, both sisters apparently closed their eyes to that idea. But early in the summer they heard the fateful news from Johnson and also their brother Charles in America. Charles wrote that *he* had heard, a full six months earlier, that their sister was married "to Captain Imlay of this country."

Eliza's instinctive reaction was stark incredulity, since such a development would mean she would lose, once and for all, any possibility of further help from Mary. (In this she was singularly prescient.)

> Mary cannot be *married*!! [she hurriedly wrote Everina] It is mere report. It is natural to conclude that her protector is her *husband*, I on reading Charles' letter for an instant believed it to be true—I would my Everina that we were out of suspense for all at present is uncertainty and the most cruel suspense. Still Johnson does not repeat things at random and that the very same tale should have crossed the Atlantic makes me almost believe it. Once Mary is Mrs. Imlay and a Mother are we ever to see this Mother and her babe. . . .

Once again Mary behaved with little imagination where her sisters were concerned. She dangled the prospect of a voyage to France before Everina ("should peace take place") and with apparently no recollection of Eliza's lost child, described her own with glowing words:

> I want you to see my little girl, who is more like a little boy— She is ready to fly away with spirits and has eloquent health in her cheeks. She does not promise to be a beauty, but appears *wonderfully* intelligent, and though I am sure she has her father's quick temper and feelings, her good humour runs away with all the credit for my nursing. . . .

Everina may have sent Eliza a copy of this letter, or else Mary wrote also to Eliza; in either case the effect on Eliza was traumatic:

> Mary's letter gave me a dreadful complaint in my [illegible] and all I felt was a degree of ill humour with the whole [world?] I never before experienced. I read her letter a dozen times yet my heart not once beat with joy on M's account I was severely hurt and really felt that every hope for ourselves were [sic] effectually blasted. . . . Mr. Imlay could he not have written to

us? If Mary was afraid to be explicit, I wonder had Mary Eliza, or poor Bess in her mind's eye when she gave her heart to this genereux—[2]

For Eliza, Mary would always remain the sister who took her away from her own child, promising her happiness and security instead. To add to her problems, Eliza was once again uprooting herself. Her employers were not only violently antirepublican, but unbearably dull. She had for some months been making weekly visits to the nearby town of Pembroke, to take French lessons from a refugee French cleric. She now decided to move to Pembroke, where she would concentrate all her time and energies on perfecting her French. Her small savings would last her for six months, and she would then be qualified for a better post. But the wrench of parting with her charge, a small boy named John, almost undermined her determination, and it was then that she resolved never again to love a small child, "while I have the power of loving!"

In November Eliza wrote to Mary and also to Imlay, in care of Johnson, asking for financial assistance. His reply, wordy and evasive, is interesting because it is the only letter from him that has yet come to light:

MY DEAR MADAM:

Mr. Johnson gave me your acceptable favour inclosing one to Mrs. Imlay, saying it was for her, which leaving me ignorant of being included, I could not return an immediate answer; since which time I have been out of town. I hope this answer will appear to you a sufficient apology for my silence, and that you will be pleased to consider it a good reason for preventing a forfeit of that claim to humanity or at least respect and esteem for a person so affectionately loved by my dear Mary as yourself, which you say had already been impressed on your mind.

As to your sister's visiting England, I do not think she will previous to a peace, and perhaps not immediately after such an event. However, be that as it may, we shall both of us continue to cherish feelings of tenderness for you, and a recollection of your unpleasant situation, and we shall endeavour to alleviate its distress by all the means in our power. The present state of our fortunes is rather [word omitted]. However you must know your sister too well, and I am sure you judge of that knowledge too favourably to suppose that whenever she has it in her power she will not apply some specific aid to promote your happiness. I shall always be most happy to receive your letters, but as I shall most likely leave England the beginning of next week, I will thank you to let me hear from you as soon as convenient, and tell me ingenuously in what way I can serve you in any manner or respect. I am in but indifferent spirits occasioned by my long absence from Mrs. Imlay, and our little girl, while I am deprived of a chance of hearing from them.—Adieu, yours truly, G. IMLAY.[3]

The letter confirmed Eliza's fears that from now on she and Everina would have to take care of themselves. Her mounting panic as her meager resources declined over the next six months is pitifully recorded in her letters to her youngest sister.

"A certain sum of money would be necessary before I could enter any situation [for clothes]. . . . Ah! Everina, what are we to hope! I never anticipated, or hoped for, the *morrow* so little as at this juncture—a kind of despair has taken stronger root than ever in *my* heart." She would remain in Pembroke until May, she told Everina—"that is, if my good fortune does not arrive from America before that period is elapsed—not that I have any objection to share in the Hundred Thousand Pounds—or to behold Imlay his friend and brat." The last four words are written in a heavy, ugly hand.

Then, at the end of April, Eliza heard once more from Mary herself. She was in London. She sent Eliza a small sum of money. And she wrote in terms that reduced her unfortunate sister to hysteria:

I have intended writing to you every day, but have been prevented by the impossibility of determining in what way I can be of essential service to you. When Mr. Imlay and I united our fate together, he was without fortune; since that, there is a prospect of his obtaining a considerable one; but though the hope appears to be well founded I cannot yet act as if it were a certainty. He is the most generous creature in the world, and if he succeed, as I have the greatest reason to think he will, he will, in proportion to his acquirement of property, enable me to be useful to you and Everina. I wish you and her to adopt any plan in which five or six hundred pounds would be of use. As to myself, I cannot yet say where I will live for a continuance. It would give me the sincerest pleasure to be situated near you. I know you will think me unkind, and it was this reflection which has prevented my writing to you sooner, not to invite you to come and live with me. But, Eliza, it is my opinion, not a readily formed one, the presence of a third person interrupts or destroys domestic happiness. Excepting this sacrifice, there is nothing I would not do to promote your comfort. I am hurt at being obliged to be thus explicit, and do indeed feel the disappointments which you have met with in life. I have not heard from Charles, nor can I guess what he is about. What was done with the £50 he speaks of having sent to England? . . .

She wrote similarly to Everina, adding that she had sent 10 pounds to their father.

Eliza herself did not reply to Mary's letter, returning it "with only these words: 'Mrs. B. has never received any money from America.'" After pouring out her fury to Everina ("Good God! what a letter! How have I merited such pointed cruelty? When did I wish to live with her? At what time wish for a moment to interrupt their *domestic* happiness?"), she demanded that Everina find her a position in Ireland, "I care not where. Dear Everina, delay not to tell me you can produce bread, with what hogs I eat it, I care not. . . ."[4]

Meanwhile, Eliza had word from another unhappy member of the Wollstonecraft family. James had apparently heard from Mary of their bitter exchange; he had also tried to use what influence he could command with his eldest brother concerning the latter's treatment of their father. In the only glimpse we have of the feelings of this least articulate of the Wollstonecrafts, James wrote Eliza:

This is the fourth time I have attempted to write to you. I never could get through a letter fearing to give you pain, I thought silence best. Mary says you returned her letter. She appears less composed and happy than formerly. I have done everything in my power with Ned. I begin to place some hopes in him. It was not in my power to send my father more mony [*sic*] for though I have made a great deal of prize money yet it is all in Spain and I may not receive it these six months and then owing to the continuance of the war [lose?] considerably in remittance at home. I sent my father five pounds. . . . God bless you, when writing you and Everina there are always such conflicting passions struggling about my heart I am almost deprived of reason I am very unhappy. Yours affectionately J. W.

With Eliza's resources now at vanishing point, an old friend came forward. George Blood was still in Dublin and living in modest comfort with his mother. He wrote urging Eliza to stay with them and offered to meet her after her crossing from England. Instead of accepting this kindness, Eliza perversely elected to beg Mary once again for help. She wrote twice, little dreaming of Mary's real situation—her attempted suicide and sudden plan to go to Scandinavia. As late as June 9 Eliza was appealing to "Mrs. Imlay" and expecting a reply. But on June 6 Mary had left London, and was even then waiting in Hull to board ship.

At long last, not hearing from Mary, Eliza gave up and crossed the Irish Sea, her bitterness compounded by hearsay: A friend had written her of a remark by Joseph Johnson that he had never seen Mary looking so well or so happy![5] The move to Ireland did not immediately solve her problems. She failed to find a position quickly and was still staying with the Bloods two months later.

Nothing in Mary's stormy life is more difficult to understand than her treatment of her sisters during this period. Granted that she felt a desperate need to salvage some remnants of her pride, that after the Fuseli episode she could not bear to admit even to her own kin the extent to which Imlay had also failed her. Nevertheless, how could she hold out to the two desperate women—especially Eliza—the possibility of "five or six hundred pounds" from a man of whose love she was now unsure and who had shown complete disinterest in her family? Was Mary still deluding herself, as well as her sisters, regarding his prospects and his feelings for her? There is no simple answer.

Her next step, motivated, no doubt, by a desperate desire to regain Imlay's love, is also difficult to understand, but it does show vividly the qualities she inherited from her father—rashness, ad-

venturousness, and intrepidity. One must still recognize her essential courage in launching out into a region relatively unknown in
England, with a small child and a maid who (as Mary's letters to
Imlay show) had proved her devotion but who was a poor
traveler, prone to seasickness and fearful of coach travel on bad
roads!

Throughout her three months' journey in Scandinavia, Mary
carried a heavy burden of anxiety, resentment, and passionate
longing. The letters she sent to Imlay are almost too painful to
read. Yet in the back of her mind lurked a remnant of canny
shrewdness inherited from old Edward Wollstonecraft. To maintain her daughter and herself, she would put to use the magnificent scenery she was viewing and her experiences as a traveler in
places usually visited only by merchants who braved the lonely
and nearly impassable roads and the often primitive inns. Quite
early, Mary wrote Imlay that she was recording her impressions,
which were published the following winter as *Letters Written
During a Short Residence in Sweden, Norway and Denmark.*
Some of the material came directly from her own letters to Imlay,
since there are abundant references to him and to her unhappiness on his account. More of the material may have been put
down in a journal or as notes; the incidents and scenes are described too vividly to have been written from memory alone.

In Hull she waited almost two weeks for a favorable wind, during which time she suffered from constant depression. The
journey across the North Sea lasted six days and was stormy and
uncomfortable. Her arrival in Sweden was not propitious, and
from the outset Mary's initiative and imagination were challenged. The boat could land neither at Arendal nor at Gothenburg, her destination, and she finally gave the captain money to
put her ashore in a ship's boat near a lighthouse, on a bleak and
dangerous coast some twenty miles from Gothenburg. After many
hours in the open boat and several landings in search of a pilot,
they were finally met by the officer in charge of that stretch of
coastline. To her maid's horror, Mary transferred her little party
to his boat solely on the strength of his speaking some English.
He took her to his home, and the next day she traveled to
Gothenburg by coach, but not before she had sustained a bad

fall on the rocky shore, which sorely frightened the good Marguerite and which Mary herself later described as caused by a "convulsion."[6]

From Gothenburg Mary traveled over only a small portion of southern Sweden and adjacent Norway. After a fortnight in Gothenburg (the headquarters of Elias Backman), she went to Strömstad, and then on to Tønsberg, in Norway. Anticipating a somewhat longer stay in Tønsberg, she left little Fanny, who was having a painful time teething, behind in Gothenburg in Marguerite's care, only to discover when she arrived in Tønsberg that she would actually have to stay there a month or more in order to accomplish her mission.

The details of that business remain obscure; certainly Mary made every attempt to carry out her share of the bargain with fidelity. She missed Fanny painfully; to add to her depression, Imlay's letters arrived irregularly and varied sharply in tone. He was again ambivalent and ambiguous, and although Mary's own letters fluctuated between promises not to ask or expect any more love from him and pleas for renewed affection, Imlay gave her little help in cutting off the relationship. "You need not continually tell me that our fortune is inseparable, *that you will try to cherish tenderness* for me. Do no violence to yourself!" she once blazed at him, but the fact that he frequently declared such sentiments continually renewed her hopes.[7]

Nevertheless, by spending most of her time in Tønsberg outdoors, with plenty of exercise and sleep, she regained something like normal health for the first time since her child had been born. She also recovered her normal level of energy and took an adventurous journey, mostly by boat, along the southern coast of Norway, visiting the offshore islands and stopping at their tiny settlements. One was a tiny isolated, clifflike fishing village where she was marooned for four days. Without any books to read and with writing as her sole pastime, Mary recorded her vivid impressions of life in such a spot:

> We were a considerable time entering amongst the islands, before we saw about two hundred houses crowded together, under a very high rock—still higher appearing above. Talk not of bastilles! To be born here, was to be bastilled by nature—

shut out from all that opens the understanding, or enlarges the heart. Huddled one behind another, not more than a quarter of the dwellings even had a proper view of the sea. . . . A few planks formed passages from house to house, which you must often scale, mounting steps like a ladder, to enter. The only road across the rocks leads to a habitation, sterile enough, you may suppose, when I tell you that the little earth on the adjacent ones was carried there by the late inhabitant. A path, almost impracticable for a horse, goes on to Arendall, still further to the westward. I enquired a walk, and mounting near two hundred steps made round a rock, walked up and down for about a hundred yards, viewing the sea, to which I quickly descended by steps that cheated the declivity. The ocean, and these tremendous bulwarks, enclosed me on every side. . . .

From Tønsberg Mary went inland to Christiania (now Oslo), and finally returned to Gothenburg. There, on August 25, she was reunited with little Fanny.

I arrived here last night, and with the most exquisite delight, once more pressed my babe to my heart. We shall part no more. You perhaps cannot conceive the pleasure it gave me, to see her run about, and play alone. Her increasing intelligence attaches me more and more to her. I have promised her that I will fulfil my duty to her, and nothing in future shall make me forget it. I will also exert myself to obtain an independence for her, but I will not be too anxious on this head. I have already told you that I have recovered my health. Vigour, and even vivacity of mind, have returned with a renovated constitution. As for peace, we will not talk of it. I was not made, perhaps, to enjoy the calm contentment so named.[8]

In Gothenburg she found letters from Imlay which made it clear he had no intention of joining her in Hamburg or in Switzerland, although he continued to equivocate about their relationship. The remainder of Mary's journey was clouded by this uncertainty and her inability either to reach a decision herself or to get Imlay to make one.

Early in September she arrived in Copenhagen, to find that a quarter of the city had recently been destroyed by fire. She did little visiting or sight-seeing, remaining in her room where she struggled to solve the problem of her own and Fanny's future.

I do not understand you [she wrote Imlay on September 6 from the Danish capital]. It is necessary for you to write more explicitly, and determine on some mode of conduct. I cannot endure this suspense. Decide. Do you fear to strike another blow? We live together, or eternally apart! I shall not write to you again, till I receive an answer to this. . . .

But she did write again. From Copenhagen she traveled to Hamburg, where she was supposed to take care of more business matters for Imlay. No instructions awaited her there. Two days later a letter of his once again reduced her to desperation:

By what criterion of principle or affection you term my questions extraordinary and unnecessary, I cannot determine. You desire me to decide. I had decided. You must have had long ago two letters of mine, to the same purport, to consider. In these, God knows! there was but too much affection, and the agonies of a distracted mind were but too faithfully pourtrayed [*sic*]! What more then had I to say? The negative was to come from you. You had perpetually recurred to your promise of meeting us in the autumn. Was it extraordinary that I should demand a yes, or no? Your letter is written with extreme harshness, coldness, I am accustomed to, in it I find not a trace of the tenderness of humanity, much less of friendship. I only see a desire to heave a load off your back. . . . It depends at present on you, whether you will see me or not. I shall take no step till I hear from you.

Unfortunately it was not in the man to make such decisions; once again he put it up to her. From Dover Mary wrote that it would be her choice that they continue to live together, mostly for the sake of the child, but that his letter had suggested to her that Imlay had already formed "some new attachment":

If it be so, let me earnestly request you to see me once more, and immediately. This is the only proof I require of the friendship you profess for me. I will then decide. . . . You have told me, that you would make any sacrifice to promote my happiness—and, even in your last unkind letter, you talk of the ties which bind you to me and my child. Tell me that you wish it, and I will cut this Gordian knot.[9]

She begged him, once again, to see her, either in Dover or on the road to London.

We know almost nothing of the events of the next few weeks. Imlay did provide Mary and Fanny with "a lodging," though he had already installed his current mistress in a house. But he kept this fact from Mary, and eventually she extracted the confirmation of her fears from her servant. Characteristically, she went at once to Imlay. There was no escaping the finality of the interview; the rejection this time was total—and annihilating.

Not even Fuseli's rejection went so deep, perhaps because with Imlay she had glimpsed the possibility of what real fulfillment could be. The author of *A Vindication of the Rights of Woman*, who had argued that education and the development of their intelligence would enable women to live mature and creative lives, now decided that she could no longer live an existence which inflicted such suffering on her as she experienced the night after her interview with Imlay.

In an agonized letter she tried to assure at least the future of their child:

> I write you now on my knees; imploring you to send my child and the maid with —— to Paris, to be consigned to the care of Madame ——, Rue ——, Section de ——. Should they be removed, —— can give their direction.
>
> Let the maid have all my clothes without distinction.
>
> Pray pay the cook her wages, and do not mention the confession I forced from her; a little sooner or later is of no consequence. Nothing but my extreme stupidity could have rendered me blind so long. Yet, whilst you assured me that you had no attachment, I thought we might still have lived together.
>
> I shall make no comments on your conduct or any appeal to the world. Let my wrongs sleep with me! Soon, very soon, I shall be at peace. When you receive this, my burning head will be cold.
>
> I would encounter a thousand deaths, rather than a night like the last. Your treatment has thrown my mind into a state of chaos; yet I am serene. I go to find comfort, and my only fear is that my body will be insulted by an endeavour to recall my hated existence. But I shall plunge into the Thames where there is the least chance of my being snatched from the death I seek.
>
> God bless you! May you never know by experience what you

have made me endure. Should your sensibility ever awake, remorse will find its way to your heart; and, in the midst of business and sensual pleasure, I shall appear before you, the victim of your deviation from rectitude.[10]

Having dispatched the letter or left it where it could be promptly found, Mary went the following evening to the Thames at Battersea Bridge. This was beyond the city limits, but there were too many passersby for her purpose, and so she hired a boat and rowed up the river to Putney, against the current, by herself. She had learned to row, with great delight, during the long days she spent in Tønsberg, and now she put her skill to this desperate use. She knew the Putney Bridge from happier days when she had lived at Walham Green with Fanny Blood and her family.

The heavy rain that had begun by the time she reached her destination suggested to her the idea of soaking her clothing so that she would sink more rapidly. For half an hour she walked up and down the shore or across the bridge; no one came by to question her presence in that lonely spot or try to dissuade her from her purpose. At last she threw herself from the bridge into the black river.

She did not sink immediately; afterward she remembered trying to hasten the process by pressing her wet clothing closer to her body, before she lost consciousness. She also remembered the frightful pain when the water invaded her lungs, as a sufficient reason for never attempting such an ending again.

She was rescued, whether from a boat or by a passersby who swam out from the shore is unclear. Again we know no details beyond the fact that having heard of her attempt, Imlay sent a physician to care for her and also asked Mrs. Christie to take Mary into her home in Finsbury Square until she had recovered from the aftereffects of exposure and near drowning.[11]

At the time, the accepted explanation of an attempt at self-destruction such as Mary's was the suicide's unwillingness or inability to live in a state of extreme unhappiness (as distinguished from intractable pain or the fear of torture or execution). In Mary's case it would have been her refusal to live without Imlay's love, that need for "particular affection" which recurs like a leit-motiv all through her life. But today attempted suicide is seen as the product of far more complex, largely unconscious motivation, frequently a deeply suppressed anger which has accumulated over a long period of time and which is so overwhelming and frightening that the suicide dares not vent it on the real object but turns it against himself. Intense anger demands punishment as retribution, and what better punishment than inflicting endless remorse for having been the cause of the suicide's death? "Remorse will find its way into your heart," Mary had written Imlay in her farewell letter, "and in the midst of business and sensual pleasure, I shall appear before you, the victim of your deviation from rectitude."[12]

But Mary was not trying to punish Imlay alone. All her life she had been angry, and always for the same basic reason—rejection, the denial of love, by her father, by Fuseli, and now by the man who was the father of her child. From childhood she had also been unable to express her anger and had thus been denied an escape valve for her emotions. Her earlier attempt at suicide before her journey to Scandinavia and the second abortive attempt from the Putney Bridge were the outcome of a lifetime of frustrated rage, in which the past merged into the present, and one figure—father, friend, lover, and husband—loomed as the hated object of her desire to retaliate.

It is only in the light of such modern psychological insight that we can understand Mary's renewed attempts, once her feelings had been to some extent relieved, to win back Imlay. Otherwise, it seems utterly irrational that she should so quickly fall back into the same pattern of appeal, argument, and complaint shown in the letters she wrote to him throughout the months of November and December, 1795. She rejected his offers of financial assistance but reiterated her love for him and insisted that "I know you are not what you now seem, nor will you always act or feel as you do now. . . ."

Despite all that had happened, Mary once again proposed not only that they live together, but that Imlay's mistress, too, live under the same roof with them—the old idea of the trio she had first conceived four years earlier, but this time with herself cast in the role she had originally envisaged for Sophia Fuseli. Imlay was sufficiently bemused by this proposal ("extraordinary and injudicious," as even Godwin termed it) to agree and take Mary to look at a house he was on the point of leasing; then he thought better of it and withdrew his consent, angering Mary anew. Shortly thereafter he left for Paris with his mistress, but Mary's letters followed him, still alternating between reproach and appeal:

> I am stunned! Your late conduct still appears to me a frightful dream. Ah! Ask yourself if you have not condescended to employ a little address, I could almost say cunning, unworthy of you? Principles are sacred things, and we never play with truth with impunity. The expectation (I have fondly nourished it) of regaining your affection, every day grows fainter and fainter. Indeed, it seems to me, when I am more sad than usual, that I shall never see you more. Yet you will not always forget me. You will feel something like remorse for having lived only for yourself, and sacrificed my peace to inferior gratifications. In a comfortless old age, you will remember that you had one disinterested friend, whose heart you wounded to the quick. The hour of recollection will come, and you will not be satisfied to act the part of a boy, till you fall into that of a dotard, I know that your mind, your heart, and your principles of action are all superior to your present conduct. You do, you must, respect me—and you will be sorry to forfeit my esteem.

In the same letter she reproached him with lavishing money after she went to Sweden, yet neglecting her request that he assist her father and sisters, "and some other people, whom I was interested about . . . some trifling debts were not discharged, that now come on me. . . . Still I have an affection for you. God bless you!"[13]

By now Imlay earnestly wished to bring matters to a conclusion. He accused Mary of tormenting him. He refused to see her. He was at this time involved in some business with Christie (a member of his father-in-law's carpet manufacturing concern). On one occasion when Mary and Fanny came to visit the Christies, they found Imlay and other gentlemen there. Mrs. Christie begged Mary not to confront Imlay, but Mary insisted on taking Fanny in to see her father, and as usual her actual presence annihilated Imlay's resolution.

He agreed to see her again the next day and came to her lodgings, where they had a friendly encounter. Once again he was the gentle and considerate man Mary so deeply cherished. The interview completely undid all her efforts at self-mastery. She began to hope for a reconciliation and with such visions left the next day on a month's visit to an old friend, a Mrs. Cotton, in Berkshire. It was there, Godwin thinks, that she received a letter from Imlay which made her realize at long last that she could never count either on his retaining the winning manner he displayed on occasion or on his continued presence. He would always be off and away again; there could be no peace, no stability, in the relationship.

It seems probable therefore that it was at this time that she wrote him the last in the series of seventy-seven letters, which finally terminated the liaison:

> You must do as you please with respect to the child. I could wish that it might be done soon, that my name may be no more mentioned to you. It is now finished. Convinced that you have neither regard nor friendship, I disdain to utter a reproach, though I have had reason to think that the "forbearance" talked of has not been very delicate. It is, however, of no consequence. I am glad you are satisfied with your own conduct. I now solemnly assure you, that this is an eternal farewell. Yet I flinch not from the duties which tie me to life. . . . It is strange that, in spite of all you do, something like conviction forces me to believe that you are not what you appear to be. I part with you in peace.[14]

CHAPTER XIV

The Golden Hours (1796-97)

IN NOVEMBER, 1795, when she was still struggling to free herself from her infatuation with Gilbert Imlay, Mary wrote asking him to return her letters, and he complied. Now she drew extensively on them for *Letters Written During a Short Residence in Sweden, Norway and Denmark*. It is unique among her writings in its descriptions of the magnificent coastal scenery, written with the detailed observation and lyricism that flowered only a few years later in the early romantic writers. In Mary's case we can truly say that loneliness and tragedy had sharpened her perceptions of sounds and colors as she watched, with little benefit of human companionship, the dramatic panorama of sea, mountains and sky:

> Sometimes [she wrote] when the sea was calm, I was amused by disturbing the innumerable young star fish which floated just below the surface; I had never observed them before; for they have not a hard shell, like those which I have seen on the sea-shore. They look like thickened water with a white edge; and four purple circles, of different forms, were in the middle,

over an incredible number of fibres or white lines. Touching them, the cloudy substance would turn, or close, first on one side, then on the other, very gracefully; but when I took one of them up in the ladle, with which I heaved the water out of the boat, it appeared only a colorless jelly.

Because of the varied reading Mary had done for the *Analytical Review*, she was also at ease in writing about history, the condition of farming and trade, the level of social development in each country, and in describing people. Moreover, for the first time since *A Vindication of the Rights of Woman* four years earlier, Mary showed a lively interest in the situation of women. There had been a notable absence of any reference to the subject in her book on the French Revolution. Now, again facing the necessity of supporting not only herself, but little Fanny, her concern was renewed, focused this time not on affluent ladies, but on working women:

> The wages [of servants] are low, which is particularly unjust, because the price of clothes is much higher than provisions. A young woman, who is wet nurse to the mistress of the inn where I lodge, receives only twelve dollars a year, and pays ten for the nursing of her own child; the father had run away to get clear of the expense. There was something in this most painful state of widowhood which excited my compassion, and led me to reflections on the instability of the most flattering plans of happiness, till I was ready to ask whether this world was not created to exhibit every possible combination of wretchedness. I asked these questions of a heart writhing with anguish, whilst I listened to a melancholy ditty sung by this poor girl. It was too early for thee to be abandoned, thought I, and hastened out of the house, to take my solitary evening's walk. . . .

Letters Written . . . in Sweden has a philosophical framework. The author sees individual people as part of the historical process and is concerned with their corporate as well as personal destinies. She shares the optimistic belief in human perfectibility which is a hallmark of the age, but the excesses of the French Revolution have taught her that gradualism is the only way to lasting progress:

As a person of any thought naturally considers the history of
a strange country to contrast the former with the present state
of its manners, a conviction of the increasing knowledge and
happiness of the kingdoms I have passed through, was perpetually the result of my comparative reflections. . . . Inumerable
[*sic*] evils still remain, it is true, to afflict the human investigation,
and hurry the benevolent reformer into a labyrinth of error, who
aims at destroying prejudices quickly which only time can root
out, as the public opinion becomes subject to reason.

An ardent affection for the human race makes enthusiastic
characters eager to produce alterations in laws and governments prematurely. To render them useful and permanent, they
must be the growth of each particular soil, and the gradual fruit
of the ripening understanding of the nation, matured by time,
not forced by an unnatural fermentation. . . .

Mary also put into *Letters Written . . . in Sweden* the most
explicit statement she ever wrote of her religious disillusionment.
The depth of her despair had been evident in her attempt at
suicide; there is pathos in the often-repeated conclusion of her
letters to Imlay—"God bless you"—when she had obviously lost
all belief in a God that blessed anyone. Now she made it clear
that as far as she was concerned, there was no hope or comfort
for individual human beings in the teachings of Christianity.
There was indeed a deity, but his "grand plan of the Universe"
was not concerned with individuals; so she thought as she
watched the training of mercenary soldiers in Schleswig-Holstein
on her way back to England through northern Germany:

I viewed with a mixture of pity and horror, these beings
training to be sold to slaughter, or to be slaughtered, and fell
into reflection on an old opinion of mine, that it is the preser-
vation of species, not of individuals, which appears to be the
design of the Deity throughout the whole of nature. Blossoms
come forth blighted; fish lay their spawn where it will be de-
voured; and what a large portion of the human race are born to
be swept prematurely away. Does not this waste of budding life
emphatically assert, that it is not men, but man, whose preser-
vation is so necessary to the grand plan of the universe? Children
peep into existence, suffer and die; men play like moths about a
candle, and sink into the flame; war, and the "thousand ills

which flesh is heir to," mow them down in shoals, whilst the more cruel prejudice of society palsies existence, introducing not less sure though slower decay.

Mary's frequent allusions, not always indirect or veiled, to her personal situation appealed to the sentimental, even melancholy taste of her readers. Godwin remarked of *Letters . . . in Sweden* that "If ever there was a book calculated to make a man in love with its author, this appears to me to be the book." He was, of course, writing after the event, but many readers must have been tantalized by her direct appeal in at least one instance, to Imlay's former love and better nature:

> Situation seems to be the mould in which men's characters are formed . . . men entirely devoted to commerce never acquire, or lose, all taste and greatness of mind. . . . You will say that I am growing bitter, perhaps, personal. Ah! Shall I whisper to you, that you,—yourself—are strangely altered, since you have entered deeply into commerce, more than you are aware of— never allowing yourself to reflect and keeping your mind, or rather, passions, in a continuous state of agitation—Nature has given you talents, which lie dormant, or are wasted in ignoble pursuits—you will rouse yourself, and shake off the vile dust that obscures you, or my understanding as well as my heart, deceives me, egregiously—only tell me when?[1]

Was Mary once again deliberately wooing the man who had turned a deaf ear to her pleas—or trying to embarrass him, since all literary London knew of their affair and its tragic ending? Or was she perhaps displaying a canniness worthy of old Edward Wollstonecraft, in turning her anguish to account?

Letters . . . in Sweden was evidence of the resiliency of body and spirit with which Mary overcame her despair. She had the help of staunch friends. Joseph Johnson stood ready to publish her book. When she finally left the Christies' home, she settled nearby at 16 Finsbury Place. She also saw Mary Hays, the intense little woman who collected literary celebrities but whose devotion to Mary Wollstonecraft grew into real friendship.

But most of the time she spent in "entire solitude." Her hopes for a reconciliation with Imlay had died, but her bitterness was still not dissipated. In January she wrote to Archibald Rowan, who was then in America and had seen Charles:

> . . . I am unhappy—I have been treated with unkindness— and even cruelty by the person from whom I had every reason to expect affection . . . I looked for something like happiness— happiness! in the discharge of my relative duties—and the heart on which I leaned has pierced mine to the quick—I have not been used well—and I live, but for my child. . . . I still think of settling in France, because I wish to leave my little girl there —I have been very ill—Have taken some desperate steps—But now I am writing for independence—I wish I had no other evil to complain of than the necessity of providing for myself and my child—do not mistake me—Mr. Imlay would be glad to supply all the pecuniary wants; but unless he returns to himself I would perish first—Pardon the incoherence of my style . . . for me there is nothing good in store, my heart is broken. Adieu! God bless you!

The letter, signed "Mary Imlay," shows her still obsessed with the belief that in returning to her, Imlay would have been returning to his real—and better—self and reveals her continued preoccupation with death, since one consideration in going to France would be to "leave" Fanny there, in a free nation.

Now she turned once again to Fuseli, ostensibly to ask him, as she had asked Imlay, to return the letters she had written him:

> When I returned from France, I visited you, Sir, but finding myself after my late journey in a very different situation, I vainly imagined you would have called upon me. I simply tell you what I thought, yet I write not, at present, comment [*sic*] on your conduct or expostulate. I have long ceased to expect kindness or affection from any human creature, and would fain tear from my heart its treacherous sympathies. I am alone. The injustice, without alluding to hopes blasted in the bud, which I have endured, wounding my bosom, have set my thoughts adrift into an ocean of painful conjectures. I ask impatiently what—and where is the truth? I have been treated brutally; but I daily labour to remember that I still have the duty of a mother to fulfil. I have written you more than I intended—for I only meant to request you to return my letters. I wish to have them, and it must be the same to you! Mary

Why she would have expected a visit from Fuseli, now or at any other time, is difficult to fathom; why he did not return her letters is more easily explained. He would not care to have it known, by either accident or design, how friendly he and Mary had been for so long a time, especially after her recent affair. Moreover, had Mary received the letters and kept them, Godwin would have been able to publish them as he did her letters to Imlay. Fuseli was a friend of Godwin's, but economic necessity might have overcome discretion.[2]

Nevertheless, the slow process of Mary's separation from Imlay and of healing took its course. In the same month that her book was published, she went to Mary Hays' for tea and there once again met William Godwin, whom she had not seen in four years. It did not appear to be a significant encounter at the time, but for Godwin it served to erase the irritation of earlier meetings with Mary; his interest was aroused since he too knew her story.

Mary's stay at Mrs. Cotton's had done her a great deal of good. Long walks through the Berkshire fields and lanes did their healing work for a woman who was always happiest when out of the city and taking vigorous exercise. When she returned to London, an unexpected encounter with Imlay failed to upset her. "They met by accident upon the New Road," says Godwin, "he alighted from his horse, and walked with her for some distance, and the encounter passed, as she assured me, without producing in her any oppressive emotion."[3]

Mary was now settled in lodgings in a part of London called Pentonville, not far from what is now Paddington Station; Godwin was living in nearby Somers Town. With her physical and mental health renewed, she found her greatest need to be stimulating companionship, and she was having difficulty finding it. The Barlows were no longer in London. Sometime during 1796 Thomas Christie died while on a voyage to the Far East. The old circle at Johnson's had changed. Confined for the most part to the society of a two-year-old child and a maid, Mary had to find new friendships. On April 14 she called on Godwin, an unconventional step completely in character for her. It has been suggested that she was already looking for a man to replace Imlay in her affections, but since she was planning as late as mid-May to leave England, it seems more likely that she was looking for friendship.

Godwin, however, was searching for a wife. At the moment he was pursuing Amelia Alderson, the lively young daughter of a Norfolk physician. But he was a kind man, and in addition to recognizing Mary's loneliness, he enjoyed her company. He invited her to dinner the following week as one of a large party and thereby, in one gesture, opened to Mary the kind of company—and pleasure—she had been denied for more than three years.

In writing about Godwin's relationship with Mary Wollstonecraft, biographers have allowed their image of the Godwin of 1796 to be obscured by the later Godwin: his well-known financial difficulties; his complex and unhappy relationship with Shelley; his humorless pedantry, benign but prosaic; his idealism in large issues offset by his profound egotism, his inordinate awareness of his merits and past achievements. He has been granted an always brilliant mind but charged with clumsy social behavior, a lack of charm, and morbid sensitivity.[4]

But this was not the Godwin of the 1790's, who, whatever his social defects, attracted—and held—the friendship of many talented men and women. We have to fall back on the explanation of a biographer, George Woodcock:

> . . . he seems to have had some charm which his enemies could not detect or his friends define, but which had a real influence on those who attained his close friendship. Nothing else will explain the fact that he enjoyed the affection of men as varied in their natures as Coleridge, Lamb, Hazlitt, Curran and Holcroft, that men like Samuel Rogers and Northcote spoke of him always with esteem, and that so many charming women should have been willing to accept his friendship.

Even before he knew Mary, he was the escort of some of the most gifted and beautiful women in London: the tragic actress Mrs. Siddons, Elizabeth Inchbald and Maria Reveley, and Amelia Alderson, who later married the painter Opie. On occasion each and all of them thought Godwin comical, but they were also sufficiently pleased with his attentions to be mildly jealous of one another.

James Northcote's portrait shows a striking face with "noble eyes," also the large nose (something he had in common with Fuseli) which obsessed Robert Southey: "A nose—oh, a most abominable nose! Language is not vituperatious enough to describe its downward elongation . . . I never see it without longing to cut it off."[5]

When Mary called on Godwin, he was the foremost radical philosopher in England and an established writer, with a philosophical treatise, a successful novel, and effective polemical journalism to his credit. Yet like Mary, he had had a difficult time before being recognized in London intellectual circles, and some aspects of his early life offer an interesting parallel to Mary's— both of them, for instance, came by their liberal educational ideas because of a coercive atmosphere at home.

Godwin was then forty years old, the son and grandson of Dissenting ministers, and his childhood was shadowed by the extreme harshness of his father, whom he hated. His mother was gentler, and Godwin remained in close and affectionate communication with her in later years.

In preparation for the ministry he was sent to a Dissenting college at Hoxton for five years and came under the influence of the liberal theologian Andrew Kippis. Kippis' freethinking carried over into the fields of social and economic thought and laid the foundations for his pupil's later radicalism. Godwin's religious faith gave way gradually; he held two ministries but does not seem to have been ordained and was finally expelled from his pulpit at Stowmarket because of theological differences with his congregation. (Recently discovered evidence suggests that his loss of belief was a difficult and painful process which constituted a major crisis in his life.)[6]

His attempt to launch a school was unsuccessful because his educational ideas were too radical for the time. He came to London in 1782 for a literary career which began inauspiciously: a dull life of Chatham, a volume of sermons, and, for a few pounds apiece, potboiler novels turned out in weeks or even days. In 1785 through Andrew Kippis he attained a modest degree of security writing the historical sections of the *New Annual Register*.

Meanwhile, he was making friends in a steadily growing circle of liberal writers and thinkers. Like them, he felt the tremendous impetus of the French Revolution and became increasingly convinced that advocating the end of monarchic rule and calling for "the rights of man" was not enough. Just what were those "rights"? What kind of society should replace that being overthrown in France and challenged in England? On what principles should it be based?

An extraordinary piece of good fortune enabled Godwin to develop and enunciate the new philosophy he believed essential. The publisher George Robinson agreed to subsidize him while relieving him of his assignment for the *New Annual Register* so that he could write a book. The result was his famous *Enquiry Concerning the Principles of Political Justice, and Its Influence on General Virtue and Happiness*. Something of the scope of Godwin's vision and of his own self-confidence can be found in his account of the book's inception:

> My own original conception proceeded on a feeling of the imperfections and errors of Montesquieu,* and a desire of supplying a less faulty work. In the first fervour of my enthusiasm, I entertained the vain imagination of "hewing a stone from the rock," which, by its inherent energy and weight, should overbear and annihilate all opposition, and place the principles of politics on an immoveable basis.[7]

Even the most cursory summary of the main ideas in *Political Justice* will explain Godwin's sudden emergence from obscurity to preeminence as a philosophical thinker, as well as his intellectual compatibility with Mary Wollstonecraft. His whole thought was grounded on the belief that human beings are "developmental" organisms, who grow according to the influence of their environment, mentally as well as physically. Education is the major influence, for better or worse, and the state, because it is a determining factor in the nature of society, is also a major element of the educational process.

The great political and social inequities in society arise from

---

* This would have been Montesquieu's *Esprit des lois*, published in 1748, which had a profound effect on eighteenth-century liberal thought.

economic inequality, whose most glaring manifestation is private property. The rewards and oppressions of rank and wealth, force of any kind, war, or fear have no place in a justly ordered society, whose foundation must be individual liberty.

Government should be as simple and direct, as unencumbered as possible, to permit the direct expression and exercise of the people's will and to remove from unproductive work the vast numbers involved in what today would be called bureaucratic employment.

Godwin was at one with the spirit of his age in his essential optimism. Truth being monolithic and open to all, man's free exposure to it would eventually assure its universal acceptance. Man, as an individual and in his social existence, is, therefore, perfectible. Progress is slow, but it is also inevitable. The vista of amelioration is gradual and long but is proved by the experience of history; progress has occurred, is even now taking place.

All of Godwin's ideas on the institutions of society, the forms of government, the manner in which education is to be carried out, the relations between individual human beings such as marriage flow from these few basic ideas.

Political Justice is a long and complex work, but it is written with beautiful order and clarity and occasional passages of great eloquence. Godwin drew not only on years of reading and thought, but on discussions with friends and some of the best English minds of the day.

Mary was in France when *Political Justice* appeared in 1793 and made Godwin famous in a matter of weeks. The following year he published the successful novel *Caleb Williams*, in which he incorporated some of the ideas in *Political Justice*: the irresistible power of moral enlightenment and truth; the oppressive nature of existing social institutions; the brutality and injustice of many laws; the tyranny of private wealth. (Its indictment of the English penal system antedated Dickens' *Barnaby Rudge* by almost fifty years.)

One reason for the powerful writing in *Caleb Williams* was Godwin's personal involvement with institutional justice during the period of political repression developing in England as a reaction to events in France. In 1793 and 1794 the government, apprehensive at the influence of revolutionary ideas on British radicals, moved toward censorship with a series of arrests and trials for conspiracy. The target was the Corresponding Societies, which were little more than debating societies keenly interested in revolutionary ideas (such as universal suffrage), but which, to the government, seemed akin to the Committees of Correspondence that had played so effective a role in the inception of the American Revolution.

Godwin wrote a letter to the *Morning Chronicle* on behalf of the defendants in the first trial, but they were found guilty and sent out to the notorious penal colonies in Australia. Several died, including Godwin's friend Joseph Gerrald. The next trial moved even closer to him, for its defendants included writers and thinkers like John Horne Tooke and Godwin's close friend Thomas Holcroft. The author of *Political Justice* obviously stood next in line, particularly if he spoke out again on behalf of the accused.

Godwin did so. Although he shielded himself to the extent of using anonymity, his authorship would have been easy to trace. When Lord Chief Justice Eyre made his notorious charge to the jury, Godwin wrote a courageous attack which demolished the prosecution's contention that although no overt acts had been committed, it was the London Corresponding Society's intention to proceed to treasonable acts. Godwin argued that it was impossible to commit a crime except by transgressing a specific law. He turned the tables on the government by charging that its own intention was harassment and proscription and drew the profile of innumerable "witch-hunts" to come:

> . . . the authors of the present prosecution probably hope that the mere names of Jacobin and Republican will answer their purposes, and that a jury of Englishmen will be found who will send every man to the gallows without examination to whom these appellations shall once have been attributed. . . . Let these men be put on trial for their lives, let them and their friends be exposed to all the anxieties incident to so uncertain and fearful a condition; let them be exposed to ignomiy, to obloquy, to the partialities, as it happen, of a prejudiced judge, and the perverseness of an ignorant jury; we shall then know how we ought to conceive of similar cases.[8]

Overnight public opinion veered to sympathy for the defendants. The first three were acquitted, further prosecution was abandoned, and all prisoners were released. Godwin's reputation and prestige reached new heights.

But by nature Godwin was primarily an observer, a student, and a philosopher. Furthermore, his independence of thought was sufficient to extend to criticism of those he had just defended. Like Mary, he was profoundly disturbed by the excesses of the Terror; in 1795 he wrote a pamphlet which found fault with the Revolution and with such unquestioning supporters as, among others, the London Corresponding Society. The radicals were outraged, and Godwin's popularity among them began to decline along with his eminence as a political controversialist.

When Mary Wollstonecraft called on him in the spring of 1796, Godwin had been living in very simple circumstances:

> He rose between seven and eight, and read some classic author before breakfast. From nine to twelve he occupied himself with his writing. He found that he could not exceed this measure of labour with any advantage to his health or to the work in hand. . . . The rest of the morning was spent in reading and seeing his friends. When at home he dined at four, but during his bachelor life he frequently dined out. His dinner at home at this time was simple enough. He had no regular servant; an old woman came in to clean and arrange his rooms, and if necessary she prepared a mutton chop, which was put in a Dutch oven.

Such a life, although basically to Godwin's taste, required considerable discipline. Because he saw his mission as living "for the general good," he believed he must make the most of every hour of the day. His attitude and carefully planned existence appealed to Mary. Moreover, there was in Godwin no suggestion of the "money-getting face" she had found so dismaying in Imlay, nothing of the rolling stone. Godwin loved London and its literary circles in which he was solidly established, surrounded by a host of friends and acquaintances.

To understand Godwin's appeal for Mary and the rapid development of their relationship, it must be remembered how much else they had in common. Both were reformers, but also gradualists who respected freedom, individual human dignity, and the power of reason. Both had come to a position of skepticism from deep religious commitment. Hard work, thought, and writing were at the center of their lives; they respected each other's need for privacy and the long hours of uninterrupted work they both required.

In addition, each brought the other something new. Godwin was touchingly grateful to Mary for opening up to him a whole new dimension of human experience. Passionate love and the deep affection which grew from it had a literally overwhelming effect on the "philosopher," who had previously underestimated (to put it mildly) the very nature of love between human beings. Judging by his discussion of "benevolence" in *Political Justice,* he had a good deal to learn:

> A disposition to promote the benefit of another, my child, my friend, my relation, or my fellow being, is one of the passions; understanding by the term passion, a permanent and habitual tendency towards a certain course of action. It is of the same general nature, as avarice, or the love of fame. The good of my neighbour could not, in the first instance, have been chosen, but as a means of agreeable sensations. . . .

In the same work he had been profoundly critical of the institution of marriage. Not only did it often take place between people insufficiently acquainted with one another, but was "an affair of property, and the worst of all properties," a sentiment in which he antedated Karl Marx by more than half a century. But instead of recognizing, as Mary Wollstonecraft had, that marriage in its existing form too often debased the emotion on which it should be founded, Godwin denied the very existence of the emotion. He did not recognize love as something of value in itself:

> I shall assiduously cultivate the intercourse of that woman whose accomplishments shall strike me in the most powerful manner. "But it may happen that other men will feel for her the same preference that I do." This will create no difficulty. We shall all enjoy her conversation; and we shall be wise enough to consider the sensual intercourse as a very trivial object. . . . It is a mark of the extreme depravity of our present habits that

we are inclined to suppose the sensual intercourse anywise
material to the advantage arising from the purest affection.
Reasonable men now eat and drink, not from the love of pleasure, but because eating and drinking are essential to our health-
ful existence. Reasonable men will then propagate their species,
not because a certain sensible pleasure is annexed to this action,
but because it is right the species should be propagated; and
the manner in which they exercise this function will be regu-
lated by the dictates of reason and duty.[9]

After Mary's death, Godwin made changes in successive editions of *Political Justice* which brought it into line with his own
experience of marriage. He even projected a work whose aim
would be to correct *Political Justice* in its failure to give "proper
attention to the empire of feeling." The book was never written;
instead, he wrote the novel *St. Leon*, which pays eloquent tribute
to marriage as it could be and as he found it to be in his brief
experience with Mary.

He made his own vital contribution to their relationship: a kind
of sturdy objectivity and reassurance which Mary sorely needed.
In addition, his understanding of the basic importance of economic factors in society deepened her own approach to social
problems, including those of women. He was able and willing to
talk with her about her work as no one else had been, not even
Fuseli.

Yet even in the late spring of 1796 Mary had still not outgrown her longing to win Imlay back again. According to a letter
she wrote Von Schlabrendorf on May 13, signed "Mary Imlay,"
she still expected to leave England:

> I wrote to you, my dear Sir, some months ago, and I think
> you would have answered my letter had you received it—for I
> wrote you in quest of your comfort and I am sure you would not
> have neglected a wounded spirit. I felt inclined to address you
> because I thought there was some similarity in our feelings—
> the attention of friendship is a moral want that torments us
> both. I was led to expect that I had found it, only to be cruelly
> deceived. . . . The man on whom I relied with the utmost con-
> fidence has betrayed me, used me illness [*sic*], dishonourably—

and ceasing to esteem him I have almost learned to hate mankind—yet I will live for my child. This explanation entre nous
. . . I wish to leave England forever, yet have not determined
where to direct my wearied feet—what Place can please when
we are tired of ourselves? Philosophy cannot fill though it may
in a degree calm an affectionate human heart—If the calmness
does not rather deserve the name of despair which flows from
such a cruel disappointment.[10]

She and Godwin were now seeing each other frequently. Although Godwin was still courting Miss Alderson, he apparently
suspected that he would not be successful and was hedging his
possible losses by writing poetry to Mary! She was candidly critical of his effort:

> . . . I want besides to remind you, when you write to me in
> *verse,* not to choose the easiest task, my perfections, but to dwell
> on your own feelings—that is to say, give me a bird's-eye view of
> your heart. Do not make me a desk "to write upon," I humbly
> pray—unless you honestly acknowledged yourself *bewitched* . . .
> I have observed that you compliment without ryhme or reason,
> when you are almost at a loss what to say.[11]

A week after he received this letter Godwin proposed to Amelia
Alderson and was rejected. Three days later in a letter by turns
ironic, coy, and practical, he served notice on Mary that she had
now become the object of his serious attentions ("Cause Margaret to drop a line in my letter box, signifying . . . that I
expect to arrive on this day sennight at seven o'clock in the
morning, to depart no more. . . .") If Godwin appears to us to
have been unduly hasty in turning from one lady to another, we
must realize that he never expected to unleash emotions he
did not know himself capable of. In those days, as now, middle-aged men—and women—often sought marital companionship as
they sought friendship—because life without it was bleak and
impractical.

It was only three more weeks "before the sentiment which
trembled upon the tongue, burst from the lips of either. There
was no period of throes and resolute explanation attendant on the
tale. It was friendship melting into love." But Godwin is not a

reliable witness on the course of his love affair. He might have wished to draw an idyllic picture, but the truth was that Mary did not find it easy to stake her trust once again (and so soon) on a man's love. It appears from Godwin's diary that they became lovers in mid-August. On the sixteenth, Mary wrote him a brief note, ending with "*Entre nous*, did you feel lonely last night?"[12] But her next reaction was shock, even fear, of being once again wounded and disillusioned:

> . . . Could a wish have transported me to France or Italy, last night, I should have caught up my Fanny and been off in a twinkle, though convinced that it is my mind, not the place, which requires changing. My imagination is for ever betraying me into fresh misery, and I perceive that I shall be a child to the end of the chapter. You talk of the roses which grow profusely in every path of life—I catch at them; but only encounter the thorns.—I would not be unjust for the world—I can only say that you appear to me to have acted injudiciously: and that full of your own feelings, little as I comprehend them, you forgot mine—or do not understand my character. It is my turn to have a fever to day—I am not well—I am hurt—But I mean not to hurt you. Consider what has passed as a fever of your imagination; one of the slight mortal shakes to which you are liable—and I—will become again a *Solitary Walker*. Adieu! I was going to add God bless you!

Godwin answered with understanding and tact, attempting to convince her not only of his integrity, but of the need for her to put the past, once and for all, behind her:

> Do not cast me off. Do not become again a *solitary walker*. . . . It is best that we should be friends in every sense of the word; but in the mean time let us be friends. . . . I will be your friend, the friend of your mind, the admirer of your excellencies. All else I commit to the disposition of futurity. . . . Be happy. Resolve to be happy. You deserve to be so. Every thing that interferes with it, is weakness & wandering; & a woman like you, can, must, shall, shake it off. . . . Call up, with firmness, the energies, which, I am sure, you so eminently possess. Send me word that I may call on you in a day or two. . . .

At last a way was opening up before Mary which led away from the bitter past. Moreover, Godwin was offering a relationship which promised to be mutual on all levels. This was what she had clamored for in *A Vindication of the Rights of Woman*: love grounded in respect for her as a *person*, which also challenged her intellect. Since she was essentially an adventurous woman, eager and hopeful, her response, at first slow because of her lacerating struggle with Imlay, was unequivocal. Within a few weeks she and Godwin were riding a new wave of experience whose felicity astounded and enchanted them both:

> Now by these presents let me assure you that you are not only in my heart but in my veins this morning [Mary wrote him]. I turn from you half abashed—yet you haunt me, and some look, word or touch thrills through my whole frame—yes, at the very moment when I am labouring to think of something, if not somebody, else. Get ye gone Intruder! though I am forced to add dear—which is a call back—When heart and reason accord there is no flying from voluptuous sensations, I find, do what a woman can—can a philosopher do more?
>
> . . . I read this morning—reminding myself every now and then, that the writer *loved me*. Voluptuous is often expressive of a meaning I do not now intend to give. I would describe one of those moments, when the senses are exactly tuned by the rising tenderness of the heart, and according reason entices you to live in the present moment, regardless of the past or future. . . . It is not rapture—It is a sublime tranquility. I have felt it in your arms—Hush! Let not the light see, I was going to say hear it—These confessions should only be uttered—you know where, when the curtains are up—and all the world shut out—

Godwin was incapable of such letters and fell back on French, as he often did when deeply moved or secretive, and on his confessed inability to put his feelings into words: "Adorable maitresse! . . . You are—but I cannot tell you what you are. I cannot yet find the circumstance about you that allies you to the frailty of our nature. I will hunt it out."[13]

He found it soon enough—in Mary's inability to overcome a lifelong sensitivity to the slightest hint of neglect, in her detection of slights where none existed or was intended, in her wearying insistence on attention or reassurance. A rapturous letter could be quickly succeeded by one written in petulance or anger which showed her once again struggling with her own particular furies.

At such times Godwin was usually patient and understanding, but sometimes he rebelled and called her to account for her peevishness:

> You treated me last night with extreme unkindness; the more so, because it was calm, melancholy, equable unkindness. You wished we had never met; you wished you could cancel out all that had passed between us. Is this—ask your own heart—Is this compatible with the passion of love? Or, is it not the language of frigid, unalterable indifference?

Nevertheless, each misunderstanding was followed by explanations, and the tie between them was never ruptured but grew steadily stronger. Any threatened interruption to their pattern of frequent afternoons or evenings together threw Mary into distraction: "Mrs. Cotton comes tomorrow, should it prove fine, or Saturday. She talks of a *few* days. Mon Dieu! Heaven and Earth!"

One reason why their relationship prospered was their compatibility of interest and intellectual conviction. They met on the same level and discussed each other's work, often reading it aloud to each other. Although Mary at first found it difficult to accept Godwin's candid criticisms, she ended up by valuing them. He was not afraid to challenge both her style and subject matter, and Mary tried, after at first flinching and flaring out at him, to make the most of his suggestions: "You are to give me a lesson this evening . . . now that you have led me to discover that I write worse, than I thought I did, there is no stopping short— I must improve, or be dissatisfied with myself."

Godwin must have tried to free her from the continuing use of her family as subject matter, particularly her hatred of her father; judging by the opening chapters of *Maria, or The Wrongs of Woman*, which was all that she finished before her death, he was not successful.

Both Mary and Godwin continued to live a social life largely independent of each other and succeeded so well that none of their friends seems to have guessed at the relationship. Godwin escorted Mrs. Inchbald and called on Fuseli and other friends; both of them dined at Johnson's, but never together. Mary went out with John Opie (who at one point was rumored to be on the verge of marrying her), dined with Mrs. Christie, and saw much of Mary Hays.[14] Mary also began to make some of Godwin's friends her own.

Mary herself was once again financially harassed. Although Imlay had given her a bond to provide for Fanny, she was receiving nothing from him. Her father's affairs were causing her so much anxiety that she wrote to Charles in America asking him to contribute to Edward John's maintenance, a request seconded by Johnson but never answered by her brother.

In February Mary had to endure a difficult three-week visit from Everina, whom she had not seen in six years. In that interval her sister had changed from the lighthearted, vivacious girl whom Mary had scolded but loved to an embittered, taciturn woman. "The evenings with her silent, I find very wearisome and embarrassing," Mary complained to Godwin. Everina was on her way from Ireland to a branch of the Wedgwood family, and despite the fact that she was leaving one position and going to another, she left behind her with Mary an unpaid bill from the cloakmaker for three pounds four shillings which Mary felt obliged to pay, because the woman "seemed so much distressed to pay her rent"; she gave her remaining cash to another friend of Everina's who was also in need and complained bitterly to her sister of "always getting . . . into scrapes of this kind."[15]

When Godwin offered to borrow some money from the Wedgwoods, Mary demurred. She had renewed her connection with the *Analytical* as a reviewer, and she may also have been earning a stipend as a kind of assistant editor, for she seems to have assigned some reviews as well, at least among her friends.

By January, 1797, Mary's irritability had reached a new pitch, and the reason soon became clear: She was pregnant: "I am still an invalid—Still have the inelegant complaint, which no novelist has yet ventured to mention as one of the consequences of sentimental distress." She put herself under the care of Dr. Fordyce, whom she had known at Johnson's, but the situation raised more than mere physical problems. Was she ready to enter a lasting relationship with a man she had known only a few months, so soon after her shattering experience with Imlay? On the other hand, did she want to bear yet another child whose father accepted no responsibility for it before society?

Godwin's situation was also complicated. He was on record as opposing, even condemning, the institution of marriage. On the other hand, his personal conduct had plainly demonstrated not only his willingness, but his desire for matrimony; less than six months earlier he had proposed to another woman.

Nevertheless, he and Mary decided to marry and, having done so, went about it promptly and in great privacy. Only Godwin's friend James Marshal was present as a witness, along with the parish clerk, when he and Mary were married at St. Pancras Church on March 19, 1797. Within ten days they moved to the Polygon, a large block of attached houses in Somers Town, and set about the business of acquainting their friends with varying degrees of defensiveness and inconsistency.

Godwin wrote Thomas Wedgwood in terms that make one wonder how he would have gone about explaining his marriage if Amelia Alderson had accepted him the preceding summer:

> . . . You have by this time heard from B. Montague of my marriage. . . . Some persons have found an inconsistency between my practice in this instance and my doctrines. But I cannot see it. The doctrine of my "Political Justice" is, that an attachment in some degree permanent, between persons of opposite sexes is right, but that marriage, as practiced in European countries, is wrong. I still adhere to that opinion. Nothing but a regard for the happiness of the individual, which I had no right to injure, could have induced me to submit to an institution which I wish to see abolished. . . . Having done what I thought necessary for the peace and respectability of the individual, I hold myself not otherwise bound than I was before the ceremony took place.

To Mary Hays he wrote with hardly less self-consciousness:

> My fair neighbor desires me to announce to you a piece of news, which it is consonant to the regard both she and I enter-

tain for you, you should rather learn from us than from any other quarter. She bids me remind you of the earnest way in which you pressed me to prevail upon her to change her name, she directs me to add, that it has happened to me, like many other disputants, to be entrapped in my own toils: in short, we found that there was no way so obvious for her to drop the name of Imlay, than to assume the name of Godwin. Mrs. Godwin (who the devil is that?) will be glad to see you at No. 29, Polygon, Somers Town, whenever you are inclined to favour her with a call.

Mary was also no less defensive when she wrote to Amelia Alderson:

The wound my unsuspecting heart formerly received is not healed. I found my evenings solitary, and I wished while fulfilling the duty of a mother, to have some person with similar pursuits bound to me by affection; and besides, I earnestly desired to resign a name which seemed to disgrace me.

She even alluded once again to former dazzling courtships, which must have caused Miss Alderson some mirth:

I have had it in my power, more than once, to marry very advantageously . . . had fortune or splendour been my aim, they have been within my reach, would I have paid the price. Well, enough of the subject, I do not wish to resume it. . . .

And she signed her letter "Mary Wollstonecraft, femme Godwin."

The astonishment of friends, who did not even suspect the couple were lovers, was compounded by their domestic arrangements. "We do not entirely cohabit," Godwin wrote Mr. Wedgwood; he had taken rooms nearby in the Evesham Buildings, where he wrote and read the greater part of each day. He and Mary had concluded that their marriage would succeed only if they respected each other's individuality and privacy. Godwin's views on "cohabitation" were a matter of record—he held that it made superhuman demands on the two partners which could never be met short of human perfection. Unused as he was to the proximity of small children, the desire to get away from the turbulence of a lively three-year-old, with another child on the way, was no small factor in his thinking. Mary's motives were somewhat different:

My conduct in life must be directed by my own judgement
and moral principles: it is my wish that Mr. Godwin should
visit and dine out as formerly, and I shall do the same; in short,
I still mean to be independent, even to cultivating sentiments
and principles in my children's minds (should I have more)
which he disavows.[16]

Today such an arrangement for a couple who are both writers
or artists is nothing unusual, but then it drew almost as much
comment, kindly or otherwise, as the actions of a philosopher
who had condemned marriage and a woman who had disre-
garded it. The couple's announced intention of going out in
mixed society without each other's company also aroused attention. Here Godwin himself missed the real issue. "We agreed in
condemning the notion, prevalent in many situations in life, that
a man and his wife cannot visit in mixed society, but in company
with each other," he wrote in retrospect; "and we rather sought
occasions for deviating from rather than complying with, this
rule." Whatever the rule, the practice had been for men to go
into mixed company or indeed any company, without their wives
while married women usually stayed home. But Mary had gone
out from the beginning of her life in London and would not have
been ready to abandon the practice now.

In general Godwin's male friends accepted the marriage with
better grace than the women. Mrs. Siddons, Mrs. Barbauld, and
Mrs. Inchbald all were apparently more shocked at Godwin's
marrying a woman with Mary's past than they had been unwilling to be her friend as long as she remained single; in the case of
Mrs. Inchbald this may have been due to injured pride, if not
outright jealousy. Fuseli was wry: ". . . the assertrix of female
rights has given her hand to the balancier of political justice . . .";
but Holcroft was delighted: "From my heart and soul I give you
joy. I think you the most extraordinary married pair in existence."

None wrote more warmly to the couple than Godwin's aged
mother:

. . . shall be glad to see you and your wife in Norfolk, if I am
spared. You must not expect great exactness, as I have a young
servant, and myself able to do nothing at all. . . . I intend send-

ing you a few eggs with this in Hannah's* box. Could send you
a small fether [*sic*] bed, would do for a servant, by wagon, if
acceptable. . . . My dears, whatever you do, do not make invitations and entertainments. . . . Live comfortable with one another.
The Hart of her husband safely trusts in her. I cannot give you
no better advice than out of Proverbs, the Prophets, and New
Testament. My best affection attend you both—A Godwin[17]

It seems likely that they accepted and were delighted with the
"fether bed," but they did not accept her exhortation to make no
"invitations and entertainments." There came to the Polygon a
growing number of writers, painters, and those with a taste for
lively and liberal conversation, to tea or dinner, over which Mary
Wollstonecraft presided with glowing warmth. The twenty-three-
year-old Robert Southey, still in his radical youth, declared that
she was ". . . of all the literary characters the one I most admire
. . . a first-rate woman, sensible of her own worth, but without
arrogance or affectation." Most of her remarks he found "wise
and true."[18] Coleridge took away "a very high idea of Mrs.
Wolstonecraft's [*sic*] powers of conversation, none at all of her
talent for book-making." Hazlitt saw her only once, very briefly,
but remembered long afterward the deft ease with which Mary
fended off one of Godwin's dogmatic pronouncements.[19]

Opie and Northcote were old artist friends of Godwin's. Thomas
Lawrence came. Even Fuseli accepted an invitation to dine;
although he found a less appreciative company than he thought
was his due, it included such Irish liberals as Henry Grattan and
the barrister John Philpot Curran (who had defended Archibald
Rowan's sedition case) and Horne Tooke. What, we may wonder, was in Mary's mind as she entertained at Godwin's dinner
table the man she had loved so desperately five years earlier?

Meanwhile, she also maintained her friendships with women:
Mary Hays, Amelia Alderson, the novelist Eliza Fenwick, and
Maria Reveley—all, with the exception of Miss Hays, originally
friends of Godwin's. Maria Reveley's little boy Henry was a play-
mate of Fanny's and gave her a rake and pitchfork, which she
used for haymaking in the open fields across from the Polygon. It

---

* Godwin's sister.

was a life that seemed in another world from that Mary had led with Imlay. Still, matters did not always go smoothly. Periodically Mary would lose patience with Godwin—sometimes over a domestic problem (Godwin had not spoken firmly to the landlord about the state of the kitchen sink, and he was unfortunately no better than Mary at coping with tradesmen to whom they might be in debt):

> Mr. Johnson, or somebody, has always taken the disagreeable business of settling with trades-people, off my hands—I am, perhaps, as unfit as yourself to do it—and my time appears to me as valuable as that of any other persons accustomed to employ themselves. Things of this kind are easily settled with money, I know; but I am tormented by the want of money—and feel, to say the truth, as if I was not treated with respect, owing to your desire not to be disturbed—

More serious was a falling out that resulted from a fortnight's jaunt he took with young Montagu, from which he returned several days later than he had promised. At first he and Mary had exchanged happy letters, and he had teased her lovingly: "And now, my dear Love, what do you think of me? Do you not find solitude infinitely superior to the company of a husband?" He exhorted her to take care of herself and "William," the son they both expected.

But instead of returning straight from Staffordshire, where Montagu and he had visited the Wedgwoods, and arriving in London before the weekend, Godwin paid two other visits en route. He wrote explaining that he would arrive later than anticipated and exhorted Mary: "Be happy; be in health and spirits. Keep a lookout, but not an anxious one. Delays are not necessarily tragical: I believe there will be none."

But the old wounds of apprehension and dismay reopened at the uncertainty and the thought that he could prefer seeing others to being reunited with her. Just before midnight on Monday, when he had still not returned, she lost her self-control and wrote him a bitter letter:

> . . . In short—your being so late tonight, and the chance of your not coming, shews so little consideration, that unless you

suppose me a stick or stone you must have forgot to think—as well as feel—since you have been on the wing. I am afraid to add what I feel—good night—[20]

Once again the impasse was resolved. Nor was there a breach after a more prolonged period of irritation, owing to his attentions to a Miss Pinkerton, who visited and dined at the Godwins' and whom he called on at her home. Mary began to feel the lady was a threat and an intruder and wrote her a sharp note but submitted it to Godwin for his approval:

> Miss Pinkerton, I forbear to make any comments on your strange behaviour; but, unless you can determine to behave with propriety, you must excuse me for expressing a wish not to see you at our house.
>
> MARY GODWIN

Godwin crossed out the words "strange behaviour" and substituted "incomprehensible conduct" and, after holding it for a few hours, sent the note to its destination. The lady acquiesced in the rebuke, and no more is heard of her. The episode demonstrated that the wheel had come full circle with Mary now playing the role of Sophia Fuseli to Miss Pinkerton's Mary Wollstonecraft and doing so with a poise and assurance that came from a feeling of security and a new kind of maturity. Godwin responded in kind, moved no doubt in part by the knowledge that Mary was near her confinement.

The couple were together even more than usual during July and August. Mary had spent the summer working, and now she awaited the child without fear. Her first childbirth had been relatively easy. She was sure now of Godwin's love. She was, in fact, secure for perhaps the first time in her life. Godwin, too, was transformed, tender and solicitous: "I think it not right, mama, that you should walk alone in the middle of the day. Will you indulge me the pleasure of walking with me?"[21] Together they looked forward to the arrival of the child with a serenity new in both their lives and with unbounded hope in the future.

CHAPTER XV

Birth and Death (1797)

"WHAT DO YOU THINK of the present state of Europe?" Mary wrote to Archibald Hamilton Rowan in September, 1796. "The English seem to have lost the common-sense that used to distinguish them."

French republican armies were victorious. Defeat and danger abroad were bringing repression at home. The government's defeat in the trial of Horne Tooke and others on whose behalf Godwin had so effectively intervened in 1794 was to be the last gasp of British liberalism for a decade. That same year Pitt had been able to suspend habeas corpus, and in 1795 two acts were passed by Parliament forbidding speech or writing against the government or any kind of public meeting without permission. Such legislation was, of course, accompanied by enforcement through police action, including spies; Wordsworth and Coleridge were being watched by Home Office informers in the summer of 1797, because they were tramping the Quantock Hills without apparent legitimate purpose. It is not surprising that Mary Wollstonecraft, now carrying a second child and cautiously testing the solidity of her newfound happiness, turned to uncontroversial subjects for her writing—literature, the care of chilren, and another novel.

In April, 1797, she published her first piece in a publication other than the *Analytical*, a letter "On Poetry, and Our Relish of the Beauties of Nature," which appeared in the *Monthly Magazine*.[1] It is closely related to the book of letters from Scandinavia. Although she had spent the greater part of the last ten years in cities, Mary had never outgrown her childhood love for the countryside. The weeks in Norway and Sweden walking or on the water in a small rowboat had powerfully reawakened her love of the outdoors and her awareness of natural beauty, and it is this experience which she urged on her readers in her little essay. Sophisticated human beings, when they lose touch with nature, themselves become false and trivial:

> . . . the beauties of nature are not forcibly felt, when civilization, or rather luxury has made comfortable advances . . . in the present state of society the understanding must bring back the feelings, or the sensibility must have such native strength, as rather to be whetted than destroyed by the strong exercise of the passions.

Poetry is best inspired by what the poet has seen and felt in nature rather than by what he has learned from books. Clearly Mary would have welcomed Wordsworth's criteria that poetry is "the spontaneous overflow of powerful feelings," the outgrowth of "emotion recollected in tranquility," and "the image of man and nature."[2] Although Mary Wollstonecraft had not yet attempted really informed and serious literary criticism, "On Poetry" suggests that she might have done so, given the congenial works of the rising school of Romantic writers as subjects for her study and consideration. Perhaps the essay struck sparks from the young men who were working on *Lyrical Ballads*; Coleridge was a dinner guest of the Godwins, and Mary may have met Wordsworth through Joseph Johnson.

While she watched over and played with Fanny, Mary was also ordering her ideas about the upbringing of children, in which she had already served a long apprenticeship. What she put down on paper were mere fragments which Godwin preserved as "Letters on the Management of Children." They show vividly her gift for perceiving and communicating with the individual child, and her belief, often expressed, that love is the key which will unlock a child's mind, heart, and will.

Another fragment called "Lessons" was to be read by a small child, increasing in complexity as the child's reading power and understanding developed. The emphasis is not only on teaching the child to *think* (Mary's old preoccupation). It should learn to think, not just in terms of itself, its growing powers and sensations, but of others—the expected baby brother, its parents, the poor.

Neither the "Letters" nor the "Lessons" runs to more than a few pages, but they show that here too Mary was far ahead of her time. She was not the originator of the tenet that a child's dignity and individuality must be respected no less than that of an adult, which she had inherited from Fenelon, Locke, and others. But because of her gift for relating to the individual child as unique, in the same way that an adult woman or man is unique, Mary Wollstonecraft might have made her own contribution to the development of child pedagogy as the precursor of Montessori and Froebel.

Her unfinished novel holds primacy of place among her unfinished writings of this year, and it absorbed by far the greatest portion of her time. Already in *A Vindication of the Rights of Woman* she had shown her awareness of the need for a "particular investigation [of] the laws relative to women" and had promised to carry it on in a second volume. But Godwin found and published only a handful of "hints" which he thought related to such a volume, and none of them has any bearing on the legal position of women. The real sequel to the *Vindication* would have been the completed *Maria, or The Wrongs of Woman*, and it is only as such that the fragment is of any real interest.[3]

Where the main emphasis of the *Vindication* was on the need for education and job opportunities for women who must earn their way either because they are single or widowed, *Maria, or The Wrongs of Woman* focuses on the additional handicap of legal inequities. Moreover, rather than concern itself primarily with the woman of some means or from a "good family," the novel shows the greater injustices faced by poor women, those at the very bottom of the heap, not from lack of virtue or ability but because they had never had a chance—for education, for health and decency, for carrying out the simplest, most basic responsibilities of motherhood. These were the worst sufferers from the inhuman debtors' laws, which trapped women like her characters Jemima and Peggy in a rat race against prostitution and complete moral disintegration and which had threatened Mary Wollstonecraft herself.

Mary had already written of the hazards facing poor women in *Original Stories*; there is a similar episode in *Maria* in the story of young Peggy, whose plight rouses the sympathies of the heroine, Maria. But it is Jemima, Maria's servant and "nurse" in the asylum where Maria's brutal husband commits her, who becomes the center of interest in the fourteen chapters which are all we have of the novel.

Jemima is something new in English fiction, the kind of character who did not really come to life till the advent of Dickens, a woman who had been "hunted from hole to hole as if she was a beast of prey, or infected with a moral plague." Unfortunately, because she was no novelist, Mary made Jemima the victim of every misery common to a class which society thrust aside because it did not even consider its members human. Certainly they had never been admitted to a place in fiction, any more than to society at large. If Mary had been capable of really "writing" Jemima, she would have earned herself an honorable place in the history of the English novel. Even in failing, she heralded the existence of the Jemimas and demanded that society recognize their plight and its responsibility for them.

Maria is another rather lifeless character whose role is to demonstrate the laws which gave a husband control over the children and over his wife's inheritance and which even denied her the right to sue in court on her own behalf or for the children's custody because, once married, a woman had no further legal identity. It would be another forty years in England before the sensational case of Caroline Norton led to the challenge of such laws by a victim who had the advantages of social position and influential connections—as well as beauty and a gift for pamphleteering!—and to eventual passage of an Infants' Custody Act in 1839, giving a wronged mother certain rights in the custody and care of young children. It would be much longer before the many other disabilities which accompanied marital status were removed from women.

Mary worked hard at her novel and, as Godwin recorded, rewrote it freely:

> . . . impressed, as she could not fail to be, with the consciousness of her talents, she was desirous, in this instance, that [her talents] should effect what they were capable of effecting. She was sensible how arduous a task it is to produce a truly excellent novel; and she used her faculties to grapple with it. All her other works were produced with a rapidity, that did not give her powers time fully to expand. But this was written slowly and with mature consideration. She began it in several forms, which she successively rejected, after they were considerably advanced. She wrote many parts of the work again and again, and when she had finished what she intended for the first part, she felt herself more urgently stimulated to revise and improve what she had written, than to proceed, with constancy of application, in the parts that were to follow.

It is tragic to know the pains Mary went to in writing this book, for even in its unfinished state it demonstrates that she had no talent whatever for writing fiction. She was still trapped in her own past (as the account of Maria's early life shows), and where she tried to break away from the accepted norms of the sentimental novel, as in the character of Jemima, she showed as little ability to bring her characters to life as she did with the conventional figures of Maria Venables and Henry Darnford. She found it downright impossible to create character through action or conversation, one means by which Jane Austen, Maria Edgeworth, and Dickens, among so many others, brought the nineteenth-century novel to its magnificent development. All Mary was able to do was to tell, through first-person accounts and flashbacks, what happened; always she was the reporter of past events. Like Mrs. Mason in *Original Stories* or herself when she traveled through Scandinavia, she could write, sometimes very movingly, *about* people, but she could not bring them to life.

Mary was clearly aware that something was wrong with her novel. She discussed it with Godwin; she also sent the first fourteen chapters to their friend George Dyson, who had no literary qualifications for criticism but might have been chosen because he typified the general intelligent reader. Dyson was critical; he found no basis in George Venables' behavior for Maria's passionate dislike of him, a reaction which outraged the author:

> . . . I am vexed and surprised at your not thinking the situation of Maria sufficiently important, and can only account for this want of—shall I say it? delicacy of feeling by recollecting that you are a man. . . . I should despise such a husband as I have sketched—yet you do not seem to be disgusted with him!!![4]

Dyson also found fault with "the style of Jemima's story," perhaps on the ground that her speech was too unladylike; the real problem, however, must have been that characters such as Jemima were simply not found in the novels of the period, and Dyson recoiled at such an intrusion into the comfortable literary staple of sentiment and cant.

In addition to the fourteen chapters which were to constitute Part I of the book, Mary also wrote part of Chapter XV, and Chapters XVI and XVII, as well as a summary of the remaining two parts. Deserted by Darnford after they were free of the asylum, Maria was to attempt suicide and had already swallowed laudanum when Jemima arrived with the child Maria had thought dead. She was forced to vomit the poison and declared "the conflict is over—I will live for my child!" Would continued marital happiness with Godwin have enabled Mary to find new channels of self-expression or at least rid her of her dependence on what was tragic in her own past as subject matter for her novels? Would there have been more Jemimas and fewer Maria-Marys and Darnford-Imlays? Would she have found her place or been submerged by the new fiction, heralded in 1800 by *Castle Rackrent* and followed a decade later by the first novels of Jane Austen and Walter Scott?

In her *Vindication of the Rights of Woman*, Mary Wollstone-craft had deplored the fact that women were being driven from one of the few remaining occupations open to them, that of mid-wife, and she decided to have a woman perform the delivery of her child. The woman she chose, a Mrs. Blenkinsop, was highly experienced and worked for the Westminster Lying-In Hospital; she was no doubt better equipped than most such practitioners. Mary sent for her after her labor pains began early in the morn-ing of Wednesday, August 30, and she arrived about nine, but Mary did not go to her room until two o'clock in the afternoon. Meanwhile, Godwin waited in his rooms in the Evesham Build-ings, at Mary's request; she did not wish him to come to her, she said, until she could present their child to him.

Delivery proved to be painfully slow. Godwin received three notes during the day, all reassuring in tone, but the child, a girl, was not born until after eleven that night. Still Godwin was not summoned. At last, after 2 A.M. on Thursday, the midwife sent for him with the alarming news that the afterbirth had not pro-ceeded in the usual manner; the placenta was adhering to the womb, and she was unable to remove it.

Godwin rushed out to fetch Dr. Poignand, a physician also attached to the Westminster Hospital, and he performed an operation, removing the placenta in stages, an agonizing pro-cedure. Mary bled heavily, fainted time and again, and suffered excruciating pain; never before, she told Godwin later, had she known what bodily pain was. It was after four when he was finally admitted to her room and found her more dead than alive.

Godwin was shaken by Mary's ordeal, but not sufficiently so; when Mary asked, later in the day, to see Dr. Fordyce, who even by the inadequate standards of that day was no obstetrical specialist, Godwin complied, despite Poignand's objections that there was no need for a consultation. Fordyce was also reassur-ing, and when Mary began to recover on Friday from the exhaus-tion following the birth, Godwin left her for several hours.

On Saturday Mary's condition was not quite as encouraging, but Dr. Fordyce saw no cause for alarm; neither, apparently, did Anthony Carlisle, the ablest of the medical men whom Godwin knew, but whose first visit was apparently only a friendly one.

But Godwin was worried; Miss Nicholes has pointed out that of the string of visits he paid that Sunday, two were on friends with earlier medical experience. When he returned, it was to find that Mary had suffered a severe chill (the first overt sign of fever caused by an infection) and that she had been uneasy at his prolonged absence. A penitent Godwin hardly left the house for the rest of the week.[5]

On Tuesday evening Fordyce was thoroughly alarmed; he brought in Dr. Clarke, the most distinguished childbirth specialist in London. But if there had been any idea of a further operation, Dr. Clarke apparently felt it was too late and that in her weakened condition Mary could not survive it. Little Fanny and the newborn child had been sent to Maria Reveley's. Eliza Fenwick had assumed charge of nursing Mary, aided by Mary Hays. Four of Godwin's closest friends—James Marshal, George Dyson, Basil Montagu, and John Fenwick—were on hand for errands or assistance. Callers came each day, Joseph Johnson among them.

But the medical knowledge of that time was helpless against the massive infection. The doctors could only prescribe wine to counteract Mary's growing weakness, while puppies were used to draw the milk from her breasts. It was Godwin's assignment to administer the wine, an excruciating task for a man of his nature:

> . . . for me, totally ignorant of the nature of diseases and of the human frame, thus to play with a life that now seemed all that was dear to me in the universe, was too dreadful a task. I knew neither what was too much, nor what was too little. Having begun, I felt compelled, under every disadvantage, to go on. This lasted for three hours.

At this point, he gave up; either Mary was refusing the wine or unable to retain it. In despair, Godwin sent young Montagu all the way across London to Brixton, on the south side of the Thames, to fetch Anthony Carlisle from a dinner engagement and bring him to Somers Town. And for the rest of the week Carlisle stayed at the Polygon, although he too was helpless. He thought Mary would die Thursday night, but the extraordinary constitution which had brought her through so many crises stood up for two days and three nights longer.

The women who nursed her and tried to give her such comfort as cleanliness and quiet and their presence might afford bore witness to the complete absence of the petulance which had so often harassed Mary during her life:

> . . . though I have had but little experience with scenes of this sort [wrote Mary Hays to Hugh Skeys] yet I can confidently affirm that my imagination could never have pictured to me a mind so tranquil, under affliction so great. She was all kindness and attention, and cheerfully complied with everything that was recommended to her by her friends. In many instances she employed her mind with more sagacity on the subject of her illness than any of the persons about her. Her whole soul seemed to dwell with anxious fondness on her friends; and her affections, which were at all times more alive than perhaps those of any other human being, seemed to gather new disinterestedness upon this trying occasion. The attachment and regret of those who surrounded her appeared to increase every hour, and if her principles are to be judged by what I saw of her death, I should say that no principles could be more conducive to calmness and consolation.

By Friday Mary herself had some idea that she was dying and "occasionally spoke as if she expected it." An entry for that day in Godwin's terse diary says "Solemn communication." Despite the fact that Mary was by then so ill that any kind of coherent conversation must have been impossible, Godwin attempted it; he was obsessed by the responsibility for two small children which Mary's death would leave him and well aware that she had ideas about their upbringing that differed in some respects from his own. He felt obliged, therefore, to try to ascertain any wishes she might have and phrased his questions to cover the possibility that she would be ill for a protracted period. Some of the man's pedantry breaks through here, for despite her apparent inability or unwillingness to discuss the subject, he persisted:

> After having repeated this idea to her in a great variety of forms, she at length said, in a significant tone of voice, "I know what you are thinking of," but added, that she had nothing to communicate to me upon the subject.

It is the clearest indication of the degree of happiness she had found with Godwin that Mary fought hard for life and bore her sufferings with such patience. Mary Hays was not the only witness of her fortitude. The distracted Godwin remembered later that "nothing could exceed the equanimity, the patience and affectionateness of the poor sufferer."

He also took pains to record that religion was not a factor in Mary's last days: "Her religion . . . was not calculated to be the torment of a sick-bed . . . during her whole illness, not one word of a religious cast fell from her lips." Even supposing that she knew her situation and that her thoughts did turn back into religious channels, she would also have remembered that Godwin could have little sympathy with such beliefs. Why therefore should she distress him or lay herself open to argument, however kindly? The truth is that no one can know what went through Mary's mind as she drifted from weakness and sleep into coma. It is not beyond the bounds of possibility that some of her earlier trust in a loving and forgiving Father came back to her at this time and helped preserve the serenity her husband and friends marveled at. We do not know. Her last testament was of Godwin: "He is the kindest, best man in the world," she whispered to Eliza Fenwick just before she finally lost consciousness. She died on Sunday morning, September 10, just before eight.[6]

Godwin was prostrated by Mary's death. He did not even attend the funeral. It was held in St. Pancras, the church where they had been married only five months earlier, and Mary was buried in the churchyard; only a few friends were present. Meanwhile, Godwin sat in James Marshal's lodgings, writing a letter of deep gratitude to Anthony Carlisle, whose devotion had kept him with Mary from Wednesday night until Sunday morning.

Friends shared the burden of notifying others, and Mrs. Fenwick, despite her exhaustion after nursing Mary, undertook the task of writing to Everina Wollstonecraft:

> I am a stranger to you, Miss Wollstonecraft, and at present greatly enfeebled in mind and body; but when Mr. Godwin desired that I would inform you of the death of his most beloved and excellent wife, I was willing to undertake the task. . . . Mrs.

Godwin died on Sunday, September 10, about eight in the morning. I was with her at the time of her delivery, and with very little intermission until the moment of her death. . . . No woman was ever more happy in marriage than Mrs. Godwin. . . . I know of no consolations for myself, but in remembering how happy she had lately been, and how much she was admired, and almost idolized, by some of the most eminent and best of human beings. The children are both well, the infant in particular. It is the finest baby I ever saw.—Wishing you peace and prosperity. . . . Mr. Godwin requests you will make Mrs. Bishop acquainted with the particulars of this afflicting event. He tells me that Mrs. Godwin entertained a sincere and earnest affection for Mrs. Bishop.

Although in some respects Godwin's situation was grim, he was fortunate in the friends whose love and help surrounded him and the two children. Fanny was brought back to the Polygon apartment from the Reveleys' the day after her mother's burial and baby Mary only a day later, with Mrs. Fenwick caring for them. Godwin himself moved back from his lodgings in the Evesham Buildings the following week. He looked first for a capable nurse for the two children, then began very slowly to pick up his old rhythm of study and writing. Within a few weeks he had launched on the memoirs of his wife, to be followed by the publication of her remaining work. But he was haunted, not only by the children's plight, but the realization of what he had lost. Weeks later he wrote to Mrs. Cotton, whom Mary had chosen to be the new baby's nurse:

> . . . I partook of a happiness, so much the more exquisite, as I had a short time before no conception of it, and scarcely admitted the possibility of it. I saw one bright ray of light that streaked my day of life only to leave the remainder more gloomy, and, in the truest sense of the word, hopeless. . . . The poor children! I am myself totally unfitted to educate them. The scepticism which perhaps sometimes leads me right in matters of speculation, is torment to me when I would attempt to direct the infant mind. I am the most unfit person for this office; she was the best qualified in the world. What a change. The loss of the children is less remediless than mine. You can understand the difference.

He was even more outspoken in writing Thomas Holcroft on the day Mary died: "I firmly believe that there does not exist her equal in the world. I know from experience we were formed to make each other happy. I have not the least expectation that I can now ever know happiness again." That, for the author of *Political Justice*, was saying a great deal; he was very nearly right.

His biggest immediate problem was the care of the children, for which he knew himself totally unsuited, and their support, for which he did not have sufficient income (Fanny Imlay was, of course, receiving nothing from her father). The first few years after Mary's death were difficult, although the *Memoirs* sold well. After the death of Edward John Wollstonecraft in 1803, Godwin seems to have had the sole management of the Primrose Street houses whose income was ostensibly divided among the brothers and sisters. But he may have withheld a portion, only a part of it Mary's share, for the care of her daughters. There were complaints from Everina that the others were not getting their fair share and also that Godwin was putting too much of the income back into repairs.[7]

Soon after Mary's death, Godwin set about finding another wife. He was lonely and haunted by his concern for the girls. However, his search was unsuccessful until 1801, when he married Mary Jane Clairmont, a widow with a son and daughter of her own. Contemporaries disagree on her character and influence on the family, but Godwin's devotion to her was steadfast, and it can be argued that whatever her shortcomings of temperament and sensitivity, the girls were better off under her care than if Godwin had remained a widower and brought them up single-handedly. Although he was a kindly father to the girls, at least during their youth, he progressively became the Godwin disparaged by his later critics: petulant, egotistical, and wildly erratic in his financial dealings.

His later novels are inferior to *Caleb Williams*. He remained remote from the urgencies of the developing Industrial Revolution with its massive exploitation and inhuman working conditions, and never went beyond the thinking of *Political Justice* in the remaining years of his life. Edna St. Vincent Millay might have been thinking of him, no less than of Tennyson's old age, when she wrote:

Growing old is dying young . . .
When the brown and tepid tide
Closes in on every side.
Who shall say if Shelley's gold
Had withstood it to grow old?

Who shall say likewise if Godwin might have withstood mediocrity if Mary Wollstonecraft had survived to spark his imagination and courage? He died in 1836 and was buried beside her in St. Pancras Churchyard.[8]

The greatest tragedy to flow directly from Mary's death was that of her daughter Fanny. Mary's letters contained many references to the little girl's bouncing good health and high spirits. She turned for compensation from her unhappiness with Gilbert Imlay to the warm and responsive child. Fanny was certainly aware of her mother's unhappiness, and a close relationship grew up between them. Fanny could hardly have remembered her father and may not have been told until much later who he was.

A child, psychologists now tell us, is deeply influenced by the emotional climate of its earliest months, even weeks. This period is crucial, and while adverse influences at this time can be overcome, they can also be aggravated by later circumstances. Unfortunately, in Fanny's case there were such circumstances, for the mother who was her entire world died when she was only three and a half years old. To a child, death can be a form of rejection, and Mary Wollstonecraft's death in the course of bringing another life into the world must have seemed the ultimate rejection.

Fanny grew up to be very different from the sparkling baby Mary described: a quiet, patient, conscientious girl, dutifully anxious to please and serve, deeply introspective and sad. Her stepfather was kind and there is no evidence that her stepmother actually ill-treated her, although they did not get on together. But the cloud of her mother's achievements and fame (or notoriety) hung over her, and her younger sister's beauty and intelligence added to Fanny's sense of inferiority.

As she grew older in a household racked by debt and consequent insecurity, her mother's tendency to melancholia and instability of disposition reappeared in Fanny. She loved her stepsister and was fond of the young poet Shelley who became a bright addition to the family dinner table. But in July, 1814, Shelley and Mary eloped, and Fanny was left to bear the brunt of her father's bitterness. She also faced having to earn her living in a world no less hostile to a woman in her position than it had been during her mother's youth. But Fanny lacked Mary's intrepid spirit, the ability to take her life into her own hands and make something of it despite the obstacles. She was frightened and overwhelmed by her inadequacy.

There was a glimmer of hope when the Wollstonecrafts' old friend George Blood came to London for the first time in more than twenty years and suggested that Fanny come live in his home in Dublin. She had a heartwarming talk with him about her mother, of which she wrote to Mary Shelley:

> Everything he has told me of my mother has increased my love and admiration of her memory. He has given me many particulars of the days of his youth and serene life. George Blood seems to have venerated and loved her as a superior being; to have been most devotedly attached to her memory ever since her death, and to have ventured to hope that her daughters were not unworthy of her. This has in some degree roused me from my torpor. I have determined never to live to be a disgrace to such a Mother. I have found that if I will endeavor to overcome my faults I shall find beings to love and esteem me. George Blood is not a man of superior intellect, but has great warmth of feeling and great goodness of heart. The manner in which he has spoken of my mother has been a great balm to my heart, and has endeared him much to me. He had not been in London for twenty years, and our Mother then bid him adieu at the coach-door. . . .

But her spirits soon wilted again. Then there was a chance she might teach in a school conducted by Everina Wollstonecraft and Eliza Bishop in Dublin. In July she wrote to Mary:

> My Aunt Everina will be in London next week, when my future fate will be decided. I shall then give you a full and clear account of what my life will be spent in, etc. . . . you know that I have not a sou of my own. . . . I am not well; my mind always keeps my body in a fever; but never mind me. . . .

However, the aunts decided against taking Fanny into their school, presumably because of the notoriety now connected with the Godwin household, from which one daughter had eloped with Shelley and another—Claire Clairmont—was pregnant by Lord Byron; at least this was what acquaintances of the sisters in Dublin told Shelley's biographer Edward Dowden many years later. There is no further written evidence. We do not know whether Fanny had any fixed destination when she left London on October 9, 1816, in a coach bound for Bristol—whether she was going to Dublin, to visit either her aunts or George Blood, or to stay with other, shadowy relatives in Wales, as has been suggested. From Bristol she sent warning notes (reminiscent of her mother) to Shelley, who with Mary was nearby in Bath, and to Godwin: "I depart immediately to the spot from which I hope never to remove."

On receiving her letters, both men rushed to Bristol. Godwin arrived just in time to read the newspaper account which reported that the body of a young woman had been found in her room alone at the Mackworth Arms Inn in nearby Swansea. Beside her bed were an empty bottle of laudanum and a note from which the signature had been torn away and burned:

> I have long determined that the best thing I could do was to put an end to the existence of a being whose birth was unfortunate, and whose life has only been a source of pain to those persons who have hurt their health in endeavouring to promote her welfare. Perhaps to hear of my death will give you pain, but you will soon have the blessing of forgetting that such a creature ever existed as. . . .

The story went on to describe the victim's clothing, which lacked any identification except the letters *G* on her stockings and *M W* on her stays. That was enough for Godwin. He returned quietly to London without claiming the body. Neither did Shelley, although he went to Swansea to seek further information. From London Godwin wrote Mary Shelley urging them to refrain from any action that might unseal the anonymity which Fanny had so earnestly wished:

My advice and earnest prayer is that you would avoid anything that leads to publicity. Go not to Swansea; disturb not the silent dead; do nothing to destroy the obscurity she so much desired that now rests upon the event. It was, as I said, her last wish; it was the motive that led her from London to Bristol and from Bristol to Swansea. . . .[9]

In consequence Fanny was buried nameless in a pauper's grave, and the inquest verdict was simply "Found dead." The long-suppressed anger at both the father and mother who had deserted her finally turned against herself.

That father outlived his daughter by twelve years. Gilbert Imlay died on the Channel Island of Jersey on November 20, 1828, and was buried in the graveyard of St. Brelade, one of the island parishes, four days later. He may have learned of the island's commercial possibilities, especially its flourishing smuggling activities, when he was first living at Le Havre with Mary and Fanny and eventually settled there.

Before the gravestone became undecipherable or was removed, someone copied its lengthy inscription; lacking any personal tone, it suggests that Imlay died among strangers who knew only that he had lived in some proximity to the great events of his time.[10]

Mary Godwin was more fortunate than her gentle stepsister. Godwin had remained devoted to his first wife and did everything he could to make her image present to Mary as nearly a living reality as he could. She also had her mother's books, which she read and reread. Most important, she enjoyed her father's deep affection throughout her childhood, during the years when it counted most. Even when he turned against her at the time of her elopement with Shelley and became more embroiled and angry with the latter over money matters, Mary continued to love him. That relationship made all the difference to her; otherwise, like Fanny, she might have gone to pieces when tragedy struck.

As Shelley's wife she knew both love and tragedy. They were constantly harassed by debt. She lost three of the four children she bore him. Moreover, Shelley was driven by his restless genius to look for inspiration in other women. Whether his tragic drowning in the Bay of Spezia in 1822 did not preserve her from a subsequent disillusionment as painful as any her mother lived through is no idle speculation: Shelley was no Imlay, but he had already left Harriet Westbrook for Mary.

Like her mother, Mary Shelley had only her child to live for. Shelley's father declined to give her an allowance adequate for the boy's education unless Mary handed the child over to him as guardian. Mary refused. She was thrown back on her own talent to supplement the miserly sum allotted to her by Sir Timothy Shelley. That talent was considerable, as demonstrated by the extraordinary story *Frankenstein*, written when she was only nineteen years old, but she wrote nothing else to equal it. Her later novels, biographies, and travel books were second-rate or worse. Her son turned out to be a strange reversion to the earlier Shelley stock—dutiful, kind, and dull. Percy Florence Shelley married but had no children, and so we cannot know what might have emerged from the extraordinary heritage which had produced from the family of a silk weaver one of the finest woman's minds of her time, from Dissenting country parsons the leading English philosopher of the age, and from county gentry of mixed antecedents but no distinction whatever, one of the greatest English poets![11]

Mary Shelley's personality and gifts have been harshly dealt with by posterity, always in contrast with her mother. She had to struggle against some of the traits which had characterized her mother: extreme sensitivity, introspection, and melancholy. She found it difficult to make friends and was often lonely. She was acutely conscious of the contrast between herself and her adventurous mother, who, whatever her doubts and depression, always came back to renewed effort and to attack the status quo. Mary Shelley admitted to having had her fill of genius when she declared that her overriding hope for young Percy was that "he might think like other people."

When the movement for wider opportunities and greater rights for women began to stir in the 1830's, some looked to her, not unnaturally, if not for leadership, then at least for some degree of participation in "the cause." But Mary Shelley shrank from any such role, for personal as well as intellectual reasons.

She was extremely ambivalent regarding "equal rights" for
women, as her journal bears witness:

> I have so often been abused by pretended friends for my
> lukewarmness in "the good cause" . . . the cause of freedom and
> knowledge, of the rights of women, &c.—I am not a person of
> opinions. I have said elsewhere that human beings differ greatly
> in this. Some have a passion for reforming the world; others do
> not cling to particular opinions. That my parents and Shelley
> were of the former class, makes me respect it. I respect such
> when joined to real disinterestedness, toleration, and a clear
> understanding. My accusers, after such as these, appear to me
> mere drivelers. . . .
>
> I have not argumentative powers: I see things pretty clearly,
> but cannot demonstrate them. Besides, I feel the counter-argu-
> ments too strongly. I do not feel that I could say aught to sup-
> port the cause efficiently; besides that, on some topics (especially
> with regard to my own sex), I am far from making up my
> mind. . . . I can by no means go so far as my friends will
> have me. . . . If I have never written to vindicate the rights of
> women, I have ever befriended women who have been op-
> pressed. At every risk I have befriended and supported victims
> of the social system. . . . I am still reviled for being worldly![12]

Inevitably Mary Shelley's thoughts were much in the past, but
not in anger and hatred. She thought often and lovingly of the
dead: her mother, Shelley, and the children who had never grown
up. She herself died in 1851, in her fifty-fourth year.

Old Edward Wollstonecraft, the "weaver and citizen of London" who dreamed and strove to lift his family up to the level of
the gentry, would have been disappointed with his descendants.
At the death of her father-in-law Mary became Lady Shelley for
a few years, and her son a baronet, but he died without leaving an
heir. Edward Wollstonecraft's other descendants were even less
successful, with only one exception. His son, the luckless Edward
John Wollstonecraft, died at Laugharne and was buried there on
April 2, 1803. He must have been more than sixty years old, a
good record for the age and, with the punishment he inflicted on
himself, an amazing one.

We know very little more about his little-loved eldest son, Edward Bland, except that he ceased practicing law in 1807 and died sometime around 1812, leaving two children, another Edward, and a girl, Elizabeth.

His brother James, who had sat for his examinations for promotion back in 1790, after many vagaries was finally posted as lieutenant in July, 1806, but the news never reached him; he died on active service in the West Indies, in the sick bay of HMS *Shark*, probably of yellow fever. The youngest son, Charles, served in the armed forces of the United States (against Great Britain in the War of 1812) and after a checkered career died a brevet major in 1817.[13]

Everina and Elizabeth clung together and eventually opened a school in Dublin, where Eliza died some time between 1827 and 1832. Everina then moved to London, and lived until she was nearly eighty years old, dying in 1843.[14]

But the Wollstonecraft family did produce one other striking figure before it flickered out in the next generation, one which resembled in singular ways both Mary Wollstonecraft and the old man Edward himself. Strangely the wheel comes full circle in the fourth Edward Wollstonecraft, Edward Bland's son. He was nearly thirty years old when, on a trip to Cádiz in June, 1812, he met a Scottish ship's doctor named Alexander Berry. Berry asked the "tall, formal-looking young man dressed in black" whether he was related to Mary Wollstonecraft, only to be told "in a somewhat slighting manner" that she was an aunt.

The meeting grew into friendship. When Berry gave up doctoring and went into commerce, Wollstonecraft became his agent. The two men lived with Edward's sister Elizabeth in London. In 1819, by then full partners, they emigrated to Australia.

The rest of their story is Australian history. They maintained an import business in Sydney and began accumulating landholdings; Wollstonecraft became a magistrate, a prominent banker, and chairman of the Chamber of Commerce. But his real talent emerged when in 1821 the two men were granted 10,000 acres of marsh and woodland on the Shoalhaven River, south of Sydney, and the custody of 100 convicts who were to be used along with free labor to develop what became the large Coolangatta holdings, draining the swamps, cutting the valuable timber which was an important export staple and later developing tobacco as a highly profitable crop. The two men continued to enlarge their holdings—Coolangatta eventually included 60,000 acres—with Wollstonecraft the prime mover in excluding or driving out other property holders. Their goal was to build a great patriarchal domain similar to the old English country estates—the reincarnated dream of old Edward Wollstonecraft who had longed for the status and gentility conferred by landed property for his descendants.

His great-grandson struggled against ill health and a saturnine disposition (reminiscent of his father's), and relations between the partners were often strained, despite Berry's marriage in 1827 to Elizabeth Wollstonecraft. Edward never married and died in 1832 aged forty-nine, his reputation secure as one of the early builders of the great commonwealth "down under"; a suburb of Sydney bears his name. His sister Elizabeth Berry died in 1845, childless, and only two years after her aunt Everina, to whom she had stretched out the hand of family affection half a world away.[15]

Only a few weeks after Mary's death, Godwin began work on the *Memoirs*, which have been the starting point for all her later biographers. He received some measure of assistance from Everina, none at all from Eliza; the breach between the sisters was too great to be healed even by death. The *Memoirs* were published by Johnson early in 1798; that same year he issued Mary's *Posthumous Works*, of which Volume III and part of IV were devoted to her letters, only slightly deleted, to Gilbert Imlay. Whether Godwin put this tragic record of Mary's anguish into print because he really believed it a contribution to literature or because he desperately needed the money to support her children is an open question; certainly one can legitimately wish that he had waited somewhat longer after her death to publish them.

It was a full hundred years before *A Vindication of the Rights of Woman* was reissued. The Victorian image of Mary Wollstonecraft grew up from the *Memoirs* and the *Letters to Imlay*—a passionate and tragic figure outside the pale of conventional society, more significant for her transgressions and suffering than for any contribution she made to social progress, and the reason why she is often confused in people's minds with her daughter Mary Shelley or not remembered at all while the wife of Shelley is.

Nevertheless, the existence of *A Vindication of the Rights of Woman* worked a slow seminal effect. It was pored over by women on two continents whose world was beginning to assume a very different shape from that in which Mary wrote her book, a world in which women went into factories and coal mines, asked legal protection for themselves and their children, as well as the right to vote, in which the first women's schools worthy of the name began to produce women scholars to challenge the sacred precincts of university education in London and Edinburgh, Cambridge and Oxford, and break down the barriers which excluded them from the professions.

The *Vindication* nourished Frances Wright and Margaret Fuller, Lucretia Mott and Elizabeth Cady Stanton and Millicent Fawcett. The women's rights movement, which took more than a hundred years to win its major objectives in England and the United States and even longer elsewhere, was often unaware of the existence of the woman who had originally sparked it, although her first biographer, Elizabeth Robins Pennell, did her best in 1884 to place her at its source. Mrs. Fawcett also wrote the introduction for a new edition of the *Vindication* in 1890.[16]

In 1851, when the encroaching railroad threatened the graves in St. Pancras Churchyard, Percy Florence Shelley moved the remains of Mary and Godwin to lie near his mother, who had been buried that same year in Bournemouth. It was also the year in which the first serious discussion of broader rights and opportunities for women since the *Vindication* appeared in England in the *Westminster Review* in response to two woman's rights conventions already held in the United States, in 1848 and 1850. The article was by Harriet Taylor Mill, wife of John Stuart Mill. Seven years later Mill published a book called *The Subjection of Women*, which became a dynamic force in the mounting struggle.

Mill claimed to have been influenced not by Mary Wollstonecraft, but by his wife. The Mills based their argument entirely on rational, legal, historical, and practical considerations, and these were to characterize the movement for its duration. Mary Wollstonecraft had justified—and encumbered, in the opinion of the later reformers—the demand that women must be trained to use their minds to achieve their highest possible development by arguing that, because woman was a creature—the work of a divine creator—her right to self-development was also a religious and moral responsibility to herself and to society, that rights *and* responsibilities (to herself, her community, and to her husband and children as well) were indissolubly linked.

Nor is it a point of view that today commends itself to many to whom freedom is an absolute, without limits or qualifications. "Teach them to think" had been Mary Wollstonecraft's cry for women; but she also believed that the capacity of rational thought was a precious gift, the "heaven-lighted lamp in man" for whose wise use women, and men as well, were answerable. They had duties to fulfill, and the whole import of freedom—from false restraints, from discriminatory restrictions, from the enforced lassitude of empty lives—was to prepare women for the duty of being human, of being women—as mothers and wives as well as citizens. Mary Wollstonecraft's own life, except for the few occasions when she strayed to the verge of aberration, exemplified that belief. It is surely not irrelevant today.

Appendix A

Edward Wollstonecraft's Property and Will

Edward Wollstonecraft leased three plots of land from the Goldsmiths' Company, two of them for a term of sixty-one years and one for sixty-two. The agreement with the Goldsmiths' specified that the buildings he would erect were to consist of three, four, and eight "brick messuages or tenements" respectively, each with cellars, three floors of rooms, and top-floor garrets. The rentals he paid the Goldsmiths' were low—a total of £16.5.5 per annum clear of taxes or other charges—but he had to maintain and repair the properties and collect the rentals from some thirty tenants.

He also had a sixty-year lease on another plot of land on Brown's Lane (now Hanbury Street) and there are records (in the Middlesex County Record Office, London) of a speculative loan based on a real estate mortgage, to "the widow Rutson."

Wollstonecraft had at least three children who lived into adulthood: Edward John; another son, Charles, who had died by 1765, but who was survived by his wife, Mary; and a daughter, Elizabeth, married to Isaac Rutson, who had three children. Innumerable other Wollenstonecrafts are listed in the records of the London Genealogical Society and parish records (the spelling of the name varies widely), but strangely, none of them is ever mentioned in the voluminous family correspondence.

The long and minutely detailed Wollstonecraft will safeguarded the bequest to his daughter, Elizabeth, of 1,700 pounds of Bank of England stock by establishing a trust, the income to be paid to her. If she predeceased her husband, Isaac Rutson, his executors were directed to sell the stock and divide the money equally between the three grandchildren. This point is important, because Wollstonecraft not only failed to take any similar or equivalent steps to safeguard the share of his other grandson, Edward Bland Wollstonecraft, but made no provision for the latter's sisters, of whom at least two and possibly three were living by the time the will was made.

What it all added up to was the bequest of the Primrose Street leaseholds and an additional mortgage or collectible debt of 3,000 pounds to Edward John Wollstonecraft; the bank stock to Elizabeth Rutson; and the Brown's Lane leasehold, and a share (value unspecified) of an East India Merchant ship, the *Cruttenden*, to young Edward Bland Wollstonecraft, then less than ten years old.

The *Cruttenden* was leased to the East India Company from 1762 to 1772, during which time she made four voyages to China, Manila, and Bencoolen (on the west coast of Sumatra). On the first two of these voyages her first officer was one Edward Bland Wollstonecraft, presumably a cousin of Mary's family, for whom Mary's brother was named. (Information from H.M. India Records Office, *List of Marine Records* [pp. 41, 44, 46, 48], and Hardy's *Register of Ships Employed by the East India Co.* [London, 4th ed., rev., 1835], pp. 9, 23, 35, 48.)

We can hazard one highly problematical but interesting speculation with regard to this relative of the Wollstonecrafts, based on our knowledge of Mary Wollstonecraft's novels as often heavily autobiographical. In *Maria, or The Wrongs of Woman,* her last and unfinished work, the heroine has an uncle who went to India, made his fortune (as the saying went), and came home to be a source of comfort to his young niece, who was persecuted by a tyrannical father and a selfish older brother! Although there is no known documentary evidence to associate this Edward Bland Wollstonecraft with the annuities provided for Edward John's daughters, so much new evidence has turned up to enrich our knowledge of Mary and her family that we may yet find such proof; it is unquestionable that the annuities *did* exist and must somehow be accounted for.

Appendix B

Mary Wollstonecraft and Joshua Waterhouse

Miss Nitchie drew her information from articles in the Huntington *Gazette* appearing July 7, 13, 21, 28, August 4, 11 and September 8, 1827, in the London *Morning Herald* of July 21, 1827, and two other contemporary accounts, "A Narrative of the Murder of the Late Rev. J. Waterhouse, etc." (Lovell, 1827) and "A Sermon Delivered at the Dissenting Chapel, Huntington, on Sunday September 8, 1827," by W. Wright (Huntington, n.d., pub. and sold by A. P. Wood). It is noteworthy that no mention of Mary's name appears in the otherwise voluminous and detailed account of the murder and the testimony in the Huntington paper during the trial and down to the execution of the confessed murderer. Mention did occur in the London paper, since Mary's name was newsworthy in the capital. It seems possible, therefore, that the finding of one or two letters possibly quite innocent in nature from her might have been blown up into mention of "love letters" from a woman whose reputation at that particular time rested less on her writings than on her unconventional relationships with Gilbert Imlay and William Godwin.

Professor Wardle has also suggested that numerous heavily defaced passages in Mary's letters during this period (to the point where they are illegible), some of which occurred in letters mentioning the mysterious "Neptune," were crossed out with the idea of sparing her further unpleasant notoriety and were therefore passages mentioning Waterhouse. The trouble with this theory is that most of these passages occur running into or after references to Mary's relations with members of her family, especially her sister Eliza, of whom she was often critical. The letters probably came into Mary Shelley's hands from Everina, the last surviving sister, who may have wanted to obliterate traces of unpleasantness between members of the family. The defaced passages occur in letters dated August 13, 1785, May 1 and June 25, 1786, January 17, 1788, and September 16, 1789.

Appendix C

"Mrs. Mason" and Mary Shelley

Mary's radical influence on Margaret King must have come through her books. As she grew older, Margaret became deeply sympathetic to the revolutionary cause, in France and in Ireland. She must have known of her former governess' increasing fame and been powerfully affected by her writings on the rights of women, the French Revolution, and the upbringing of children. Margaret's later life belongs in a biography of Mary Wollstonecraft because it was so strangely linked to Mary's family and ideas.

A month before her twentieth birthday, on September 12, 1791, Margaret was married to young Stephen Moore, the Earl of Mount Cashell, a nearby landowner of English descent. Once again, as in the case of her parents, it was a marriage of convenience, and once again, it proved an unhappy one (the Kingsboroughs, after twenty-five tempestuous years, separated in 1794). Mount Cashell was amiable and good-tempered, but almost completely uneducated and very conservative. He and his wife developed completely opposing sympathies and interests. She not only was a radical, but preferred simple living and insisted on the education of their children, which Lord Mount Cashell considered a waste of money.

In 1804, while they were on a trip to the Continent, she became intimate with an Irishman named George Tighe. While her husband returned to Ireland with their children, she remained with Tighe and lived with him in Italy, in a *de facto* marriage, until her death in 1835.

She took the name of Mrs. Mason, the companion of the two girls modeled on the Kingsborough children in Mary's book called *Original Stories from Real Life* (see Chapter VII). She may have remembered that the girl modeled on herself in Mary's book said: "I wish to be a woman and to be like Mrs. Mason."

As Mrs. Mason she paid an old debt to Mary by befriending the Shelleys in Pisa—the poet had married, as his second wife, the nineteen-year-old daughter of Mary Wollstonecraft and William Godwin, at whose birth Mary died (see Chapter XV). Mrs. Mason became a friend in need and a stalwart prop to the tempestuous group that gathered around the poet in Pisa, where she also lived, and after Shelley drowned, she did her utmost for his bereft young widow and infant son.

Having reared ten children (two of them daughters of George Tighe), she distilled her experience into a book called *Advice to Young Mothers on the Physical Education of Children, by a Grandmother* (London, 1827). Mary Wollstonecraft would have applauded its advanced ideas on diet and feeding, exercise and discipline, which reached a much wider public than Mary's own writings on the subject. Her life story has been told in an excellent biography by Edward McAleer, *The Sensitive Plant: A Life of Lady Mount Cashell* (Chapel Hill, N.C., 1958), although I question his assignment of the authorship of the *Stories of Old Daniel* (London, 1833) and its sequel to "Mrs. Mason."

Appendix D

Mary Wollstonecraft's *Analytical* Reviews

Professor Wardle has allocated to Mary all reviews signed either M. or W. and any series of unsigned reviews followed by one signed by M. or W. (Ralph M. Wardle, "Mary Wollstonecraft, Analytical Reviewer," *PMLA*, Vol. 62, 1947, pp. 1000–9.) He has also argued that she used the initial T. as a signature, since the style, subject matter, and certain references of these reviews lend themselves to such an identification. On this basis he believes Mary to have written a total of 412 reviews for the *Analytical* (many of them admittedly brief notices of one or two sentences). This figure has been challenged by Derek Roper, who arrives at a total of 204 "signed" reviews, the remaining 208 being of "varying degrees of authenticity (*Notes and Queries*, January, 1958, pp. 37–38: "Mary Wollstonecraft's Reviews").

Even this figure seems doubtful, since no other contributor signed his own initials. Knowles says that Fuseli signed his Z. Z. Professor Eudo Mason believes that Fuseli signed some reviews R. R. and Y. Y. and used other sets of double initials on various occasions. (*The Mind of Henry Fuseli*: Appendix II: "Fuseli's Contributions to the *Analytical Review*," pp. 356–59). It also seems more likely that he rather than Mary reviewed William Gilpin's *Observations*

Relative Chiefly to Picturesque Beauty (January, 1790) which dealt with esthetics, even if it was signed W., although Professor Wardle sees this as evidence of Mary's increasing scope as a reviewer. But did she really contribute the 17-page lead review of Burney's *General History of Music*, signed M. in the following February issue, and if she did, is this evidence of her growing competence or of the *Analytical*'s lack of qualified contributors in some areas? We know that Christie, Anderson, Geddes, Hewlett, and others wrote for the magazine, but there is no assurance as to their signatures, although we can speculate, subject matter permitting, that K. was Christie and AN. was George Anderson.

Appendix E

Mary Wollstonecraft's Letters to William Roscoe ·

These letters from Mary Wollstonecraft to William Roscoe are here published for the first time, courtesy of the Liverpool City Libraries.

Be it known unto you, my dear Sir, that I am actually sitting for the picture and that it will be shortly *forthcoming*. I do not imagine that it will be a very striking likeness; but, if you do not find me in it, I will send you a more faithful sketch—a book that I am now writing, in which *I* myself, for I cannot *yet* attain to Homer's dignity, shall certainly appear, head and heart—but this between ourselves—pray respect a woman's secret!

Milton is, at present, the word. I did not answer your last letter respecting it, because I waited till the plan was shaped into proposals—and now you have received the proposal let me hear what you think of it.

I am now going to ask a favour of you—when I ask it I take it for granted that you would be glad to serve me, so you need not hesitate to say no—if you cannot say yes. But first let me tell you that the annuitant has the houses entirely in his possession, and I am glad of it—for I now know what I am about—my two sisters are settled very comfortably, and one of my brothers, who threw some money away to dance after preferment, when the fleet last paraded at Portsmouth, has, at last, condescended to take the command of a trading vessel; but, observe, it is a voyage of speculation. My present care, or rather blister, is a younger brother (he is just of age) and loitering away his time in Wales. He was bound to my eldest brother; but my father took him away, when the dispute about the property commenced—since which he has been unsettled. He was with me some time. He is a thoughtless youth with common abilities, a tolerable person, some warmth of heart, and a turn for humour. If he remains much longer idle, he will, of course, grow vicious. His boiling blood could only be cooled by employment and I cannot procure him a situation. I have been repeatedly disappointed in my endeavour to get him an appointment in the East India service—and I write to you as a forlorn hope, because I do not know what step to take. I should be glad to place him in any situation, were it but a temporary one, to employ him till something better occurred. Could you procure him any station in a counting-house, at Liverpool? I should wish him not to be left too much to himself.

yours sincerely
M. WOLLSTONECRAFT

Octr. 6th. 91
I have lately removed—but you direct to me at Mr Johnson's

DEAR SIR,

I should have written to you sooner, not only to have thanked you for so speedily answering my letter, but for your affectionate *remembrances* in Mr Fuseli's, had I not been very much engrossed by writing and printing my Vindication of the Rights of Woman, and by a standing-dish of family cares. I shall give the last sheet to the printer to day; and, I am dissatisfied with myself for not having done justice to the subject.—Do not suspect me of false modesty—I mean to say, that had I allowed myself more time I could have written a better book, in every sense of the word, the length of the Errata vexes me—as you are gentleman author you can make some allowance for a little ill humour at seeing such a blur, which would only make those who have never dabbled in ink, smile. I intend to finish the next volume before I begin to print, for it is not pleasant to have the Devil coming for the conclusion of a sheet before it is written. Well, I have said enough of this said book—more than is civil, and not sufficient to carry off the fumes of ill humour which make me quarrel with myself.—

And now, not to affront your authorship, I must tell you that I like some lines in your Revolution song, and some stanzas in your ballad.—Our friend Fuseli is going on with more than usual spirit—like Milton he seems quite at home in hell—his Devil will be the hero of the poetic series; for, *entre nous*, I rather doubt whether he will produce an Eve to please me in any of the situations, which he has selected, unless it be after the fall. When I am in a better humour I will give you an account of those already sketched—but had you not better come and see them?—We have all an individual way of feeling grandeur and sublimity.

My brother, the brother, whom I mention to you, is now in Town, and I have been repeatedly disappointed in my attempts to procure him an appointment in the service of the East India Company; or, indeed, to procure him any situation—This is a serious vexation. I did not take advantage of what you offered because I doubted about his professional knowledge, but I was not the less obliged to you for endeavouring to serve me—It is now time to bid you adieu—for after suffering a transient gust of sourish gall to flow over I must not harp on a string that is constantly out of tune.

yours sincerely
MARY WOLLSTONECRAFT

Store Street Janʸ 3, 92

DEAR SIR,

I am not a very punctual answerer of letters; but I write now to inform you of a circumstance that has afford'd me great satisfaction, and to request some professional advice. I have, at last, settled my brother, or rather put him in the way to be settled just as I could wish. He is to accompany a Mr and Mrs Barlow to America, who will endeavour to place him in a farm to obtain a little experience till he can purchase some land for himself. Mr B has lately published a sensible political pamphlet, which you will like, it has prejudised [sic] me in his favour, and Mr Paine assures me that he could not be recommended to a more worthy man, and that there is not a doubt of his earning a respectable livelihood if will he asert [sic] himself—I want now to ask you in what manner he must empower me to take possession of and sell for him the little property which he will be entitled to when my father dies, whose state of health is very precarious, and how, for I once was very much [illegible] provoked by the unjust conduct of a person with respect to a *lapsed legacy*, he could leave it to his sisters, should he chance to die before he received intelligence of my father's death—you will readily perceive that my dear-bought experience makes me anxious to guard against contingencies lest by some quirk of the law my eldest brother, *the Attorney*, should snap at the last morsel.

Well, now to talk of something else—schemes for printing works *embellished* with prints have lately been started with *catch-penny* eagerness, and such an inundation, to borrow a fashional [*sic*] cant word, has damped my hopes with respect to the success of our friend's. I love the man and admire the artist, and am sorry to find that subscribers come in very slowly. This I mention to you in confidence and make light of it to him, for on this work the comfort of his life, in every sense of the word, seems to depend. Mr Johnson the world contains not a more friendly heart, [illegible] many employments and could not condescend to use the mean arts, had he leisure, which the promoters of other plans, of a similar nature, avail themselves of, in this puffing age, and I still think, I speak without reserve, that it would have been carried on with more spirit had there been a partner or two with money to speculate with. The first number most probably will have considerable effect towards filling the subscription; but till then I am sorry Mr F. has not more encouragement, for I should be vext to see his fancy spent in brooding over disappointments. Remember me kindly to Mrs. Roscoe and her fine brood, and believe me yours sincerely

Mary Wollstonecraft

Store Street, Bedford Square. Feby 92.
Direct to me immediately. Mr J. tells me that you make the Liverpool women read my book.—

Dear Sir,

Mr Johnson tells me that he has a frank for you, and that I *ought* to write to you—I am not in a mood to chat on paper—I had rather not talk *all* myself—yet, it is a shame to be so indolently fond of my own *reveries* when I have to thank you for the kindnesses that were not lost on me.—I felt them—and that I may still continue to remember them *I will not* thank you—Debts of this kind rest lightly on my pillow, and sweeten instead of disturbing my slumbers—I love to sip the milk of human kindness, when I can, to make the bitter pill of life go down.

Unfinished; no date

DEAR SIR,

I have put off writing to you till the noon of the day of my brother's departure and I find my spirits so low that I shall not attempt to lengthen out this introductory letter; or rather I have desired my brother to call upon you as a proof of my respect, for his stay will be so short he cannot avail himself of the civilities which I know you would shew him. One word more, pray do not wait for an *excuse* when your spirit (or your heart) let Mrs Roscoe see this parenthesis, moves you to write to me, for I shall always be glad to hear from you, though I cannot promise to be, what I have never yet been, a punctual correspondent.

yours sincerely
MARY WOLLSTONECRAFT

London Octr 2, 92.——

London Novr 12th 92

MY DEAR SIR,

For your most friendly behaviour to my brother receive my sincere thanks, it is pleasant not to find oneself mistaken in a character—or rather, I am glad to hear that absence has not cooled the little kindness you felt for me when we met, for the first and last time, in Town.—When do you think of again visiting the metropolis? Not very soon, I hope, for I intend no longer to struggle with a rational desire, so have determined to set out for Paris in the course of a fortnight or three weeks; and I shall not now halt at Dover, I promise you; for as I go alone neck or nothing is the word. During my stay I shall not forget my friends; but I will tell you so when I am really there. Mean time let me beg you not to mix with the shallow herd who throw an odium on immutable principles, because some of the mere instrument [*sic*] of the revolution were too sharp.—Children of any growth will do mischief when they meddle with edged tools. It is to be lamented that *as yet* the billows of public opinion are only to be moved forward by the strong wind, the squally gusts of passion; but if nations be educated by their governments it is vain to expect much reason till the system of education become more reasonable. You are employed, however, to exhibit the glossy side of aristocracy, yet I

hope you have not quite forgot the *order* of the day, or I shall think
your praises of Liberty mere headwork; and laugh as I once saucily
did when even in rhyme you talked of *declining* a transport—but
for the *sake* of the jingle, I know the same breath must blow hot
and cold, so *beauty* must forgive the affront.

Our friend Johnson is well—I am told the world, to talk big,
married m[e] to him whilst we were away; but you [illegible] that I
am still a Spinster on the wing. At Paris, indeed, I might take a husband for the time being, and get divorced when my truant heart
longed again to nestle with its old friends; but this speculation has
not yet entered into my plan. Remember me to Mrs Roscoe and believe me yours sincerely

MARY WOLLSTONECRAFT

Appendix F

Mary Wollstonecraft's Family

One reason James Wollstonecraft's commission was not awarded after his examination may have been the rather well-known radical views of his sister Mary. James was forced back into commercial shipping and then settled in Paris (where he was living at the time Mary died), understandably embittered by the treatment he had received from the Admiralty and attracted by republicanism. But in 1798 he was arrested and imprisoned as an English spy. From prison he wrote to Talleyrand and other officials, hotly protesting his innocence and his devotion to the principles of his newly adopted country (Archives, Ministère des Affaires Étrangères, Quai d'Orsay: Correspondence Politique, vol. 92, No. 280). When he appealed to the husband of Helen Maria Williams, John Stone, the latter interceded with Talleyrand but was only partially successful: James escaped the usual fate of spies but was deported and returned to England. (Bureau des Interrogatoires, Relève Général des Affaires Instruites et en cours d'Instruction, F7, 671, Archives Nationales). He reentered His Majesty's Service and won considerable prize money but was unable to collect it and was compelled on at least one occasion to appeal to Godwin for a loan (James Wollstonecraft to Godwin, 1805, Abinger).

At the time of Mary's death, the youngest Wollstonecraft, Charles, was with Archibald Rowan in Delaware, where the latter had launched an attempt at calico printing which ended in failure. Previously Charles had already tried farming and land speculation. In 1800 he entered the service of the United States Army, serving first as paymaster and then in the Ordnance. His career was checkered—he was repeatedly under arrest and reprimanded for "conduct unbecoming an officer, disobedience of orders, and the use of bad language." Nevertheless, he was successively promoted to lieutenant, captain, and brevet major.

One description of Charles' affairs at the time of his death bears out Mary Wollstonecraft's worst fears for him: "When living, [he] appeared to be a man of great wealth, which was in good degree lost by his death; for when a speculator of many concerns dies suddenly, the thousand things which drop from his hands are with difficulty gathered up by anyone, however sagacious. . . ." (Female Biography, comp. S. L. Knapp [Boston, 1833].) Charles' matrimonial affairs appear to have been similarly confused. He was already married when Archibald Rowan knew him, but Knapp mentions a second wife, another Mary Wollstonecraft, with a literary and feminist bent (ibid). However, the widow who applied for the land bounty owing to Charles or his heirs under the Congressional Act of 1850 was one Sarah Wollstonecraft, who married him on August 23, 1804 (National Archives)!

An Educational Inquiry Commission reported in 1826 that Mrs. Bishop taught twelve girls and Miss Wollstonecraft twenty boy pupils and that Mrs. Bishop's establishment was a day school. When Edward Dowden was in Dublin in the 1880's in search of material for his life of Shelley, he talked to people who had known the Wollstonecraft sisters. Their description of Everina tallies with Mary and Godwin's impression of her—disagreeable, ill-tempered, and overbearing—according to others, "hard," "tall and formidable." What Dowden heard of Eliza is also hard to reconcile with the picture we have of her from her earlier letters; as Everina grew harsher, Eliza mellowed: "winning, gentle manners . . . a perfectly ladylike and refined person," who made peace by passing around the sweets when an argument in the sisters' parlor became too acrimonious. She must have won the hearts of at least some of her pupils; one of them who went to India supplied her for some years with an annuity of 60 pounds.

Sometime after Eliza's death, Everina wrote a desperate letter appealing for help to Lady Morgan, a quixotic literary figure with many influential connections and a philanthropic reputation; Everina begged Lady Morgan to appeal on her behalf for a pension of some sort (the letter is in the Bodleian Library). There is no indication that she received any assistance from this source. She came to London to the utter consternation of Mary Shelley. Mary had kept in touch with her aunt, although she neither liked her nor had the means to assist her, and she foresaw that Everina, alone in England without other relations or friends, could become a most unwelcome responsibility.

> Did I tell you of my misfortune [she wrote to a friend] in my Aunt, my Mother's surviving sister, coming over (from Ireland) and settling at Pentonville—Everina was never a favorite with anyone—and now she is the most intolerable of God's creatures . . . she is so disagreeable to me, that I know of no punishment so great as spending an hour in her company . . . others might like her—for she can be amusing and means well. . . . [*Letters*, Vol. II, p. 86.]

Yet she did her best, with occasional visits and notes and theater tickets when she could procure them from her friends. Surprisingly, there were people who liked Everina, among them her landlady, who did much to soften the bitterness of her closing years of infirmity. Another was her niece, Edward's daughter, who had gone out to Australia, who wrote warm and affectionate letters deploring Everina's inability to join her in Sydney, where she would have been happy to care for her, and who also occasionally sent her money. Everina lived to be nearly eighty, dying in 1843.

Bibliographical Note

BIOGRAPHERS OF Mary Wollstonecraft necessarily use as their point of departure William Godwin's *Memoirs of Mary Wollstonecraft*, written by her husband the year she died. Experience has shown that his labor of love cannot be used uncritically; for one thing, he did not have access to any of the family letters. C. Kegan Paul's *William Godwin: His Friends and Contemporaries* and Elizabeth Robins Pennell's *Mary Wollstonecraft*, written in 1876 and 1884 respectively, lack the modern scholarly approach, but both had the inestimable advantage of access to these letters, then in the possession of the Shelley family. They now belong to a collateral descendant, Lord Abinger.

A spate of Wollstonecraft biographies which coincided with the upsurge of the woman suffrage movement are of little interest today. Modern critical biography began with W. C. Durant's edition of the *Memoirs* in 1927, to which he appended a lengthy Commentary and in which he published some additional letters from Mary Wollstonecraft to her contemporaries. Durant, however, did not have access to the family papers.

Ralph M. Wardle published the first full-length critical and scholarly biography of Mary in 1951, using the family papers. A great deal of fresh light has been added to Mary's life by the publication of the first four volumes of *Shelley and His Circle*, based on the manuscript holdings of the Pforzheimer Library. Volumes I and II contain valuable commentaries by Miss Eleanor L. Nicholes and Professor Kenneth N. Cameron. The Commentary in Volume IV is by the author. *One Woman's "Situation": A Study of Mary Wollstonecraft* (Urbana, Ill., 1970), by Margaret George, while adding no new facts to Mary's life, interprets them from the viewpoint of today's feminists. *Mary Wollstonecraft: Her Life and Times*, by Edna Nixon (London, 1971), contributes no new facts and perpetuates many errors dating back to an earlier period of scholarship.

I have leaned on my predecessors while differing from them somewhat in interpretation and, I hope, adding new facts and new insights of my own. All quoted letters, unless otherwise identified, are in the Abinger Mss. collection, in the possession of Lord Abinger, Clees Hall, Bures, Suffolk, which includes the Shelley papers available to Kegan Paul and Mrs. Pennell, as well as more recent acquisitions. These have been made available to me through the courtesy of the Pforzheimer Library which has a complete microfilm of the Abinger collection.

Reference Notes

Chapter I: As the Twig Is Bent

1. According to the parish registers and poor-rate books of St. Botolph's (without) Bishopsgate, the Wollstonecrafts lived on Primrose Street from 1756 to 1761. The records are in the London Guildhall Library. On the Primrose Street houses, see Appendix A.

2. Apprentice records, Company of Weavers, Guildhall.

3. Ballyshannon has claimed Elizabeth Dickson: Hugh Allingham, *Ballyshannon, Its History and Antiquities* (1879), p. 83. A brother, Edward Stirling Dickson, rose to commander of a ship in the Royal Navy: John Marshall, R.N., *Naval Biography* (London, 1824), Vol. II, Part 1, pp. 296–98.

4. The Essex County Record Office in Chelmsford searched its records and personal names index but found no trace of the Wollstonecraft family's moves. According to Elizabeth Ogborne, *History of Essex . . .* (London, 1814), p. 161, Mary thought she lived her earliest years near Epping and in Epping Forest. See also William Godwin, *Memoirs of Mary Wollstonecraft* (hereinafter referred to as *Memoirs*), p. 9.

5. St. Margaret's parish poor-rate records, at the Town Hall, Barking.

6. See G. E. Mingay, *The Agricultural Revolution, 1750–1880* (London, 1966), pp. 58–59 and *passim*.

7. The original will, which has not been used by previous biographers, is in the Public Record Office, Registry of Wills, Somerset House, Lon-

don. For further details see Appendix A. William Godwin in the *Memoirs*, says Mary's father inherited "about £10,000."

8. "It has always been understood in Beverley that Edward John Wolstonecraft [*sic*] was farming in Walkington" (Beverley *Guardian*, April 23, 1887, which also refers to him as "a farmer living at Walkington"). This quotation came to me in a letter from Mr. C. A. Arden, a descendant of Mary Wollstonecraft's friend Jane Arden (see below). Mr. N. Higson, East Riding archivist in Beverley, found for me the Highway and Poor Rate Register which locates the Wollstonecrafts in Beverley. Charles' birth is recorded in the register of St. John of Beverley.

9. Most of the information about Mary's years in Beverley and all quotations from Mary's letters to Jane Arden are taken from the Pforzheimer Library's monumental study, *Shelley and His Circle* (Cambridge, Mass., 1961, 1970, hereinafter referred to as *SC*), Vols. I–IV, Kenneth N. Cameron, ed., who also wrote the commentary on the letters to Jane Arden, Vol. II, pp. 933–84. All but one of the fifteen letters were previously unpublished.

10. Arthur Young, *A Six Months Tour Through the North of England* (London, 1771), Vol. I, p. 148 n. On Beverley, see George Poulson, *Beverlac, or The Antiquities of Beverley* (London, 1829), and George Oliver, *History and Antiquities of the Town of Beverley* (Beverley, 1829). Local authorities prefer Poulson.

11. *Memoirs*, p. 11.

12. On Jane Arden, see Everilda

Ann Gardner, *Recollections of a Beloved Mother* (London, 1842).

13. See Appendix A.

14. *Memoirs*, p. 19.

15. Dylan Thomas, *Collected Poems* (New York, 1957), p. 17. See also Mary Curtis, *The Antiquities of Laugharne* (London, 1880).

16. *Memoirs*, p. 25. See also Mary's letter to Jane Arden, *SC*, Vol. II, p. 966. The reference to Everina's annuity occurs in Mary's letter to Henry Gabell, Sept. 13, 1787 (*SC*, Vol. IV, p. 860). See also Appendix A.

17. Marriage register, St. Botolph's, Aldgate, Guildhall.

18. London Law Society, *Law List 1779–1807*.

Chapter II: *Forge of Adversity*

1. *Diary and Letters of Madame D'Arblay* (London, 1891), Vol. I, pp. 221–22.

2. *D'Arblay*, Vol. I, p. 486.

3. Jane Austen, *Persuasion*, Ch. 19.

4. *SC*, Vol. II. As in the case of the Beverley period, these letters give a firsthand picture of Mary's life with Mrs. Dawson which had previously been lacking.

5. Abinger microfilm (see Bibliographical Note), hereinafter referred to as Abinger.

6. *Mary, A Fiction* (London, 1788), p. 16.

7. *Maria, or The Wrongs of Woman* (*Posthumous Works*, London, 1798), Vol. I, p. 174.

8. Wardle, p. 9 (see also p. 16: ". . . she died as abjectly as she had lived"); *Memoirs*, p. 9.

9. See G. E. C. Catlin's Introduction to the Everyman edition of *A*

Vindication of the Rights of Woman (p. xii): "[Mary] found herself the support of shiftless brothers and two sisters . . . both as resourceless as they were orthodox." Only Elizabeth Robins Pennell among the biographers seems to have glimpsed the essence of Elizabeth Dickson Wollstonecraft's personality (p. 22).

10. The family's stay in Enfield, the change of domicile while there, and Edward John's eventual departure are recorded in the poor-rate books for the Town Quarter of Enfield (Vols. 71, 74, 78) in the Middlesex County Record Office, London. His wife's burial in April, 1782 (two years later than Godwin's date in the *Memoirs*), is noted in St. Andrew's (Enfield) parish burial register (Elizabeth Woolstingcroft!). This drastically reduces the period during which Mary stayed with the Bloods and renders even more unlikely the theory developed by Professor Harper that Fanny and Mary spent three months in Walworth under the roof of Thomas Taylor, "the Platonist" (see *Notes and Queries*, December 1962, pp. 461–63).

11. *Memoirs*, 23. Godwin also stated that the decision was made for Edward John to "live upon the interest of his fortune." This is a strange error, for at the time he wrote the *Memoirs* he certainly was aware of the real source of Mr. Wollstonecraft's income (the Primrose Street rentals) and his children's, especially Mary's, share in managing it; Johnson's memo to Godwin (see Abinger) says so clearly.

12. *Maria or The Wrongs of Woman*, Vol. I, p. 173; Vol. II, p. 15.

13. Eliza Bishop to Everina Woll-stonecraft, May, 1791; Mr. Wollstonecraft's death and burial on April 2, 1803, are recorded in the Laugharne parish burial register (letter from the Reverend Victor H. Jones, April 16, 1966, to the author).

14. ADM. 36/9606, Public Record Office, Chancery Lane, London.

15. Fanny Blood to Everina, February, 1783.

16. The documents concerning the marriage, docketed in the proceedings of the Commissary Court of St. Katherine's (in Chancery) in the London Guildhall, were discovered by Miss E. L. Nicholes. Mr. Wollstonecraft's consent was sworn at Carmarthen, the county seat near Laugharne, October 4, 1782.

17. The series of letters begin in October and run through January, 1783. Clearly Eliza's relationship with Bishop antedates her mother's death, which we now know took place two years later than was previously believed.

18. Eliza Bishop, from Pembroke, Wales, to Everina, then in Ireland, November 17, 1794.

Chapter III: *The School on the Green*

1. This and the ensuing quotes are from a letter written by Fanny to Everina Wollstonecraft on February 17, 1783.

2. On the Newington Green community, see P. W. Clayden, *The Early Life of Samuel Rogers* (London, 1887), pp. 1–100; Michael Thorncroft, *Trust in Freedom: The Story of Newington Green Unitarian Church, 1708–1958* (London, 1958); Carl B. Cone, *Torchbearer of Free-*

dom: The Influence of Richard Price on the Eighteenth Century (Lexington, Ky., 1952).

3. Richard Price paid rent for his house "on the Green" as late as 1785 (Islington Land Tax Book, #2021, Middlesex Record Office, London).

4. Chapel records for this period show no contributions from Mary Wollstonecraft (information from Mr. Trevor Watkins, a member of the present meeting house who has worked on its archives).

5. Mary Wollstonecraft to George Blood, September, 1785.

6. Elizabeth Nitchie, "An Early Suitor of Mary Wollstonecraft," *Proceedings, Modern Language Association (PMLA)*, LVIII (1943), pp. 163–69.

7. See Appendix B.

8. Wardle, pp. 51, 76.

9. This and preceding quote, Mary to George, July 21 and 27, 1785.

10. Mary to Eliza and Everina, December, 1785.

Chapter IV: *Thoughts on the Education of Daughters*

1. *Mary, A Fiction*, pp. 36–37.

2. Mary to George Blood, February 27, 1786.

3. On Hewlett, see *SC*, Vol. I, p. 64 and n.

4. *Thoughts on the Education of Daughters*. Quotations are taken from the following pages: 7, 15, 18, 22, 22, 56, 58, 69, 72, 84, 77.

5. Mary to George Blood, May 22, 1786.

6. *Ibid.*, June 18.

7. *Ibid.* The letter is dated June 25, but internal evidence suggests that it was probably July 25; Mary frequently misdated her letters.

8. Mary to Everina, September, 1786.

9. *Memoirs*, p. 39.

10. Mary to Everina, October 9, as also the two following quotes.

11. Mary to Eliza Bishop, November 5, 1786. On Henry Gabell, see *SC*, Vol. IV, pp. 840–55 for a discussion of Mary's relationship with Gabell, by the author.

Chapter V: *Irish Crossing*

1. Mary to Eliza, December 22, 1786.

2. Mary to Everina, November 17, 1786.

3. Mary to Joseph Johnson, December 5, 1786. Printed in full, *SC*, Vol. I, pp. 66–67.

4. *Ibid.*

5. Mary to Everina, January 19, 1787.

6. Mary to Henry Gabell, some time between mid-February and mid-April, 1787. Printed in full, *SC*, Vol. IV, with commentary by the author, pp. 840–46.

7. Mary to Everina, March 24, 1787.

8. Same, February 10, 1787.

9. Same, February 12 and March 3, 1787.

10. Same, March 24, 1787.

11. Same, March 24, 1787.

12. Mary to Everina. The letter is dated March 4 of the same year, but its contents suggest that Mary misdated it, as she sometimes did, and that it was written April 4.

13. Same, March 14, 1787.

14. Quoted in Margaret Lane, *The Brontë Story* (London, 1953), p. 123 and *passim*.

15. George Eliot, *Middlemarch* (NAL ed., 1964), p. 160.

16. Mary to Everina, January 15, 1787.

17. *A Vindication of the Rights of Woman* (Everyman ed.), p. 191.

18. Mary to Eliza, November 5, 1786. On Mary's influence on Margaret King, see Appendix C.

Chapter VI: *In the Shadow of St. Paul's*

1. Mary to Eliza, June 27, 1787.

2. See J. M. S. Tompkins, *The Popular Novel in England* (London, 1932); Allene Gregory, *The French Revolution and the English Novel* (New York, 1915); B. G. McCarthy, *Later Women Novelists, 1744–1815* (Cork and Oxford, 1947).

3. Mrs. Makin, *An Essay to Revive the Ancient Education of Gentlewomen* (1673); Mary Astell, *A Serious Proposal to Ladies, etc.* (1697); "Sophia," *Woman Not Inferior to Man* (1739). Some of the better minds of the Augustan Age—Steele, Addison, and others—urged better education for women.

4. *Mary, A Fiction* (London, 1788), pp. 39, 59, 79.

5. Mary's friendship with Henry Gabell in relation to the novel *Mary* is discussed in more detail in *SC*, Vol. IV, pp. 840–60, in a Commentary by this author, in connection with four of Mary's letters to Gabell, which are reprinted in full.

6. Wardle, p. 78.

7. "As for my *Mary*, I consider it a crude production, and do not willingly put it in the way of people whose good opinion, as a writer, I wish for . . ." (Mary to Everina, March 22, 1797).

8. Published in *Posthumous Works*, Vol. IV, pp. 154, 131–32.

9. Mary to Eliza, June 27, 1787.

10. Johnson holograph, Abinger mss. microfilm, reel IX. Godwin recounts Mary's coming to London but says nothing about her being dismissed by Lady Kingsborough, since as usual he wishes to present Mary only in the best light; only when biographers began having access to the mss. letters (beginning with Kegan Paul) did a more realistic picture emerge.

11. Charlotte Brontë, *Villette* (1853), Ch. 11.

12. John Nichols, *Literary Anecdotes of the Eighteenth Century* (London, 1812–15), Vol. III, pp. 462–64; Charles Timperley, *Dictionary of Printers and Printing* (London, 1839), p. 836.

13. *SC*, Vol. I, p. 68, n. 3.

14. *Collected Letters of William Cowper*, Thomas Wright, ed. (London, 1904), Vol. III, p. 488 (Cowper to Johnson, October 3, 1790).

15. Mary to Everina, November 7, 1787.

16. Quoted in Thomas Wright, *Life of William Blake* (Olny Bucks, 1929), p. 21.

17. Timperley, *op. cit.*

18. Johnson holograph, Abinger.

19. *Annual Necrology, 1797–8* (London, 1800).

20. Mary to Johnson, Letters II and III in *Posthumous Works*, Vol. IV, pp. 64–67.

21. Mary to Henry Gabell, *SC*, Vol. IV, pp. 859–62.

22. Mary to Everina, November 7, 1787, and another undated letter but probably also November, 1787.

Chapter VII: *Johnson's Circle*

1. *Original Stories from Real Life*, p. iii. References are taken from the 2d (1790) ed.

2. Mary to Joseph Johnson, *Posthumous Works*, Vol. IV, Letter IV, pp. 67–68.

3. Wardle, p. 90.

4. *Original Stories*, pp. 171–72, 151–52.

5. Quoted in Alexander Gilchrist, *Life of William Blake* (London, 1863, 2d ed., 1906), p. 94.

6. Godwin, *Memoirs*, p. 49.

7. There is no authoritative modern biography of Fuseli to supersede John Knowles' *Life and Writings of Henry Fuseli* (London, 1831), 3 vols. Knowles was a longtime friend of Fuseli's, as well as his legatee. His work contains many inaccuracies regarding Mary's relationship with Fuseli (including the year 1790 as the date of their first meeting). There are a number of excellent studies of Fuseli's work: Eudo C. Mason, *The Mind of Henry Fuseli* (London, 1951), with an appendix listing Fuseli's contributions to the *Analytical Review*; Paul Ganz, *The Drawings of Henry Fuseli* (London, n.d.); Frederick Antal, *Fuseli Studies* (London, 1956); Ruthven Todd, *Footprints in the Snow* (New York, 1947). Peter Tomory, *The Life and Art of Henry Fuseli*, was published after this book was in type; my principal source was therefore John Knowles' *Life and Writings of Henry Fuseli*.

8. W. P. Murdoch to an unnamed friend, June 12, 1764, in the *Mitchell Papers*, Vol. 23, British Museum, Add. 6840, ff. 62 *et seq.*

9. Quoted in Knowles, Vol. III, p. 145.

10. Leigh Hunt, *Lord Byron and His Contemporaries* (London, 1828), pp. 292–93.

11. This account is taken from *Annual Necrology, 1797–98*, and the *Dictionary of National Biography (DNB)*. Professor Wardle is not entirely mistaken in describing Anderson as a "classical scholar" (he had translated from Greek and Latin), but his principal career was in government service.

12. Godwin, *Memoirs*, p. 68. The best source on Christie is John Nichols, *Literary Anecdotes of the Eighteenth Century* (London, 1812–15), Vol. IX, pp. 366–89.

13. *Letters of Anna Seward, 1784–1807* (Edinburgh, 1811), Vol. I, pp. 311–12; on André, see James Thomas Flexner, *The Traitor and the Spy* (New York, 1953).

14. Nichols, *op. cit.*, p. 374 n.

15. Mary to Everina, March 22, 1788.

16. Mary to Johnson, *Posthumous Works*, Vol. IV, Letter IV, n.d., pp. 68–69.

17. Although both Johnson and Godwin say that James went to Woolwich, it seems more likely that he received private instruction from Bonnycastle. Woolwich was primarily a military school and had stiff entrance requirements, while James does not seem to have had much formal education. Prior to the date of his examination there is a gap of four years during which James' name does not appear in Admiralty records (PRO, Chancery Lane, London, ADM 107–213); he may have been at sea on a merchant ship, and part of

the time he was living with Mary and pursuing his studies.

18. Mary to George Blood, April 16, 1788, and January 1, January 17, and February 28, 1789. In the last letter she wrote that she had paid Caroline's workhouse board because it was once again long overdue; it is the last we hear of Caroline.

19. Mary to George Blood, May 16, 1789.

20. Nichols, *op. cit.*, p. 288.

21. See *SC*, Vol. I, pp. 152–57, with a Commentary by Eleanor L. Nicholes.

22. *Posthumous Works, op. cit.*, Letter XIV, pp. 88–90.

23. *Of the Importance of Religious Opinions*, translated from the French of M. Necker, p. 151. Professor Wardle credits the *Analytical's* review (Vol. III, pp. 47–48) to Mary herself, but this would hardly square with Christie's promise that the magazine would publish only responsible criticism.

24. Wollstonecraft, *A Historical and Moral View of the French Revolution* (London, 1796), pp. 61–62.

25. According to Godwin, the *Reader* was first published as the work of "Mr. Creswick, Teacher of Elocution" (*Memoirs*, p. 45). Johnson says that Mary "compiled the *Female Reader*, introducing some original pieces and prefixing a preface to it" (holograph). Kegan Paul incorrectly referred to it as "A French Reader," and others perpetuated the error. No copy has yet come to light.

Chapter VIII: *A Vindication of the Rights of Men*

1. On Gabell, see Robert Hope, *A*

History of the Lord Weymouth School (privately published, 1961), pp. 59–62.

2. James Woodress, *A Yankee's Odyssey: The Life of Joel Barlow* (New York and Philadelphia, 1958), p. 101.

3. Thomas Christie to Joseph Banks, November 16, 1789 (Banks Collection, British Museum—Add. Mus. 33.978 ff., pp. 270–77).

4. Alfred O. Aldridge, *Man of Reason: The Life of Tom Paine* (Philadelphia and New York, 1959), p. 127; *SC*, Vol. I, p. 122, n. 2. A note in Burke's *Correspondence* (see *supra*, Vol. IV, p. 412) places Christie in Paris in mid-October. The *DNB's* account of Christie erroneously states that he went to Paris in 1789 for only six months, but he was clearly also there at various other times.

5. William Wordsworth, *The Prelude*, Book Eleventh.

6. Richard Price, *Sermon on the Love of Our Country* (London, 1789), pp. 33–34, 40–41. Quotations are from 2d ed., London, 1790. Excerpts in Alfred Cobban, ed., *The Debate on the French Revolution, 1789–1800* (London, 1950), pp. 57–64.

7. On Burke, see Carl B. Cone, *Burke and the Nature of Politics:* Vol. I, *The Age of the American Revolution* (Louisville, Ky., 1957); Vol. II, *The Age of the French Revolution* (1964).

8. *A Letter from Mr. Burke to John Farr and John Harris, Esqrs.* etc., April 3, 1777, *The Works of Edmund Burke*, Henry Roger, ed. (London, 1841), Vol. I, p. 217.

9. *Ibid.*

10. *Correspondence of Edmund Burke*, Lucy S. Sutherland, ed. (Cam-

bridge and Chicago, 1960), Vol. IV, pp. 245–47.

11. "Substance of Mr. Burke's Speech on Army Estimates, etc." *Works, op. cit.,* p. 377.

12. R. J. Fennessy, O.F.M., *Burke, Paine and the Rights of Man* (The Hague, 1963), p. 2. For selections from some of the other replies, see Cobban, *op. cit.*

13. *Memoirs,* pp. 52–53.

14. Fennessy, *op. cit.,* p. 202.

15. *A Vindication of the Rights of Men,* facsimile reproduction of 2d edition (Gainesville, Fla., 1960) with an introduction by Eleanor Louise Nicholes, pp. 7–8.

16. *Ibid.,* pp. 24–27.

17. *Ibid.,* pp. 20–21.

18. *Analytical Review,* Vol. VIII, p. 419; Cone, Vol. II, pp. 446–52.

19. *Vindication, op. cit.,* pp. 34–36.

20. That same year Anna Letitia Barbauld had written *An Address to the Opposers of the Repeal of the Test and Corporation Acts.* Earlier there had been two pamphlets by Catharine Macaulay, in 1770 and 1775.

21. Emma Rauschenbusch-Clough, *A Study of Mary Wollstonecraft* (London, 1898), Ch. IV; Nicholes, *op. cit.*

Chapter IX: *Seedtime*

1. Mary Wollstonecraft to William Roscoe, October 6, 1791.

2. Mary to George Blood; the first letter is undated but is probably September, 1789, the others dated November 19, 1789, and February 4, 1791.

3. There is doubt about who the child was. According to Godwin, Ann was "the niece of Mrs. John Hunter, and of the present Mrs. Skeys, for whose mother, then lately dead [Mary] had entertained sincere friendship." (*Memoirs,* p. 49; this would have made the child a relative of Fanny's.) But according to the *Journal* of Ezra Stiles (then president of Yale University), Ann was an orphan whom the dying mother, an East Indian, asked Mary to bring up. Stiles' source was Mark Leavenworth, a friend of Joel Barlow's.

4. This and preceding excerpts from Eliza to Everina, dated October, May, and June, 1791.

5. Johnson holograph.

6. Christian Gotthilf Salzmann, *Moralisches Elementarbuch* (Leipzig, 1785). See Rauschenbusch-Clough, p. 195 and n.

7. Hope, *op. cit.,* pp. 59–62.

8. Mary to Everina, letters dated August 23, September 7 and 10, 1790.

9. *Memoirs,* p. 62.

10. Mary to Everina, summer of 1790; Eliza to Everina, October, 1791.

11. Mason, *op. cit.,* pp. 27–28. Ganz, *op. cit.,* suggests Fuseli was primarily homosexual in his eroticism. This view is certainly supported by the tone of the twenty-two-year-old Fuseli's letters to his friend Lavater, of which Mason reprints excerpts (pp. 97–99). Later Fuseli developed into an apparently normal heterosexual, as suggested in a letter written when he was about thirty-five, about Lavater's niece. (Mason, p. 155.)

12. Allen Cunningham, *Lives of the Most Eminent British Painters, Sculptors and Architects* (London,

1829), pp. 75–76; Joseph Farington, *The Farington Diary*, James Grieg, ed. (London, 1922), Vol. I, p. 115. On Fuseli's *Analytical* reviews, see Mason, App. II, pp. 356–57.

13. Knowles, p. 165; Godwin, *Memoirs*, pp. 58, 60.

14. The bulk of Fuseli's work is not readily available. The greater part of his paintings are privately owned or in the Kunsthaus in Zurich. His drawings are represented in the print collections at the British Museum and the Victoria and Albert, London. A commemorative exhibition toured the United States in 1954.

15. For Fuseli on Mary's appearance, see Knowles, pp. 350, and 164; Robert Browning, "Mary Wollstonecraft and Fuseli," in *Jocoseria* (1882).

16. Roscoe, *Life of Lorenzo de' Medici* (Liverpool, 1795), and *The Life and Pontificate of Leo the Tenth* (Liverpool, 1805). My attention was called to the correspondence between Mary and Roscoe by Miss Nicholes (see Appendix E). There is no mention of Mary in the standard biography by Henry Roscoe (London and Edinburgh, 1833).

17. Joel Barlow to Richard Price, Bodleian Library, Oxford (Mss. Montague, d.e. fol. 13). On Barlow, see James Woodress, *op. cit.*

18. Mary to Everina, June 20, 1792. Letters from Mary to Ruth Barlow are published in *New Letters of Mary Wollstonecraft and Helena M. Williams*, Benjamin P. Kurtz and Carrie C. Autrey, eds. (Berkeley, 1937); W. C. Durant, *Commentary on William Godwin's Memoirs*; and *SC*, Vol. IV, with Commentary by the author, pp. 867–77.

19. *Thoughts on the Education of Daughters*, pp. 131–32.

20. *Memoirs*, p. 27.

21. *Thoughts on the Education of Daughters*, p. 77.

22. Mary to Henry Gabell, April 16, 1787, printed in *SC*, Vol. IV, pp. 857–58, with Commentary by the author, pp. 847–49.

23. *Thoughts on the Education of Daughters*, p. 132.

Chapter X: *A Vindication of the Rights of Woman*

1. Mary Wollstonecraft to William Roscoe, October 6, 1791.

2. *Memoirs*, p. 57. Mary wrote that she was already thinking of her book when she heard of Mrs. Macaulay's death, which took place on June 22, 1791. (*A Vindication of the Rights of Woman*, Everyman ed., 115.)

3. Archives Parlementaires, Paris, Vol. XXX (1ere série), pp. 445–511.

4. Poulain de la Barre, *L'Egalité des deux Sexes* (Paris, 1673); Condorcet, *Lettres à un Bourgeois de New-Haven*, *Oeuvres*, IX, Lettre 2, pp. 14–21.

5. *A Vindication of the Rights of Woman*, p. 69.

6. *Ibid.*, pp. 60–61, 51, 57, 70, 75.

7. *Ibid.*, p. 144.

8. *Ibid.*, pp. 129–30, 214.

9. *Ibid.*, p. 167.

10. *Ibid.*, pp. 163, 162.

11. *Ibid.*, pp. 160–61, 212, 214.

12. *Ibid.*, p. 44.

13. *Ibid.*, p. 186.

14. *Mendship Annals, or A Narrative of the Charitable Labours of Hannah and Martha More in Their Neighbourhood*, Reverend Arthur Roberts, ed. (London, 1859), pp. 6–9.

15. *A Vindication of the Rights of Woman*, pp. 186, 192, 84, 192.

16. *Ibid.*, pp. 160, 156–57.

17. *Ibid.*, pp. 60, 58–59.

18. *A Vindication of the Rights of Men*, pp. 78–79.

19. *A Vindication of the Rights of Woman*, pp. 74–75.

20. James Burgh, *The Dignity of Human Nature* (London, 1767), Vol. I, pp. 2, 3, 188.

21. Catharine Macaulay, *Letters on Education* (London, 1790), Letter XXI. Mary's review of the book appeared in the November, 1790, issue of the *Analytical*, Vol. IX, pp. 241–54.

22. Jean Jacques Rousseau, *L'Emile, or A Treatise on Education*, W. H. Payne, ed. (New York and London, 1906), p. 263.

23. Hannah More to Horace Walpole, n.d., *Memoirs of the Life and Correspondence of Mrs. Hannah More*, William Roberts, ed. (New York, 1836), Vol. I, p. 427. Walpole's famous description of Mary as a "hyena in petticoats" occurs in a letter to Mrs. More several years later (*Letters of Horace Walpole*, Mrs. Paget Toynbee, ed. [Oxford, 1905], Vol. XV, pp. 337–38).

24. *Letters of Anna Seward* (Edinburgh and London, 1811), Vol. III, p. 117.

Chapter XI: *Revolution and Renewal*

1. Mary to Everina, February 23, 1792.

2. Mary to William Roscoe, January 3, 1792.

3. Mary to Everina, February 23, 1792; to George Blood, January 2, 1792.

4. Eliza to Everina, July 3, 1792.

5. Mary to Roscoe, November 12, 1792 ("I shall not now halt at Dover"); Joel to Ruth Barlow, June 15; Mary to Everina, September 14, and to Roscoe, November 12.

6. Kegan Paul, *op. cit.*, pp. 194–95. Earlier in describing Mary's visits to him, Johnson also wrote: "F. was frequently with us"; Paul also omitted this sentence. Neither Mrs. Pennell nor Durant had access to the Johnson holograph; Professor Wardle was the first after Paul to see it and point out its significance. There seems to be no basis for Paul's statement that Mary continued her friendship with Sophia Fuseli (p. 207).

7. Godwin found only scattered notes for this period among Mary's papers after her death (*Memoirs*, p. 65; *Posthumous Works*, Vol. IV). R. R. Hare has posited Mary's authorship of Imlay's two books at this time and has published an edition of *The Emigrants* with her name as co-author along with Imlay (Gainesville, Fla., 1964) a theory I do not subscribe to.

8. *Thoughts on the Education of Daughters*, p. 88.

9. Mary to Roscoe, January 3 and February 14, 1792.

10. Knowles, *op. cit.*, pp. 163, 167; Mary to Roscoe, November 12, 1792.

11. Mary to Ruth Barlow, February, 1793 (in *SC*, Vol. IV, p. 867).

12. For instance, Mary to Godwin, July 4, 1797 (in *Godwin and Mary* [Lawrence, Kan., 1966], p. 111).

13. Mary to Roscoe, November 12, 1792.

14. Mary to Johnson, December 26, 1792 (Letter XVI, *Posthumous Works*, Vol. IV, pp. 92–95).

15. The first two are printed and discussed in *SC*, Vol. I, pp. 121–32; the third is in the Bodleian Library, Oxford, and is dated much earlier, January 10, 1793.

16. Mary to Ruth Barlow; see also *SC*, Vol. IV, Commentary by author, pp. 862–67.

17. Condorcet's essay *Sur l'Admission des Femmes, etc.* was published in Paris in 1790 and appears in *Oeuvres*, Vol. X, pp. 121–30; the *Report to the Legislative Assembly Oeuvres*, Vol. VIII (includes the memorandum "L'Education des Femmes," pp. 215–28). F. de la Fontainerie, *French Liberalism and Education in the Eighteenth Century* (New York and London, 1924), includes the English text of the report but unfortunately not of the memorandum on the education of women. The author searched the files of the Comité sur l'Instruction Publique at the Archives Nationales in Paris but found nothing that could be identified as Mary's "plan."

18. *Posthumous Works*, Vol. IV, p. 50.

19. Emma Rauschenbusch-Clough, see *op. cit.*, was the first to identify Von Schlabrendorf, pp. 200–2. See also J. C. Jochmann, *Reliquien* (1836), and H. Zschokke, *Prometheus: Zeitschrift für Licht und Recht* (Arrau, 1832): "Graf von Schlabrendorf in Paris über Ereignisse und Personen seiner Zeit," Vol. I, pp. 149–204. The only modern work on Schlabrendorf seems to be Karl Faehler, *Studien zum Lebensbild eines Deutschen Weltburgers,* *des Grafen von Schlabrendorf* (Munich, 1909). This was Part I of a PhD thesis presented to the University of Jena, which has not been drawn on previously. There are copies of Part I in the Bodleian Library at Oxford and in the University of Jena Library, but Part II does not seem to have been published, and the family papers on which Faehler drew were destroyed during World War II. It was Von Schlabrendorf, not Jane Christie, who broke their engagement.

20. Joel to Ruth Barlow, April 19 and May 2, 1793. Originals in the Houghton Library at Harvard.

21. Imlay's role in the conspiracy was examined by Ralph L. Rusk, "The Adventures of Gilbert Imlay," *Indiana University Studies* #57 (Bloomington, Ind., 1923), and G. F. Emerson, "Notes on Gilbert Imlay, Early American Writer," *PMLA*, Vol. 39 (June, 1924); the two scholars worked independently. The source material is largely in the *Annual Report* of the American Historical Association (1908, Vol. I), in Vols. I and III, *American Historical Review*, and in the exhaustive writings of Frederick Jackson Turner. See particularly "Plan for a Revolution in Louisiana," *Archives des Affaires Etrangères* in AHA *Annual Report*, 1896, pp. 945–53, which is unsigned but may have been written by Imlay, and *AHR*, Vol. III, pp. 491–94, endorsed "Citizen Otto"; Otto was the son-in-law of St. John Crèvecoeur who knew Imlay (see Emerson). A brief earlier memorandum signed by Imlay also stated that "Since the plan will be carried out by Americans, it will eventually drag that

country into actual war. . . ." (AHA *Annual Report*, 1896, pp. 953–54.)

22. "Correspondence Politique sur l'Espagne," published in *AHR*, Vol. III, pp. 494–503.

23. On Imlay, see especially Emerson, *op. cit.* I am indebted for hitherto unknown details of his life to Admiral Miles Imlay, USCG, retd., a collateral descendant who generously gave me the results of his research. Imlay's rank and length of service in the Continental Army are recorded in the company muster and pay rolls of Forman's Regiment, National Archives, Washington, D.C. The records of his land purchases were found by Admiral Imlay in the Index to Land Grants, State of Virginia (of which the Kentucky Territory was then still a part), in the State Library in Richmond. The Kentucky records have been destroyed by fire or otherwise lost. On Imlay and Boone, see John Bakeless, *Daniel Boone* (New York, 1939), p. 343. A PhD dissertation on Imlay presented by Lieutenant Colonel Joseph Fant, USA, to the University of Pennsylvania has not been available to me but will undoubtedly throw new light on the subject when it is published.

24. *Memoirs*, p. 74.

Chapter XII: *Disillusionment*

1. *Memoirs*, p. 77; reprinted in Durant, p. 265. Although he dated the letter in the fall or early winter of 1794, the Barlows had left Paris the preceding spring.

2. Mary Wollstonecraft, *Letters to Imlay*, Kegan Paul, ed. (London, 1879), Letter II. The original edition

in *Posthumous Works*, Vol. III and IV, omits the number LXXII; consequently it appears to have one additional letter, which is not the case. All citations here are from Kegan Paul.

3. Letter IV.

4. *Memoirs*, p. 77; Cecilia Lucy Brightwell, *Memorials of the Life of Amelia Opie* (Norwich and London, 1854), pp. 42–49.

5. Letters V, X, XXIII.

6. Letters IX, XIV.

7. Letters XVI, XVIII, XIX; the letter to Ruth Barlow is published in *Four New Letters of Mary Wollstonecraft and Helen Maria Williams*, Benjamin P. Kurtz and Carrie C. Autrey, eds. (Berkeley, 1937), 41.

8. Mary to Ruth Barlow, July 8, 1794, printed in Commentary, pp. 261–63.

9. Wollstonecraft, *French Revolution*, pp. 426, 161–64.

10. "John Adams's Comments on Mary Wollstonecraft's French Revolution," Bulletin of the Boston Public Library, 4th Series, Vol. 5, No. 2, (January–March, 1923), pp. 4–13.

11. Mary to Everina, September 20, 1794; *Letters to Imlay*, XXIII.

12. Woodress, *A Yankee Odyssey*, *op. cit.*, pp. 146–52. Joel and Ruth did not return to Paris until after Mary had gone back to England, and in all likelihood they never saw one another again.

13. Helen Maria Williams, *Letters Containing a Sketch of the Politics of the French Revolution* (London, 1795), Vol. I, p. 185.

14. Archibald Hamilton Rowan, *Autobiography* (Dublin, 1840), pp. 253–54.

15. *Letters to Imlay*, XXXV, XXXVI.

16. Letter XXXVIII; quoted by Mary in Letter LXXVI; her letter to Rowan is printed in Commentary, pp. 293–94 (a slightly different text appears in Kegan Paul, Vol. I, pp. 221–22).

17. *Letters to Imlay*, XXXVIII; *Memoirs*, pp. 81–83.

18. Original in Abinger; partly reprinted in Kegan Paul, Vol. I, 227–28.

19. It was also during this period that Mary must have paid a visit to Fuseli, judging by a letter she wrote Fuseli the following winter (see Chapter XIV, p. 223).

20. *Letters to Imlay*, XLII.

Chapter XIII: *Dark Passage*

1. Quoted in Eliza's letter to Everina of July 1, 1793; Eliza to Everina, November 5, and April 24, 1794.

2. Mary to Everina, March 10, 1794; Eliza to Everina, June 16; Mary to Everina, September 29; Eliza to Everina, October 2.

3. Eliza to Everina, November 7, 1794; Imlay's letter is printed in Kegan Paul, Vol. I, p. 217.

4. Eliza to Everina, March 4, 1795; quoted in full, Eliza to Everina, April 29, 1795; Eliza to Everina, May 10 and April 19, 1795.

5. Quoted, Eliza to Everina, May 10, 1795; same to same, June 13.

6. *Letters to Imlay, op. cit.*, Letters LII, LVIII.

7. Letter LXIV.

8. *Letters Written During a Short Residence in Sweden, Norway, and Denmark* (London, 1796), pp. 132–34; *Letters to Imlay*, Letter LXIX.

9. Letters LXV, LXVII, LXVIII.

10. Letter LXIX.

11. *Memoirs*, pp. 86–90. This suicide attempt is mentioned in Farington, *op. cit.*, Vol. I, pp. 170–71; there is no substantiation for Farington's statement that Imlay was already married when he met Mary.

12. Letter LXIX.

13. Letter LXXIV; *Memoirs*, pp. 90–91; Letter LXXV.

14. *Memoirs*, p. 94; Letter LXXVII: Kegan Paul dates this letter, like the two preceding ones, in December, 1795, but as noted earlier, his dating is occasionally open to question.

Chapter XIV: *The Golden Years*

1. *Letters . . . in Sweden*, pp. 97–98, 102–3, 240–41, 251–52; Professor Wardle has analyzed the similarities between Mary's book and the later Romantic writers. Certain passages have a strong resemblance to Dorothy Wordsworth's style in her diaries.

2. Commentary, pp. 300–1 (a slightly different version appears in Rowan, *op. cit.*, pp 250–51); Knowles, *op. cit.*, pp. 299–300 (this is the only letter from Mary to Fuseli which has survived). Durant tells the story (at fourth hand and therefore highly speculative) of Godwin's visiting Fuseli after Mary's death to ask for her letters. Fuseli allegedly showed him several packets of letters in a drawer and then closed it, saying, "Damn you, that is all you will see of them" (Commentary, 185–87). The letters were thought to have been in the possession of the Shelley family as late as 1884 and were then probably destroyed (Wardle, p. 350, n. 8).

3. On Mrs. Cotton, see *Memoirs*, p. 94, and Kegan Paul, *op. cit.*, p. 280. Godwin also mentions Sir William East in connection with the stay in Berkshire. Despite his radicalism, Godwin was a snob and never failed to mention any families of social standing who were acquainted with the Wollstonecrafts. On Imlay, see *Memoir*, p. 95.

4. There is no modern definitive biography of Godwin. The best is George Woodcock, *William Godwin: A Biographical Study* (London, 1946). See also F. K. Brown, *William Godwin* (London and Toronto, 1926), and R. G. Grylls, *William Godwin and His World* (London, 1953). All three draw heavily on Kegan Paul, who, as previously noted, is often unreliable on dates and other details. The *Shelley and His Circle* series will continue to publish new Godwin mss.; see in particular K. N. Cameron's introductory essay in Vol. I, pp. 7–22. There is a considerable body of criticism on Godwin's major works.

5. Woodcock, *op. cit.*, p. 42; Southey to Joseph Cottle, *Life and Letters of Robert Southey*, C. C. Southey, ed. (London, 1850), pp. 305–6; Southey was very conscious of his own oversized nose.

6. *SC*, *op. cit.*, pp. 26–34. He wrote his mother that "he was far from desirous" of relinquishing the ministry.

7. Quoted from Kegan Paul, *op. cit.*, p. 67. Paul printed a number of excerpts from "biographical notes" by Godwin which do not appear to have survived in any other form.

8. "Cursory Strictures on the Charge Delivered by Lord Chief Justice Eyre to a Grand Jury," published in the *Morning Chronicle*, October 21, 1794, then as a pamphlet.

9. Quoted in Kegan Paul, *op. cit.*, p. 79, from a note by Mary Godwin Shelley; *Political Justice*, Book IV, Ch. 9; same, Book VIII, Ch. 6.

10. Faehler, *op. cit.*, pp. 17–18; the elisions are Faehler's and the original was lost with the rest of the Von Schlabrendorf papers.

11. Brown, *op. cit.*, p. 116. No original of this letter appears to have survived. The remaining letters quoted in this chapter unless otherwise noted are published from the Abinger mss. in *Godwin & Mary*, Ralph M. Wardle, ed. (Lawrence, Kan., 1966). Godwin himself numbered and dated them. Of the 162 letters they are known to have exchanged, 9 are missing in mss. form.

12. *Ibid.*, p. 9; *Memoirs*, p. 100; *Godwin & Mary*, p. 14.

13. *Ibid.*, pp. 15, 17, 33, 41–42, 39 and 23.

14. *Ibid.*, pp. 59–60, 45, 35; Farington, *Diary, op. cit.*, Vol. I, pp. 170–71.

15. Mary to Everina, March 3, 1797; *Godwin & Mary*, 68. When Godwin visited the Wedgwoods, who were old friends of his, Mary begged him to treat her sister as kindly as he could ("a little more than her manner, probably, will call forth," p. 83). He himself noted that it was most unusual for Everina to be in good spirits (p. 91). The Wedgwoods had also known the Wollstonecrafts back in Wales when all the girls were still in their teens.

16. *Godwin & Mary*, p. 64; Kegan Paul, *op. cit.*, p. 235; *Love Letters of Mary Hays*, p. 241; *Memorials of Amelia Opie*, pp. 61–62.

17. Knowles, *op. cit.*, p. 170; Kegan Paul, *op. cit.*, pp. 240 and 237–38.

18. Southey to Thomas Southey, April 29, 1797, *op. cit.*, Vol. I, pp. 310–11. Earlier he wrote to Joseph Cottle that of all the London literati he had met, Mary's "countenance" was the best; "the only fault in it is an expression . . . indicating superiority; not haughtiness, not sarcasm . . . but still it is unpleasant. Her eyes are light brown and though the lid of one of them is affected by a little paralysis, they are the most meaningful I ever saw." (*Ibid.*, Vol. I, p. 305.) No one else has mentioned a paralysis of Mary's eyelids.

19. William Hazlitt, *Collected Works*, Waller and Glover, eds. (London, 1904), Vol. XII, p. 264.

20. *Godwin & Mary*, pp. 74–75, 80, 83, 106–7.

21. *Ibid.*, p. 118. Miss Pinkerton wrote in reply: "At length I am sensible of my conduct. Tears and communication afford me relief. N. Pinkerton."; p. 116.

Chapter XV: *Birth and Death*

1. See *SC*, Vol. I, pp. 152–57, for text of one of Mary's reviews; Godwin published "On Poetry" in *Posthumous Works*, Vol. IV, and it appears, together with a commentary, in *SC*, Vol. I, pp. 174–79.

2. Rowan, *op. cit.*, p. 253; first published in *Monthly Review*, April, 1797—see *Posthumous Works*, Vol. IV, pp. 159–75, also *SC*, Vol. I, pp. 175–79; William Wordsworth, *Selected Poems and Prefaces*, Jack Stillinger, ed. (Boston, 1965), "Preface to the Second Edition of 'Lyrical Ballads,'" pp. 443–64.

3. *Posthumous Works*, Vols. I–II.

4. *Memoirs*, p. 111; *SC*, Vol. IV, pp. 887–93 for the letter and Commentary by the author. When Godwin published Dyson's letter (anonymously) in the preface to *Maria*, he made several important deletions.

5. *Vindication*, p. 162 (Godwin states that Mary was also influenced in her choice by "ideas of decorum," but this would have been completely foreign to everything we know of Mary); on Mary's delivery and death, see *SC*, Vol. I, pp. 185–201: "The Death of Mary Wollstonecraft" by Eleanor L. Nicholes.

6. *Memoirs*, pp. 118–22, and Kegan Paul, *op. cit.*, pp. 272–75.

7. Kegan Paul, *ibid.*, pp. 282–83, 280–81, 276; Everina to Godwin, July 15, 1806, and July 3, 1807. (Since the tenements were due, under the terms of the leases, to revert shortly to the lessor, the Goldsmiths' Company may have been compelling Godwin to make substantial repairs and thus make up for earlier neglect.)

8. Edna St. Vincent Millay, *Collected Poems* (New York, 1956), p. 92; the graveyard is now a public park but the monument Godwin raised to Mary still stands there.

9. Edward Dowden, *Life of Percy Bysshe Shelley* (London, 1886), Vol. II, pp. 23, 41, 51–52, 57–58; Kegan Paul, *op. cit.*, Vol. II, p. 242 (from the *Cambrian* of October 12, 1816).

10. Parish records of St. Brelade, Jersey, C.I.; letter from Judicial Greffier of Jersey to the author, January 14, 1967; the inscription was

preserved by Richard Garnett, who wrote the biography of Imlay in the *DNB*, and published it in the *Atheneum*, August 15, 1903. It was reprinted by Durant, Commentary, pp. 245–46.

11. See *The Letters of Mary Shelley* and *Mary Shelley's Journal*, both Frederick L. Jones, ed. (Norman, Okla., 1944 and 1947). *Frankenstein* was published in London in 1818; see R. G. Grylls, *Mary Shelley* (Oxford, 1938), pp. 306–21.

12. Shelley, *Journal*, pp. 206–16.

13. Letter to author from Reverend Victor Jones *re* Laugharne parish burial register; London Law Society Law Lists; London Directories; HMS *Shark* Muster Books, Admiralty Records, PRO; "Records of Men Enlisted in the U.S. Army Prior to the Peace Establishment, 1817" and "Ditto, from May 17, 1815 to 1828 inclusive," National Archives, Washington, D.C. See Appendix F.

14. "Second Report of the Irish Commissioners of Education Inquiry" (Dublin, 1826), pp. 564–66; my attention was called to this source by Mr. Michael Quane of Dublin. See also Dowden, *op. cit.*, Vol. I, p. 462.

Shelley, *Letters*, Vol. II, p. 262; see also Appendix D.

15. See *Australian Dictionary of Biography* for both Wollstonecraft and Berry, also *Journal and Proceedings*, Australian Historical Society, Vol. 27, 1941–42, p. 26, which draws on Berry's *Reminiscences* (Sydney, 1912); James Collier, *The Pastoral Age in Australia* (London & Melbourne, 1911). There are letters from Everina to Elizabeth Berry among the Berry papers in the Mitchell Library in Sydney and from Mary Shelley to Elizabeth Berry in Shelley, *Letters, op. cit.*

16. For historical material see as follows: For the United States, Eleanor Flexner, *Century of Struggle: The Woman's Rights Movement in the United States* (Cambridge, Mass., 1959; and paperback ed. New York, 1967); Andrew Sinclair, *The Emancipation of the American Woman* (p.b., 1970); for Great Britain, Ray Strachey, *The Cause* (London, 1928), and Josephine Kamm, *Rapiers and Battle Axes* (London, 1966); for Canada, Catherine L. Cleverdon, *The Woman Suffrage Movement in Canada* (Toronto, 1950).

Index

Some other books published by Penguin
are described on the following pages.

Elizabeth Gould Davis

THE FIRST SEX

By looking at the superiority of woman to man, this unique book aims to give woman her rightful place in history. Drawing on science, mythology, and archaeology, Elizabeth Gould Davis comes up with some eye-opening facts to show that woman was first in the discovery of the arts and sciences, first in the march toward civilization, and first in physical efficiency. (Some samples: Biologically, man is a mutant of woman, since the Y chromosome is a stunted X. . . . Ancient civilizations such as the Sumerian were matriarchal societies where women ruled and men were servants.) Combining the expert documentation of *The Second Sex* with the lively controversy of *Sexual Politics*, *The First Sex* could well become the handbook of the women's movement.

Edited by Jean Baker Miller, M.D.

PSYCHOANALYSIS AND WOMEN

The articles in this volume revise the traditional psychoanalytical approach to women. Feeling that women have been too long "kept in their place" by Freudian myths about penis envy, biological determinism, dependency, and masochism, the editor aims for a more realistic view. Included are articles by such eminent figures as Karen Horney, Alfred Adler, Clara Thompson, Gregory Zilboorg, Mary Jane Sherfey, and Robert Seidenberg. Together, these writings dispel the old stereotypical attitudes with their phallocentric bias and go on to show that psychoanalysis can have a new relevance for women today. Jean Baker Miller is a practicing psychoanalyst.

Wilfred Blunt

THE DREAM KING
Ludwig II of Bavaria

This richly illustrated biography re-creates the passionate life and tragic death of Ludwig II, the "mad" king of Bavaria. Wilfred Blunt describes Ludwig's harsh and isolated boyhood, which ill prepared him for the throne he was thrust upon in 1864; his fervid patronage of Richard Wagner; his tangled emotional life; his eventual withdrawal into a lavish dreamworld; and his mysterious death. Above all, Blunt emphasizes King Ludwig's extravagant concern with architecture, music, and the other arts. The text is illustrated with nearly 150 paintings, drawings, and photographs, including forty-eight pages of color plates. These last show spectacular views of Ludwig's castles—both their breathtaking settings and their fantastic interiors. Wilfred Blunt is Curator of the Watts Gallery at Compton, England.